Will Rogers

Will Rogers

Will Rogers

His Wife's Story

By Betty Rogers

With a Foreword by Reba Collins

University of Oklahoma Press : Norman

To My Sister

Theda Blake
(Aunt Dick, as our children always called her)

ISBN: 0–8061–1526–2, cloth
0–8061–1600–5, paper

LC: 79–4743

FOREWORD

I am pleased that this biography of Will Rogers is back in print and available again. There have been many books written about Will, and there will be even more, about him as cowboy, sage, writer, philosopher, humorist, performer, ambassador, and great American. Of all those books, none has or can have the freshness, immediacy, first-hand knowledge, and private and personal perspective of this account.

It is here that we are afforded a unique insight into Will Rogers the man. We get a behind-the-scenes picture of his development from wayward youth to international celebrity, with close family ties throughout, with doubts and misgivings along the way, with failures and successes, and with an even more humane view of the man as distinguished from the image.

Here we find the youngster who signed a letter as "your True Friend and Injun Cowboy, W. P. Rogers, Oologah, I.T.," the successful man who never forgot his heritage, and who later could write, "Today, as I write this, I am out in Oklahoma among my people, my Cherokee people, who don't expect a laugh for everything I say."

It is here that we find the sensitive account of the young man who ran away from school to become a cowboy in Texas, who traveled around the world, working as a cowboy in South America and as a circus performer in South Africa and Australia, and who suffered feelings of remorse for the money he spent and the "failure" he had become. Even after he had become successful in vaudeville, he considered giving it up and settling down as a respectable rancher.

Here, also, we see the ups and downs of his careers on the stage, his mistaken efforts to acquire a "big" show rather than be the one-man performer at which he was best, his faltering experiments with a monologue to supplement his rope act, his decision, finally, to be himself, and his unique approach to life and humor. "The stage, to Will, was no different from any place else he happened to be. He said whatever popped into his head at the moment and so naturally and sincerely that it was rarely misunderstood."

Here we see the man who was the friend of presidents, royalty, the rich and the famous, yet remained as common, unpretentious, and comfortable as an old shoe. When he saw his sister described as "Mrs. C. L. Lane, sister of the famous comedian," he said, "it was the other way around. I am the brother of Mrs. C. L. Lane."

Will's life coincided with the passing of the frontier, from the man on horseback to the man in the cockpit, and he had a role in it all as working cowboy, as witness to major changes in America, as performer on radio and in the movies, and as inveterate traveler by horse, train, ship, and airplane. When he was a young ranch hand, he helped drive a trail herd from Texas to Kansas. Later, he was one of the most successful radio and movie performers, acting in both silent movies and the talkies. He was also a friend and champion of Lindbergh, Billy Mitchell, Wiley Post, and other early advocates of the airplane. When he crashed in Alaska, he was on a trip to help establish a new air route.

All his experiences helped to equip him to become such an astute commentator on humanity, civilization, and politics. If Will Rogers was short on book learning, he

was long on perception, and some of his most enduring
and endearing comments, couched in language that make
them palatable and humorous, are devastating observations about the frailties of human behavior, especially
in politics. Any political party or politician that courted
Will's endorsement did so at grave risk, for he found
politics and politicians, regardless of party, an unfailing
source of humor.

Will's relaxed and easy-going approach to life is evi-
dent here, and it extended to money, but not to those
who needed it more than he did. He could never refuse
a request for help, even if he didn't have the money, and
some of his most dedicated efforts were in behalf of
others. Few people know of the many money-raising
efforts he made, at great personal sacrifice, for good
causes, whether to help the poor or the victims of war,
floods, or earthquakes.

Betty Rogers wrote a biography from which emerges a
true picture of Will Rogers the man, an American original
who captured the imagination of the country and who
remains an intriguing figure in cultural history. Her book
was timely and important when it first appeared in 1941.
It remains timely and important today.

Reba Collins

Betty and Will *(Courtesy Will Rogers Memorial)*

Will Rogers

I owe much to Richard Adamson, who helped in the selection of my husband's writings, and who was kind enough to take time out to go over my manuscript; and I want to thank my neighbor Irvin Cobb, who encouraged me to write the story myself, and gave me much needed advice.

BETTY ROGERS

Santa Monica, California

INTRODUCTION

OF COURSE I did not know it was our last evening together. The California night was cool, and as we sat in the grandstand at Gilmore Stadium, I remember thinking there was something incongruous about a rodeo under floodlights. I missed the sunshine and the hot smell of cattle. But Will was having a good time. Since the old Indian Territory days when he had taken part in them himself, Will had never lost his delight in the rodeo contests—calf roping, bulldogging and bronk riding. Even tonight he could not stay away, although his bags were packed and he was taking the eleven o'clock plane to San Francisco on the first leg of his flight to Alaska.

Sitting there in our box under the floodlights, I watched him grin and wave to the contestants as they rode by on the tanbark. Will knew most of the boys in the show, and one by one, as the evening wore on, the old-timers came over to shake hands with him.

Someone gave Will a little wood-and-paper puzzle while we sat there. Quite unconsciously he toyed with it throughout the evening. It was a mannerism I knew so well, and which was so much a part of him. His restless hands could never stay still. Then, when the show was over, I saw him stuff the puzzle in the pocket of his coat. The printed program went there too.

Will had a habit of keeping little things. He never played a theater without saving the program, never attended a dinner or banquet without bringing home the menu card. His pockets, like those of a boy, always held trinkets or souvenirs of one kind or another.

That night in Los Angeles we drove from Gilmore Stadium to the airport. The waiting room was crowded and we slipped outside to talk until the plane was ready to go. Then we said good-by, and with his overcoat over his shoulder and a roll of midnight editions under his arm, Will stepped aboard. The plane taxied down the field, turned around and came back for the take-off. As the ship nosed up I caught a fleeting glimpse through the window—he was smiling—and I stood looking up at the red and green lights of the plane until they disappeared in the darkness.

Just ten days later he and Wiley Post crashed on the boggy tundras of Northern Alaska. An Eskimo runner brought the news to Point Barrow and a rescue expedition was sent out. In Will's pockets, when they found him, were the stub of a pencil, a picture of our daughter, Mary, clipped from a newspaper, a few coins, a knife, a dollar watch, the program of the rodeo that night, and the fragments of the little wood-and-paper puzzle.

The first time I heard the name Will Rogers was in the Fall of 1900. A severe attack of typhoid fever had left me very thin—my hair, which had been cut, was still as short as a boy's—and my family thought a change would be good for me. So I was sent to visit my oldest sister in Oologah, Oklahoma, which was then Indian Territory.

Rogers, Arkansas, where I lived, was a busy little town with considerable community and social life. Oologah at that time was little more than a train stop on the railroad, and obviously was going to be a change. My sister's letter said, "The only young people in the town are the daughters of the hotel keeper, and there is one boy, Will Rogers, who lives out a few miles on a ranch."

My brother-in-law was the station agent at Oologah, on the main line of the Missouri Pacific Railway between Fort Smith, Arkansas, and Coffeyville, Kansas. Aside from the depot and stock pens, there was a two-story frame hotel in the town, a livery stable, a church, which also served as a school, and a few little one-story frame buildings with rickety plank sidewalks in front. The buildings were scattered along on each side of a single main street until it gave up being a street and dwindled out into a dim trail over the rolling prairies. There was not a tree in sight and the country seemed desolate and barren to a girl who had been raised in the ruggedness of Northwestern Arkansas.

My sister and her husband lived in the three little rooms in the depot, and I can still remember the shrill cry of the locomotives and how the little wooden station shook when the through express trains roared past beside it.

Two passenger trains stopped daily at Oologah, one in the morning from the south and one at eight o'clock in the evening from Kansas City. When the whistle of the incoming passenger train was heard, the whole town rushed over to the depot to see the arrival and depar-

ture of the train. I used to sit on the telegraph table
in the bay window of the depot—the little bay window
common to small railroad offices—and watch the people
who clustered around the platform outside and the
passengers who sat on plush seats in the warm light of
the coaches. No one ever seemed to get off and it was
seldom anyone got on. I would watch through my bay
window, and as the train pulled out and the postmaster
hurried away with his bag of letters, everybody left
the station and sauntered back to town and up to the
post office to wait for the mail. In a little while the
depot platform was deserted. Everything was lonely
and quiet again. The train had come and gone.

One cold evening I sat in the bay window and
watched the train come in from Kansas City. This time
a lithe figure swung down the car steps before the train
had stopped. I think I must have known that it was
Will Rogers. He walked briskly into the waiting room
and up to the ticket window. My brother-in-law was
outside taking care of the baggage, so I hopped down
from the telegraph table and stepped to the window to
see what the boy wanted. I looked at him and he looked
at me, and before I could even ask his business, he
turned on his heel and was gone without so much as
saying a word.

A moment or so later, my brother-in-law came in
with the express packages. One was a banjo addressed
to Will Rogers. I knew then that he had come to get
it, but had been too shy to ask me. I hoped that he
would come back, but he didn't. He spent the night
at the hotel across the road.

Very early next morning, even before our lamp-lighted breakfast, I heard the sound of horse's hoofs on the frozen ground outside. Perhaps I was still thinking about Will Rogers. Anyway, I jumped up from my couch in the sitting room and ran to the window in my nightgown. It was the same boy I had seen the night before. He was on a little dun pony, his overcoat collar turned up against the cold, reins in one hand, a valise in the other and, absurdly enough, a derby hat high on his head.

I watched him ride down the deep-rutted road that ran through the town and out into the prairie. I watched him as far as I could see and until he was out of sight. And then I was sorry that he had not spoken to me at the ticket window, and I wondered how he would ever get his banjo.

Kate and Lil were the daughters of Mrs. Ellis, who ran the hotel. Kate was the older and taught school in the little church building. The next day—or perhaps it was the day after—Lil came to the depot with the exciting news that Will Rogers was back in town, that he had brought with him all the new popular songs from Kansas City and that her mother wanted me over for supper.

We sat down at one long table. I can recall everyone who was there: Mr. and Mrs. Ellis, Kate and Lil, Will and I, the regular boarders—Miss Lindsey, a school-teacher, and Doctor Place, Oologah's bachelor physician—and two traveling men from Fort Smith and Coffeyville. Will was awkward and very still during supper, but later, in Mrs. Ellis' little sitting room, in a low rocking chair, with a roll of music in his lap, he gradually thawed out and began to sing. He sang without any accompaniment whatever. He had a high tenor voice, and the songs, impressive to us country youngsters because they were the latest from the city, were nearly all "coon songs," so popular at the time. One of them, a lively favorite, was *Hello, My Baby, Hello, My Honey, Hello, My Ragtime Gal.* Will lost every trace of shyness and I remember my delight as he sang song after song in imitation of the way he had heard them on the stage in the city.

Outside, it was frosty, but it was warm inside the cozy kitchen where we popped corn over the hot range and where Mrs. Ellis already had a pot of sorghum molasses boiling on the stove. When everyone buttered hands and was given a plate of taffy, Will became shy again, but when he had thoroughly besmeared himself and dropped his taffy on the floor a few times, his stiffness disappeared, and before I left to go back to the depot, he gave me his new songs and asked me to learn to play them on my sister's piano, one of the few in town. He said he would be in from the ranch very soon.

He did come in, and this time got his Kansas City banjo. I am afraid I showed off a little that evening, for I could see he was impressed by my musical accomplishments. First I played the piano, then I paraded my talents by stringing and tuning the banjo. Will made a few attempts at playing, but finally gave up and handed the banjo to me. He sang while I played, and I am quite sure that I outdid myself in fancy plinking and plunking.

From the very first, our love of music was a bond between Will and me. Neither of us could imagine a better way of spending an evening than singing and playing. Will never completely mastered any instrument. He could scrape out a few tunes on the violin and he could chord on a guitar, and, I think, would rather have played an instrument well than anything else in the world. I can recall an evening not so many years ago—in fact it was on our last trip to New York—when we dined one night at Dinty Moore's restaurant. Gus Edwards was there, and Joe Howard, and they had collected around the piano on the second floor. Gus Edwards and Joe Howard are, of course, the famous song writers. Gus wrote *School Days, School Days, Dear Old Golden Rule Days,* and Joe Howard was responsible, a generation ago, for the tremendous hit, *I Wonder Who's Kissing Her Now.* Both of them wrote dozens of other tunes which my children do not know, but which bring back the whole golden past to me; the tunes run through the years like a calendar. We joined them on the second floor that night and Will sang all the old songs with them until the restaurant closed. I believe he never had a better time.

But I'm getting ahead of my story. I don't think you would call our meetings there in Oologah incidents in a courtship. We simply became very good friends.

In Oologah, my brother-in-law had a buggy and team of ponies, and when I was there, we often drove about the country visiting the different farms and ranches. One day he drove us out to the Rogers ranch, which was some four miles from town. Will had repeatedly invited us to visit him, but he had no warning of our coming that day and was away from home when we called. We were met by the farmer's wife. The house was cold, ill-kept and bare of furniture. As I remember, the whole place was run down and neglected, and I knew it had little resemblance to the hospitable home where the Rogers family had been born and raised.

I left Oologah just before Christmas, as I wanted to spend the holidays with my family in Arkansas. The trip had been a great success, and I went home in excellent health.

It was just after the new year that I received my first letter from Will. It was written when he was twenty-one years old. Here it is:

Miss Betty Blake,
Rogers, Arkansas,

My Dear Friend: No doubt you will be madly surprised on receipt of this epistle but never the less I could not resist the temptation and I hope if you cannot do me the great favor of dropping me a few lines you will at least excuse me for this for I can't help it.

Well I know you are having a great time after being out among the "wild tribes" for so long. Well I have had a great time this Christmas myself. Have not been at home three nights in a month; taken in every Ball in the Territory and everything else I hear of. I was in Ft. Gibson last week to a Masked Ball. I had a time. The Ball came near being a failure, it was managed by Sidney Haygood which accounts for it.

Say you folks never did come out as you said you would and see us "wooly cowboys" rope a steer. I

WILL ROGERS19

have some pictures of it I think and if you want them
I will send them to you if you will send me some of
those kodak pictures you had up here of yourself and
all those girls. Now isn't (?) that a "mammoth in-
ducement for you" to have your picture in a lonely
"Indian Wigwam."

I never have had that Swell Ball that we talked of
when you were here. But if you had staid we would
of had it but you would not stay long enough for us to
show you a hot time we were just getting acquainted
when you left. If you will only come back up here we
will endeavor to do all that we can to make you have
a time.

Well, I guess you have an ample sufficiency of nonsense so I will stop. Hoping you will take pity on this
poor heart broken Cow pealer and having him rejoicing
over these bald prairies on receipt of a few words from
you I remain your True Friend and
                    Injun Cowboy
                              W. P. Rogers,
                              Oologah, I. T.

As a genteel young lady of Arkansas, I must have
allowed a proper lapse of time before replying, for his
next letter was written on March fourteenth. It was
my first love letter from Will, and in the closing paragraph he said:

I am going to Fort Smith sometime soon and, if you
will permit, I can probably come up, but I know it
would be a slam on your society career to have it known
that you ever knew an ignorant Indian cowboy. I still
have lots of pretty ponies here and if you will come out
I will let you pick the herd. Now, Bettie, please burn
this up for my sake. Hoping you will consider what

I have told you in my undignified way, and, if not, please never say anything about it and burn this up. I am yours with love.

Will Rogers

Just what happened to our correspondence after this, I do not remember, but I do know that I did not burn the letter.

I saw Will later that summer. It was in Springfield, Missouri, which was near my own Arkansas town, at a rodeo given during the convention of the Elks Lodge. Rodeos were new then in our section of the country and there were special excursion trains from all near-by points. Colonel Zach Mulhall, livestock agent for the Rock Island Railroad, promoted these shows, which were not true rodeos: they were rather Wild West exhibitions. His daughter, Lucille, was a special attraction; she was the only cowgirl in the country who could rope, throw and tie a wild steer.

Will had become acquainted with Colonel Mulhall the year before at the annual fair held in St. Louis. The Colonel was putting on a riding and roping contest there and requests for entries had been sent out over the cattle country. It happened that Will had just won the steer-roping contest at a little rodeo held in Claremore. So someone sent in his name and he received transportation for himself and his pony to St. Louis. This was Will's first appearance in a contest of any importance.

He had a wonderful little dun-colored roping pony named Comanche, and after he returned from St. Louis he took his pony to every fair and rodeo he heard about.

Will had the pony with him that time we were in Springfield. Comanche was very fast, and Will's cowboy yell could be heard over all the others as he raced his pony around the arena at a dead run. It was only when Will came into the grandstand where we were sitting, that he quieted down and became timid and shy. At the rodeos Will always dressed modestly. Then, as later on the stage, he wore a small stetson; never in his life, I believe, was Will decked out in the traditional big ten-gallon hat.

My friends at home knew that I liked Will a lot and they continually teased me about my "Wild West Indian cowboy." It irked Will to know that my friends were teasing me about him. He was very proud of his Indian blood—as he continued to be all of his life— but he was very sensitive and when he was around my friends he was timid in asking me to go out with him.

We met again later that fall. This time it was at a street fair at Fort Smith. On the last night of the festivities, a big ball was given in honor of the girl who had been chosen queen of the fair. I had seen Will several times during the week and had hoped that he would come that night. I kept looking for him all during the evening, and finally, as I danced by a window, I saw him wandering around among the people outside on the cool green lawn. He was watching the dancers and sometimes glancing in my direction. But he did not come in and I did not go out.

That was the last I saw of Will Rogers for two whole years. When next we met, he had circled the globe.

CHAPTER I

THERE are many quotation marks in this story. Much of it has been told in Will's own words. His weekly articles often contained personal bits about himself. I have quoted freely from these articles; sometimes, too, from his daily wires; and from an unpublished manuscript written many years ago, long before Will could use a typewriter, or had any thoughts of becoming a newspaper syndicate writer. This was scribbled in lead pencil—on the stationery of the St. Francis Hotel, West Forty-seventh Street, New York City.

Headed "How I Broke Into Show Business," it was Will's one attempt to tell his own story. He left it unfinished. And he never tried it again, though in later years magazine editors and book publishers repeatedly asked Will to write his autobiography. Once I remember when Mr. and Mrs. George Horace Lorimer were visiting at our Santa Monica ranch, Mr. Lorimer said to him: "Will, we want you to do the story of your life for the *Saturday Evening Post*."

"Do the story of my life!" Will exclaimed. "How can I write my life? I haven't lived it yet. I've got too much life to live before I do my memoirs."

And that was Will. He was more interested in other people and in what was going on around him, and too much a part of the events himself to sit down and write about the past. Will wasted no time remembering, his

days were full and he took delight in the things he did
to fill them.

Few people, I think, could crowd more into a single
day than Will. Friends used to marvel at the amount
of work he could keep up, and without letting the work
interfere with other things he wanted to do. Besides
his daily comment in the newspaper and a long article
each Sunday, he often had, in his later years, dove-
tailing commitments for radio programs, motion picture work, concert tours, personal appearances and
charity benefits. Yet he could always find time for a
game of polo, and it was a rare evening at the ranch
when he did not rope calves until darkness.

Will had superb health, great physical energy and
mental vitality; and along with this, an inner serenity
that was seldom ruffled. Through his whole life, including those years when his activities multiplied and
every minute was crowded with action, he was un-
hurried, and worry was unknown to him. If things
went wrong they just went wrong and were forgotten
with a new day.

From the beginning Will was ambitious. On tour
during the old vaudeville years, our little hotel room
was always littered with ropes. He practised roping
day in and day out, creating new tricks or perfecting
the old ones. Later, when talking became a part of
his act, Will exercised the same thoroughness in keeping himself posted on what was going on. He strove
for perfection in whatever he tried; he was restless and
impatient when he felt he had fallen into a rut and
that he wasn't going ahead fast enough. And he was

keenly alert when a new opportunity presented itself.

It was not so much that he sought the new opening as that he never failed to seize it when it came his way. His whole career was the development and unfolding of a personality through the various vehicles that seemed to be constantly and almost miraculously presenting themselves. His comment on the stage during his roping act was incidental at first, if not accidental. His writing came the same way. His entrance into the movies, too, was not of his own seeking. But once started in these new fields, he made the most of each, giving to them the same enthusiasm and energy he had given to the rope in the early days.

No one ever wrote so much as a line for Will. His material was entirely his own; he even did his own typing. Taking care of his mail was the most that was ever done for him. And he never missed a newspaper deadline, though it was seldom that his articles were filed at the telegraph office or dropped into the mail an hour too soon. Most syndicate writers have articles written for weeks ahead, but Will never did. He carried a portable typewriter in the back of his car, had the faculty of being able to do his work wherever he happened to be, and always waited until the last minute.

Will's appetite for newspapers was, of course, proverbial. Newspaper reading was an important part of his work, and newspapers became almost a part of him—extras, out-of-town papers, metropolitan dailies and country weeklies. He seldom entered a restaurant without a rolled-up paper in his hand. Newspapers, magazines and books were stacked on the desk in his dressing room at the studio, strewn in the back of his automobile and piled high on the table beside his bed.

"I can fall asleep and never drop my paper," Will said. "My closest friends can't tell if I'm reading or sleeping. They say, 'Will, you read a lot,' and I say, 'No, I sleep a lot.' I can be sitting around anywhere and reading a newspaper and doze off. I'll even take the papers and go to bed and then to sleep still holding the paper out at arm's length, and the lights burning and my glasses on."

And how many silent meals I had to sit through because Will liked to read a newspaper while eating. In folding and refolding the sheets, he usually managed to knock over the salt cellar. And then, as naturally as anything he ever did, he would shake out a little salt in the palm of his hand and throw it over his left shoulder.

Will was not really superstitious, but like most people of the theater, he went through the rituals of superstition. He would never walk under a ladder, he was always flipping a coin in moments of decision, and from the very first of his stage career, he never stepped out before an audience or up to a radio microphone without first knocking wood.

With all his activity—and he played as hard as he worked—Will was never tired. He had amazing recuperative powers. If he sat down he relaxed completely. When he was not doing anything he was always resting.

That was Will's secret. He either worked at something or he rested. There was no spending of nervous energy in worry or the futile threshing of a problem. When he had a job to do, he did it. But when the job

was done he was able to turn off a faucet of energy
or to turn it in a different direction. He could fall
asleep in a chair for only a few moments and wake up
refreshed. This happy gift of being able to doze off
and snatch a bit of sleep anywhere, any time, no matter
what the circumstances, was one thing that enabled him
to maintain the heavy schedules he set himself.

I remember that during the three-week drought-
relief tour through the South in 1931 for the Red
Cross, he gave performances in three or four different
cities every day. Appearing in one town early in the
morning, he would dash off to another for the afternoon program—then into a plane again and off to the
next city in time for his evening engagement. A stren-
uous schedule, but Will loved it. Not simply because
it was a job he could do and do well, but because he
was giving his time and talent for a worthy purpose.
And because he liked the people he met while doing it,
and because they liked him.

Most of us stand in awe of celebrities, but no one
ever stood in awe of Will. There was something neigh-
borly about him, something that made you feel as though
you had always known him. And it was this something,
of course, that had been in a measure responsible for his
success—success that had come in a natural sort of way,
out of little things that just seemed to grow into larger
things. "I am just an old country boy trying to get
along," he once said. "I have been eating pretty regular, and the reason I have been is because I stayed an
old country boy."

Will, in his career, had enough praise to turn anyone's head. In the old days, during his vaudeville beginnings, he was flattered by audiences and reviewers alike. And later, as everyone knows, he had a speaking acquaintance with many of the great of the earth. But there was never a time when Will could not stand off and take a cool, appraising look at himself.

I suspect that Will's modesty had its origin in a tremendous respect for his father and a knowledge that, at least in early manhood, he was a disappointment to his family. Will was a restless boy who dodged his responsibilities and would not go to school. Instead, he went traipsing off to the ends of the earth. He hated routine, he loved freedom, and he finally shocked his family and friends by joining a Wild West circus in South Africa. Even when he was made a star in the Ziegfeld Follies, Will knew that his father's cronies were not impressed, and he used to tell the story of a few old-timers who watched him perform in New York. When they returned to Oklahoma, another old-timer asked for news.

"Well, what's Willie doing now?"

"Oh," said the others, "just acting the fool like he used to do around here."

Will's father, Clement Vann Rogers—"Uncle Clem" as he was affectionately called and generally known— was one eighth Cherokee Indian. He was a farmer and a rancher and took a leading part in the affairs of the Indian Territory. Thousands of head of cattle had grazed across his acres, and Will remembered seeing as many as fourteen binders working at one time in his father's open wheat field.

According to Indian Territory standards, Uncle Clem was a wealthy man, and when he gave up ranching, it was to organize and become vice-president of the First National Bank of Claremore. Before Oklahoma became a state, he served for four terms as a senator in the Cherokee Nation; he was a judge of the Cooweescoowee District, and a member of the commission appointed by President Cleveland to appraise the improvements of the white settlers in the Nation. Then, in 1898, he was one of the Cherokee delegates chosen to safeguard Indian interests before the Dawes Commission, the Federal agency which broke up and allotted the Indian lands preparatory to statehood.

When at last, in 1906, Congress authorized the Territory to qualify for admission to the Union, he was elected by a large majority as a member of the Constitutional Convention. Sixty-eight years old at the time, he was the oldest member of the body, and former Governor William Murray ("Alfalfa Bill") was the youngest. Rogers County was named in his honor—not in Will's honor, as some people mistakenly believe—and Claremore became the county seat. Will used to say that the crowning achievement of the convention was that of compelling hotel owners to have their bed sheets nine feet long, and he added: "Papa said he didn't know why they did it—so few of the delegates ever had much contact with sheets."

Because Will was careless about his speech, just as

he was careless about his dress and careless about his manners, some people believe that he was a poor, uneducated cowboy who struggled to the heights from obscure beginnings. Will, of course, did not have a college education, but that was only because he would not go to school; his difficulties grew out of temperament and not out of environment. As for his being a poor boy, the truth is that, as the only surviving son of an indulgent father, Will had everything he wanted. He had spending money and the best string of cow ponies in the country. No boy in the Indian Territory had more than Uncle Clem's boy.

CHAPTER II

MANY years ago the Indian Territory was absorbed
into the State of Oklahoma, but when Will was a little
boy, it was an unsettled and extraordinary country and
the home of the Five Civilized Tribes—the Cherokee,
the Choctaw, the Chickasaw, the Creek and the Sem-
inole Indians.

Each tribe, by treaties with the United States Government, was established as a separate nation. They
were actually five nations within a nation. Each tribe
made its own laws, held its own courts and built its own
schools.

And each tribe, of course, had its own allotted land.
Will was about fourteen years old at the time of the
Cherokee Payment—the eight and a half million dollars paid to the tribe by the United States Government
for land known as the Cherokee Strip—and he remembered the excitement in Claremore when the paymasters
visited that district. Children shared equally with their
parents, each Cherokee on the tribal rolls collecting
$265.70.

There were lively days both before and after the payment. Weeks ahead, in wagons and on horseback,
Indian families had come into town, and waiting for
them were the peddlers selling goods on credit—cook
stoves, pianos, musical instruments and cheap jewelry
by the ton. It was a high holiday, in hot July, and
Will remembered the merry-go-rounds, the sideshows

30

and the eating booths that offered such delicacies as "fried catfish and ice cream."

Because of the difficulties of extradition, the Indian Territory from the very first had been a haven for criminals of all kinds. After the United States courts took such matters as murder out of the hands of the Indian courts, it was a common sight to see United States marshals riding around the country in search of some outlaw. Since it was difficult for the Government to find men bold enough to go after these desperadoes, some of the United States marshals were ex-bandits themselves, and characters about as desperate as the men they hunted.

"In the old days in the Indian Territory," Will once said, "there were so many United States marshals and so many whisky peddlers, that they had to wear badges to keep from selling to each other."

Members of the Dalton gang, four of whom were shot down in the celebrated Coffeyville, Kansas, raid, and other outlaw gangs used to hide out in the hills near the Rogers ranch. Two of the Dalton boys—and this is illustrative of the unsettled times—formerly had been deputy United States marshals.

Most of the young boys knew these outlaws by sight, but Will said they certainly didn't try to learn too much about them. Of all the outlaws, the dark and sullen Cherokee Bill was the most desperate and the most dreaded. He came from Fort Gibson and was a cruel and vicious killer.

One night when Will was home on vacation from one or another of his numerous schools, he and a couple of ranch hands were eating supper. Uncle Clem was away from home. The door slowly opened and Cherokee Bill walked into the dimly lighted room. He pulled out a chair, sat down at the table and said, "Willie, I'm going to have supper with you." No one made a move or said a word. Cherokee Bill didn't want to talk and the boys were too frightened to make a sound. When Cherokee Bill got up to leave, he said, "I want a good horse; mine is leg-weary. Take good care of him and I'll be back and get him some day."

When the outlaw had galloped off, the boys went out to see which horse he had chosen. Cherokee Bill knew a good horse when he saw one, and had picked the best pony on the ranch. Early one morning a few weeks later, when the boys went to the corral, they found that Cherokee Bill had been there during the night. His horse was gone and Will's horse, tired and lame from hard riding, was standing in the corral with the others. It was not long afterward that Cherokee Bill was caught and hanged.

The original home of the Cherokees was east of the Mississippi, in what is now Georgia, Tennessee, the Carolinas and Alabama. Early white settlers soon discovered that they were the most intelligent and ambitious of all the American Indians. Many soldiers and white traders became members of the tribe by marrying half-breed daughters of earlier frontiersmen, or the full-blood daughters of Indians.

The Cherokees were not savage or warlike, nor did they dress in blankets and wear feathered bonnets on their heads. They had been in contact with white cul-

ture for generations. They were farmers, merchants
and cattlemen; they lived in houses, not wigwams. Their
leaders had been educated in the best eastern schools
and as long as a century ago it was found that half of
the adult male population of the Cherokee Nation could
read and write.

Will's pride in the fact that he was part Indian in-
spired a story that has been repeated as often as anything he ever said. He was appearing on one of his
lecture tours in Boston's hallowed Symphony Hall, not
long after his return from a trip abroad. With a ram-
bling beginning Will solemnly announced to the distinguished audience that he was honored by the presence
of so many descendants of the pioneer Americans, and
admitted that his forefathers had not come over on the
Mayflower—"But," he said, "they met the boat."

Little is known definitely of Will's great-grand-
father, Robert Rogers. But it is said that he was an
adventurous Irishman, the son of a British officer, and
that he settled in Georgia among the Cherokees and
became a member of the tribe when he married Betty
Cordray, the daughter of another Irishman whose wife
was a full-blood Indian.

Three sons were born of this marriage, Robert, John
and James. Robert, the eldest, married Sallie Vann, the
daughter of a well-known Cherokee family—and these
were the paternal grandparents of Will Rogers.

Long before the Cherokees were compelled by force
to leave their country, many Indians took advantage
of the Government's offer to exchange their Eastern
land for land in the West. Robert and Sallie Rogers,

with many other Cherokee families, ventured first as far
as the Territory of Arkansas. Later they moved on into
the Indian Territory where Robert built his home near
the Baptist Mission of the Going Snake District, one
of the nine districts in the Cherokee Nation West. (This
was near what is now Maysville, Oklahoma.) Will's
father, Clem Vann Rogers, was born there, January
11, 1839.

The Cherokees maintained good schools, supported
by the interest from funds held in trust for the tribe by
the United States Government. Clem Rogers attended
the Indian schools in his district and the male seminary
at Tahlequah, capital of the Nation, and had an education well above the standard of his time. His father
died when he was very young, and his mother married
William Musgrove.

Clem liked to handle stock and was a natural horseman. I've heard Will say that his father could get
more out of a horse than any man he ever knew.

"Riding along with papa," Will told me, "I never
could keep up with him. Papa could ride all day long
and his horse would never be out of a little fast walk or
dogtrot. We'd start out in the morning side by side, but
my horse was soon lagging way behind and I'd have
to kick him in the sides to catch up. At the end
of the day I was plumb played out and my horse was
in a lather, but papa wasn't tired and his horse had
never turned a hair."

Clem handled his bridle reins lightly, and he moved
"free and easy" in his saddle. He rode wherever a
saddle horse could pass and was known as a man of long,

hard rides. Among Will's papers I find this story of an early trip made by his father:

"One time papa told me that he drove a bunch of cattle for his folks up to Kansas City. When they got there they found there was no market for them, so papa said, 'Well, what other town have you got around here that wants two thousand head of cattle?' He was told St. Louis was a great market, so papa and his gang lit out for there—only 250 miles away. Now, if I wanted to make a scenario out of this, instead of the truth, I would tell you that they couldn't sell in St. Louis and had to go on to Chicago. But such is not the truth. They just didn't happen to meet anyone with a sense of humor, so they drove their cattle on to the St. Louis market and lost only one steer on the trip. He jumped off the boat as they were crossing the Mississippi taking them over to the stockyards in East St. Louis. Papa said the last he saw of the old steer he was floating down the river and I don't know at that if he ever drowned. Mark Twain just as likely as not picked him up with one of those old steam shovels of his.

"It took them four months driving their cattle to market, but they were only nine days making the trip home. After they sold their cattle they all had to ride home to the Indian Territory on horseback. Papa rode a mule on the whole trip—not much romance in that— that's why he came back single."

Clem was still in his teens when he made this overland cattle drive, and after he returned, his mother gave him two Negro boys, Rabb and Houston, and with a few herd of cattle and some horses, he started out on his own in the Cooweescoowee District, near what is now Oologah, Oklahoma.

Under Indian law, all land was held in common by the tribe. Thousands of acres were open and free, and as a Cherokee citizen Clem was entitled to settle upon and have for his own use any unoccupied land he cared to improve.

In his school days Clem had met Mary Schrimsher, a tall, slender girl with dark hair and flashing black eyes. Mary was pretty, witty and a graduate of the Indian female seminary at Tahlequah. Clem was in love with Mary and after he got settled at his place and began to feel a sense of independence, he and Mary Schrimsher were married. From her comfortable home in old Fort Gibson the young husband and his bride drove away along the dim wagon road to the isolation of Clem's farm in the Cooweescoowee District. The next year a daughter was born; they named her Elizabeth.

Clem ran a trading post and worked at farming and stock raising. He had the reputation of being an industrious, reliable man whose word could be depended upon. But not long after the birth of Elizabeth, the Civil War broke out and the whole Territory was disorganized. One section of the Cherokee Nation upheld the cause of the North, the other that of the South, and a rich and fruitful country was laid waste. Horses and cattle were driven away for military supplies or, as sometimes happened, for profit.

Clem's farm was near the Kansas border where Northern soldiers were stationed. Early in the conflict he became uneasy about his young wife and her baby,

and sent them, accompanied by a trusted Negro slave,
to her parents in old Fort Gibson. It was a long, hard
trip on dim prairie trails and, as they jogged along the
sixty miles on horseback, Mary Rogers and the Negro
boy took turns holding the fretful baby in their arms.
They arrived safely, but shortly afterward the baby
became ill and died. Mary soon left with the Schrimsher
family who fled to Bonham, Texas, with all they could
carry away and stayed there for the duration of the
war.

Meanwhile Clem Rogers had enlisted in Company
G, of the Cherokee Mounted Volunteers. Later he became a captain under the great Cherokee soldier, Brigadier-General Stand Watie, and served with distinction
through the four years of the war. Stand Watie
surrendered June 23, 1865, the last Confederate general to relinquish his command.

Then Captain Clem went to Texas to get Mary and
her baby Sallie who was born in Bonham in 1863.
Clem's cattle had been confiscated. His improved land
had gone back again to wilderness. But Clem was
young and in a young country. He needed money to
restock his ranch and he chose a hard and hazardous
occupation to get it—wagon freighting. For several
years he drove a six-horse team in a wagon train and
saved his money carefully. On his last freighting trip,
he carried a stock of goods to the Choctaw and Chickasaw nations, and traded for cattle which he drove back
to the Verdigris River bottom lands only a few miles
from their first home. It was there finally, now with
a family of three children (Sallie, Maude and Robert),
that Mary and Clem returned to begin life anew.

With the coming of the railroads, the Indian Territory began an era of steady development. Clem fenced thousands of acres of rich grassland, introducing, I have been told, the first barbed wire into the Indian Territory. He bought cattle in adjoining states in the spring, fattened them on the fine grass of the Territory, and shipped them in the fall to the Kansas City and St. Louis markets.

As Will's father prospered—he had the use of all the land he could fence and maintain—he built a big two-story house with a portico and two broad stone chimneys, one at each end. Neighbors came to help him hoist the heavy walnut logs that had been cut from the river bottom and which workmen had spent two years in selecting, hewing and seasoning. The house was weatherboarded outside and plastered inside, and it stands as solidly today as the day it was finished, some seventy years ago.

It was in this house that Will was born on November 4, 1879. He was named William Penn Adair Rogers for Colonel William Penn Adair, a distinguished Cherokee who served as his people's delegate in Washington for many years. Colonel Adair had soldiered with Uncle Clem under Stand Watie and was a guest at the ranch the day Will chose to arrive.

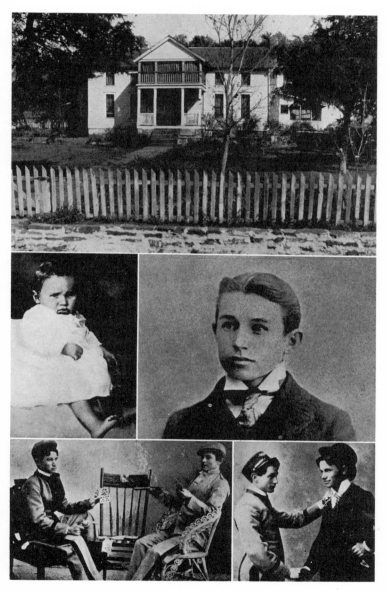

Top: Birthplace of Will Rogers. *Middle left:* A tintype of Will as a baby. *Middle right:* Will at twelve. *Bottom left:* High life at Kemper Military Academy. *Bottom right:* Will and Houston Paine

Top left: Sister Sallie and her husband Tom McSpadden. *Top right:* Uncle Clem Rogers, Will's father. *Bottom left:* Sister May as a young girl. *Bottom right:* Sister Maude.

Top: Will in vaudeville, 1913. *Bottom:* Will (second from right, first row) as a member of the Kemper football team, 1897

Betty Blake of Rogers, Arkansas. *(Courtesy Will Rogers Memorial)*

CHAPTER III

MARY ROGERS had lost two more babies, Zoe and Homer, in the six years before Will was born, and during his babyhood she watched over him anxiously. To her great joy, he grew into a healthy, sturdy youngster. Will and his mother were very close. Her face and her voice always stayed with him. He remembered her doctoring the Negro help, and he remembered the slow Southern sweetness of her voice. In his mind's eye he could see her sitting in her chair, smiling at him and lifting her hand to the gray-streaked, black hair that she always wore in a knot at the back of her head. She had called him "Willie" and among his family and old friends he was always known by that name.

Clem was blustery and loud, but as far back as Will could remember, his mother's soft voice and calm, sweet, unruffled manner remained always the same.

Everyone loved Mary Schrimsher Rogers. She was the sister of Judge John G. Schrimsher, a prominent man in the affairs of the Nation. Mary was a quarter-breed Cherokee, and the daughter of well-to-do and religious parents. Her father, Martin Schrimsher, was of Holland Dutch descent; her mother, Elizabeth Gunter, a half-breed Cherokee Indian.

The story of Mary's full-blood Indian grandmother, Catherine, is a part of the family tradition. Mary's grandfather was John Gunter, a white man of Welsh ancestry, who had settled in the old Indian country, in

Alabama, at what became known as Gunter's Landing. He was a trader and gunpowder maker and controlled a salt claim. When the chief of the Paint Clan came to barter for salt, he brought along his fifteen-year-old daughter Catherine. Gunter saw her and there the bargaining ended. Gunter took Catherine in marriage and the Paint Clan was promised salt as long as the grass grew and the waters flowed.

Catherine was timid and shy, and felt out of place in her husband's big house. When children came, Gunter, with his own ideas about their education, first turned them over to the Negro mammies on the place and later sent them away to boarding school.

Aunt Martha Gulager, Will's mother's sister, told me the story and showed me a lock of Catherine's coarse black hair that she kept in the locket of a gold clasp pin. Aunt Martha told me that Catherine could not even talk to her children—she spoke no English and they spoke no Cherokee—and how, as she grew older, she would often disappear for weeks at a time to stay with her own people. Then, driven with the frantic desire to be near her children, the unhappy little squaw would quietly slip back into the big house almost unnoticed by her husband and the children.

Mary Rogers was proud of her home on the Verdigris River. She herself had planted the rows of cedars on either side of the broad stone walk that led from the portico to the front gate. The cedars have long since disappeared, but they used to meet in a cool green arch overhead.

She had a way with flowers and never came home

without bringing seeds and cuttings from her neighbors. Will's sister Sallie told me that in the spring people would come from miles around to see the yellow jonquils and white and lavender hyacinths, planted just inside the white picket fence Clem had built around a patch of clover and Bermuda grass at the front of the house. And Will remembered helping her cover, on frosty nights, the tender plants, set out in tin cans, which she kept on a narrow shelf in the sunshiny window of her room.

Will's mother was forty when he was born. Her life had not been easy—she had borne eight children and had buried three. Will was the youngest. Sallie, the oldest, was away at boarding school. Next there was Robert, a husky boy of twelve, and then ten-year-old Maude, who, like Will, had her father's strong features and crinkling blue eyes. Sister May was six and was the infant of the family until Will came along.

At an age when most youngsters are looking at the world from the security of a gocart, Will was riding on a pillow tucked behind the saddle horn, with any cow hand willing to swing him aloft. And these early associations, I suppose, were responsible for the affection for horses that remained with him through life. Will has told me that he never saw a "top horse" without wanting it for his own, and the size of our feed bills in later years should indicate how often he got what he wanted.

Will was just two years old when his brother Robert died and he could hardly have been conscious of the solicitude that began to be shown him as the only boy in the family. He remembered but vaguely his early childhood—he always said that he had gone from long baby dresses right into long pants—but he did recall distinctly his first pony, a little sorrel mare who would rear up on her hind legs and plunge when he tried to pull himself into the saddle. The frisky little pony alarmed his mother. She would cover her face with her hands and call to his father, who stood proudly by, "Clem, you're going to get my boy killed."

Nothing happened, however. The pony was gentle enough, simply head-shy. Someone always had to hold her. Will said that as soon as he was in the saddle she would throw up her head and trot off beside the other horses, but when he came to dismount, it would be the same performance all over again.

Mary was a busy, old-fashioned mother, and ministered herself to the illnesses that come to a family of many children. There was malaria in the Verdigris bottoms, and many times the lid from the hot kitchen stove was put in Willie's bed when he shook with a chill. And he remembered the calomel and the quinine that his mother always kept handy in bottles on the kitchen shelf, and meted out to the children on the blade of a knife. "The minute you would take it," Will said, "you'd eat something right quick to take away the taste, but you never could do it quick enough."

There had been no neighbors during the early, hard years, but now many Cherokee families were moving into the surrounding country. Across the river were the Lanes and the Foremans, some six miles away. Nearer were the Lipes, the McClellans and the Musgroves.

But distances still were very great in the Indian Territory. "Coffeyville, Kansas, used to be our post office from our old home," Will said. "It was forty miles away, but then we didn't get much mail anyhow. In fact I have known some of us to make the whole trip and never get a circular."

Between the Cherokee families there was more the feeling of kinship than of just being neighbors. Everybody was "Aunt" or "Uncle." Homes were hospitable, warm and friendly. Often a whole family would drive for miles over the dim wagon trails to spend a few days with Aunt Mary and Uncle Clem. When Clem was a judge of Cooweescoowee District, farmers and ranchers from many miles around came to him with their problems.

Will was six years old when his sister Sallie married, and he said the only thing he could remember about the festivities was the big bird on Sallie's going-away hat. Afterward, and even before their mother's death, it was Maude who more or less looked after Willie. Despite a difference of ten years in age, Maude and Will were much alike. She had his sense of humor and his warm friendly personality.

It was Maude who told me how difficult it had been to separate Willie from his baby bottle. Even at the age of two or three years he still protested when offered milk in a glass. It took a rising of the Verdigris, Maude said, to wean him. Going to a neighbor's house one day, Maude and the little boy had to row across the river, which was then very high. A floating log struck the boat as they reached the swift current in the middle of the swollen stream. The boat gave a sudden jerk, and Willie, who had been hanging onto his bottle with grim determination, suddenly lost his hold. The bottle fell overboard. Willie was stunned but he didn't cry. Silently and philosophically he watched his bottle float out of sight downstream. And that was the end; he never asked for it again.

Willie always had a strong, stubborn will of his own, Maude told me, and was harder to manage than the average child. Once she recalled that she was leading him across a big pasture when their father galloped up on his horse and called to them to run quickly to the fence. A wild bull was loose and coming their way. Maude fled, but Will refused to budge. Uncle Clem came roaring back across the field on his horse and barely had time to reach down and yank the screaming boy to his saddle and safety. Will never forgot the spanking his father gave him, once the two of them were safely on the other side of the fence.

It was difficult for Clem to be patient with the contrary, stubborn little boy, and in exasperation he used to shake his head and say, "There's a lot of mule in Willie."

When it was time for Will to go to school, he was sent to stay with his sister Sallie and her husband, Tom McSpadden. Their place was across the river from the Rogers ranch, and near Drumgoul, Will's first school.

"Drumgoul was a little one-room log cabin built of post-oak logs, four miles east of Chelsea," Will said. "The school stayed with such books as Ray's Arithmetic and McGuffey's First and Second Readers. We had a geography around there, but we just used it for the pictures of cattle grazing in the Argentine and the wolves attacking the sleighs in Russia.

"It was all Indian kids that went there, and I, being part Cherokee, had just enough white in me to make my honesty questionable. There must have been about thirty of us in that room that rode horseback or walked miles to get there. We got to running horse races and I had a little chestnut mare that was beating everything that any of them could ride to school and I was losing interest in what we were really there for. I could run pretty fast and my nickname was 'Rabbit.' I could never figure out if that referred to my speed or to my heart.

"Thousands and thousands of acres surrounded us," Will explains, "with not a thing on them but cows—no stadium and not a concrete seat for a spectator to set on. We had Indian boys there that could knock a squirrel out of a tree with a rock, but the regents didn't know enough to get Pop Warner to teach them to hide a ball under their jersey. No, they just had the old-fashioned idea that the place must be made self-sustaining by learning alone, and you see where their ignorance got them. Now the weeds are higher than the school-house."

Apparently Uncle Clem was not satisfied with Willie's progress at Drumgoul, for after the first year he was shipped off to Harrell Institute in Muskogee, a boarding school for young ladies where Will's four-teen-year-old sister, May, was finishing her training. Willie was eight years old and was allowed to attend the girls' school because the president, Doctor Brewer, also had a little boy of Willie's age. It was decided, after considerable correspondence, that the two boys could learn their lessons in a strictly feminine regime without imperiling their manhood. Willie studied music and art along with the young ladies who were being genteeled. He showed some talent in drawing, and did well at the piano, or so he always maintained, until an exasperated teacher slapped him off the stool. His sister, May, as well as all the other young ladies, spoiled him, just as his family did.

The summer of Willie's second vacation home from Harrell was a tragic one for him, a summer that he never forgot. His mother became ill with typhoid fever. Uncle Clem was away from home at the time, and a Negro boy was sent to fetch him. That night, with a lantern tied to the tongue of his buggy, Clem drove his team from sundown to sunup, the sixty miles back to the ranch.

There had been much sickness in the family that year. Sister Sallie had lost a baby. Will had had the measles. And now Mary Rogers was dying.

There was little anyone could do. Clem kept wagons continually on the move, bringing ice to the ranch from Coffeyville, but ice was not enough, and even Doctor Lane, who had brought Mary's children into the world, was unable to save her. Mary Rogers died and was buried on the ranch beside her son Robert, in the little family cemetery with its twisted cedars and crape-myrtle bushes enclosed within an old-fashioned iron fence.

Will never quite got over his mother's death. He cried when he told me about it many years later. It left in him a lonely, lost feeling that persisted long after he was successful and famous. "My mother's name was Mary," he wrote, "and if your mother's name was Mary and she was an old-fashioned woman, you don't have to say much for her. Everybody knows already."

It was a sad little boy of ten who left home that fall to stay with friends and go to school in Tahlequah. He did not make a good record there. During the period of Willie's adolescence Uncle Clem became accustomed to reports that Willie was not doing well. Willie grew careless and untidy and his manners were those of a spoiled, impetuous boy who had inherited a natural restlessness and love of freedom that would not submit to discipline of any kind. This made him slow in his studies, and his teachers thought he was careless and lazy.

From Tahlequah he moved on to Willie Halsell College at Vinita, some twenty miles from home. Most of the boys and girls at Willie Halsell College were from around the neighborhood and Will had grown up with many of them. I think the four years he spent there gave him his happiest schoolday memories.

Then Will changed schools again and left Willie Halsell for Scarritt College in Neosho, Missouri. These "colleges," I should explain, were colleges only by courtesy; they were really academies—private boarding schools with grade-school and high-school curricula. As far as the family could find out, Willie seemed to be doing all right in Scarritt, but a few weeks before the term closed, he was unexpectedly sent home. His passion for rope throwing was responsible.

As a very little boy, Will had been taught by the family ranch hands to throw a lasso. He was determined to be a "top steer roper" and he spent every idle moment improving his skill. One lariat after another was taken away from him at school. Once he managed to smuggle in a thin one by wrapping it around his body under his shirt, but this, too, was discovered and confiscated in time.

An old mare, owned by the headmaster at Scarritt, ambled onto the campus with her colt one day. And on a dare, making a lasso out of some stuff that had been used to tie a trunk, Will roped the colt. His catch was all right, but in the excitement he lost his hold on the improvised lariat and things got out of hand. The frightened mare and her colt—the trunk rope still dangling from about its neck—bolted, tore through the tennis-court net, jumped a fence, and, still running, disappeared down one of Neosho's quieter streets. The headmaster decided then that maybe Willie couldn't do without his lariat, but that the school could do without Willie.

When Robert died, Uncle Clem had known there would be no more sons, and he early drifted into the habit of giving Willie everything he wanted. There were frequent trips to St. Louis and Kansas City, and during one school vacation there was a trip to the Chicago World's Fair. Willie had one of the first rubber-tired buggies in the country and always the best ponies to be had. Three of his horses, Comanche, Robin and

Monte, were considered by the punchers of the time, as one of them has since told me, to be the "three outstanding horses in the Indian Territory, or anybody else's territory."

But the richness and warmth of family life had disappeared from the Rogers ranch in the years since Mary's death. All three sisters were married now and raising families of their own, and Uncle Clem had married again and set up a home in Claremore.

Will was interested only in ranching, and the open range was even then disappearing. He made his friends among the cowboys—that was the life he wanted and the life he chose to follow. Cowboys are usually lonely men and much of the time Willie was a lonely boy. Old friends say he always talked to himself in the saddle. They used to wonder what he talked about, they said, but whatever it was, he kept it to himself.

CHAPTER IV

Will's abrupt return from Scarritt College apparently gave his father occasion for serious thought, and with the hope that the strict discipline of Kemper Military Academy, at Boonville, Missouri, would do what the other schools had failed to do, Will, at seventeen, was packed off and buttoned into the stiff uniform of a cadet. He entered Kemper at what would now be called the Sophomore year of high school.

At first, military discipline was a novelty. Will liked his gun and he liked to parade in his new school uniform and he was extremely proud of the dress regalia with its brass buttons and a high, tight collar with the school insignia embroidered in gold.

Even after his first year at Kemper, Will continued to be fascinated by military routine, and once during vacation when he was showing off at the ranch, he borrowed a rifle from one of the cow hands and, shouting his commands in a loud voice, marched, halted, shouldered arms, presented arms and what not. Then, in obedience to his own gruff command, he grounded arms with such military snappiness that there was a deafening discharge. It was nearly a fatal accident. His hat spun in the air. The bullet had just grazed his face and he bore always on the side of his forehead a long white scar.

From Kemper records it is possible to trace his wavering interest in study. One month he scored 100 in

history, the next month 68. Will's term grades taken
together were about average for the school; but his ups
and downs, not only from month to month, but from
subject to subject, were drastic. His studies at Kemper
included arithmetic, grammar, bookkeeping, history,
elocution, algebra, letter-writing, composition, physics
and political economy. In history, political economy
and elocution, Will was generally good.

During his first month at Kemper, he had the highest grade in elocution. The school was small at this
time—only fifty-two cadets being enrolled in Will's
first year—and a fourth of the student body each Saturday would take its turn in declaiming, with the rest
making up an audience. Elocution then, of course, was a
matter of memorizing and delivering with standardized
gestures the time-honored classics, such as "Spartacus
to the Gladiators" and Patrick Henry's "Give me
liberty or give me death." Naturally, it was impossible
for Will to resist the temptation to declaim for laughs.
The strange thing is that the elocution teacher, recognizing that the purpose of oratory, after all, is to sway
the audience, would give Willie good marks when he
succeeded in getting his laughs.

Bookkeeping, however, held no interest for Willie—
neither did physics; and in these subjects his grades
were uniformly bad. But grades, so far as Willie was
concerned, were just another form of bookkeeping, and
of no more interest than the subject. According to
classmates, he never worried about his grades.

Like many boys of his temperament, he learned
easily, and in a few minutes, if so inclined, could memor-

ize what others struggled with for hours. With no effort at all, probably unconsciously, he memorized the name of every boy in school. Years later, when a name sounded familiar, I have heard him recite the whole Kemper roll call to see if he and the man had gone to school together. And he always knew.

Although Will's studies suffered—many younger boys were ahead of him in school—he had a good record in sports. He played baseball and was a member of the football team. The school's social activities didn't interest him, but he was popular with his classmates. Many of them have told of his constant roping; and his regular request, with the lasso ready, for somebody to "stoop over, run, and bawl like a calf." Will's nickname at Kemper was "Swarthy."

Traits that matured in later years were clearly established in these school days. Fellow students remember his talent for clowning. When called upon to recite, he had no need to say a word to send the class into hysterics. A lifted eyebrow, a turn of the head or a shrug of the shoulders as he dragged himself slowly from his seat, and the entire class was disrupted.

Summing up his school career, Will said, "I spent two years at Kemper, one in the guardhouse and one in the fourth grade. I spent ten years in the fourth grade and knew more about McGuffey's Fourth Reader than McGuffey did."

One of Will's friends at Kemper was Billy Johnston from the Texas Panhandle. He, too, was a ranch boy, and the tales he told of the big outfits in Texas proved more than Willie could stand.

It was early spring, glories of the uniform had begun to fade, studies grew irksome and he could no longer stay tied to his desk. Besides, there seemed to be something in the wild nature of the boy that made it difficult for him to submit to the discipline of school routine. So he borrowed ten dollars from each of his three sisters, on the plea of some mysterious necessity, and left school to become a cowboy.

"There has always been some curiosity," Will wrote, "about how I left Kemper Military Academy—whether I jumped or was I shoved. Well, I can't remember that far back. All I know is that it was a cold winter and Old Man Ewing's ranch on the Canadian River near Higgins, Texas, wasn't any too warm when I dragged in there."

Young Frank Ewing, about Will's age, was a friend of Billy Johnston's. Also, Mr. Ewing knew Will's father, and he wrote at once to tell Uncle Clem that Willie was there. But before an answer came from Clem, asking Mr. Ewing to put the boy to work, Will had bought a horse and outfit from one of the cowboys on the ranch and had started cross country for Amarillo, Texas.

"All I had was the clothes I had on and a few dollars in money," Will said, "so I bought an old, spoiled horse that had been eating loco weed, and he was just as spooky as they made 'em. It was still pretty cold and somebody around the ranch gave me two old comforters—we called 'em sugans. The cook gave me a sack of grub. I rolled it up in my sugan and tied it on behind my saddle, and one morning lit a shuck for Amarillo.

"Late one evening I rode up to a drift fence. These fences were built by the big cow outfits on the south side of their pastures, to keep their cattle from drifting off too far during a blizzard. The drift fence was going in the direction I wanted to go and I'd been following it for about fifty miles. Just about sundown I rode up to a little cabin where there was a windmill and a well. I didn't see anybody around, so I watered my horse and rode off a couple of hundred yards, found some grass for my old horse and started to make camp for the night.

"I staked out my horse with a long stake rope I had, ate my jerky and biscuits out of a paper bag, rolled up in my sugans and went to sleep. Pretty soon I woke up and the rain was hitting me in the face. I'd never seen such lightning or heard such loud thunder in my life. A big bunch of range horses that had become frightened at the storm, had come aflyin' down the drift fence, and when they hit the rope that my old horse was tied with, they turned somersaults and fell all over the place. When it would lightning, I couldn't see my old horse anywhere and I knew he'd broken loose and run off with the others.

"I dragged myself out of there and started back to the cabin. I began hollering 'Hello, hello.' I thought maybe the man that lived there was away and his wife was afraid to let me in, so I said, 'Lady, I'm no thief or burglar; I'm just caught out in the rain.' Nobody answered, so I opened the door and kept talking all the time. It was nice and warm in the room. I found a table and laid down on it and soon fell asleep.

"Next morning the sun was shining bright and I found there wasn't a soul in the place. It was a one-room shack used as an outpost for line riders. There was a cook-stove and plenty of grub was stored there and over in the corner was a nice bed and plenty of blankets. I knew my old horse had run away, so I started out to get my saddle and outfit and bring 'em back, but I hadn't gone very far when I saw this old jug-headed pony still tied to the stake rope and grazing around as good as ever."

When Will arrived in Amarillo, he temporarily shelved his ambition to be a cowboy. The Spanish-American War had just started, and in Amarillo, as all through the cattle country, there was brisk recruiting for Colonel Theodore Roosevelt's regiment of cavalry. Will had told me how frightened he was and how his hand shook as he went up to open the door and volunteer. But boys of eighteen, freshly escaped from Kemper Military Academy, were not the material needed for the Rough Riders. And Will, humiliated and indignant, was declined with thanks.

So he went through town asking everyone about a job. Finally, one morning, a merchant told him that a trail boss had sent word that he was in need of a man. And though the merchant had already spoken to another boy who was looking for work, he told Will he'd better be on hand in case the other boy failed to show up.

Will was on hand. "And right there," he said, "I saw a fellow talk himself out of a job. This boy started telling what a good cowboy he was. The trail boss listened to him till he had his say, and then he told him,

'I'm in need of a hand all right, but I think you'd suit me too well.' He told me to get on my horse and come on out to the camp.

"He put me to wrangling horses," Will said. "That's the lowest job with any outfit, but it wasn't long before he put me on as a regular hand."

Will helped drive a trail herd to Western Kansas, and after he returned, continued to work with the same outfit in Texas. At last his dream had come true. He was a real cowboy now, working on a real ranch for thirty dollars a month. With a bedroll and a horse and saddle of his own, he was up and riding early seven days a week, rounding up, roping and branding calves, along with old seasoned cowhands. It was hard work for a boy of eighteen, and June, July and August are hot in Texas, but Will stuck it out and loved it.

"No greater, no happier life in the world," he wrote long afterward, "than that of the cattle man. I have been on the stage for twenty years and I love it, but do you know, really, at heart, I love ranching. I have always regretted that I didn't live about thirty or forty years earlier, and in the same old country—the Indian Territory. I would have liked to have gotten there ahead of the 'nesters,' the barbed wire fence and so-called civilization. I wish I could have lived my whole life then and drank out of a gourd instead of a paper envelope."

Will could seldom resist an opportunity to get back in the cattle country. Visiting with the old ranchers and the real cowhands remained one of his greatest delights. Early in the summer of 1934, the summer before his flight to Alaska, he described a trip back to the same country where he had worked as a boy.

"I flew all night just to get over to the 'Mashed O' outfit [he wrote] to the calf branding at Ewing Halsell's, an old boyhood friend. My youngest kid Jimmie and my nephew Jim Blake were there learning to be cowboys. I got to Amarillo at 4 o'clock in the morning. It's about 100 miles from there to the ranch, down at a town named Muleshoe. Well I got in a taxi and lit out. I didn't know the road, but I did know the direction. We were driving over a country where 36 years before, as a boy 18 years old, I had helped to drive a bunch of cattle to Western Kansas. That was the prettiest country I ever saw in my life, flat as a beauty contest winners stomach, and prairie lakes scattered all over it. And mirages! You could see anything in the world—just ahead of you. I eat out of a chuck wagon and slept on the ground all that spring and summer of '98 and my pay was $30 a month. Well here I was 36 years later driving out to a ranch, to eat at another 'Chuck Wagon,' and do a little roping."

Will had just finished a series of talks over the radio and had made a moving picture at the same time. So Ewing forewarned his cowboys. "Mr. Rogers is coming over to the ranch for a few days' rest and vacation," he told them. But on a good cow pony and in the corral with the other hands Will worked as hard as anyone. He would rope and drag his calf out from the herd to the branding fire and, after the brander had slipped the rope from over its head, go back for another. The heat of the fire had not added to the comfort of an extremely hot day, but Will kept on. He was hot, dirty and dog tired and the sweat was pouring down his face, when he overheard an old slow-talking cowboy say to another, "Some folks sure got a hell of an idea about a vacation."

Will was a good hand and a hard worker in his young days too—after he left the Texas outfit, he drifted on to New Mexico and had no difficulty getting jobs on other ranches. He liked the life and was doing the thing he wanted to do; he often told me that he would probably have stayed in that country, and eventually become a rancher, if it had not been for what happened that winter, when he and an older cowboy were sent to California with a trainload of cattle consigned to the Hearst ranch.

When the cattle had been delivered at San Luis Obispo, Will and his partner went to San Francisco to see the sights. They put up the first night at a small hotel, "where," Will said, "something happened." Will was tired and went right to bed, but the other cowboy went out to see the bright lights.

The boys were fresh from the kerosene country. Will said, "I was asleep when he came in. He says he didn't blow the gas out—maybe there was a leak. Anyhow, next morning they dug us out of there and hauled us to a hospital and, believe me, I didn't know a fighting thing until late that night, and that was just bull luck.

"The main doctor gave me up, but a lot of young medical students, just by practising on me, happened to light on some nut remedy that no regular doctor would ever think of and I came to. I landed back home in pretty bad shape. The stuff had located in my system and papa sent me to Hot Springs, Arkansas, to take the baths."

Most of the country in the Cherokee Nation had been free range and grassland during Will's early boyhood. But in 1889 the Indian Territory began to be opened up to homestead settlement, and the ten-year period of Will's varied and unsatisfactory schooling almost coincided with the passing of the frontier. Cattlemen were being crowded out by farmers, limitless grazing lands broken up by fences. Uncle Clem's own ranch now was little more than a good-sized farm.

The great days of the cattlemen in the territory were past. But so far as Uncle Clem could see, nothing worthwhile interested his son except cattle.

Gradually Will recovered his health and was soon on his way back to Texas, but this time his stay was brief, and when he returned home his father knew more schooling was out of the question, and he felt, too, that it was high time the young man was settling down. So Clem gave Willie a bunch of cattle for his own and sent him out to the old place on the Verdigris River.

A tenant farmer and his wife now occupied the big house on the ranch. It was neglected and run-down, and Willie did not find living there particularly pleasant. Nor did he get along well with the farmer's family—"nesters" he called them.

Once his relations with the "nesters" became so strained that Willie decided to move out and build a place of his own. With the help of a Negro boy on the place, he prepared logs and, with a catch-rope tied to his saddle horn, dragged them to the location he'd picked

near a spring in one of the pastures where some longhorn steers were grazing. When he had the four walls
of his cabin up, he sawed out a doorway and moved in,
planning to put on a roof and hang the door some other
time.

About a week later he was awakened in the night by
a strange noise. Peeking out from under the cover, he
saw by the dim light of the stars that one of his longhorn steers was in the cabin with him. The steer was
almost as big as the entire room, and the peculiar noise
that Will had heard was the old steer licking salt off
the table. Willie knew he must be very quiet and not
make a sound, for if the steer became frightened, he'd
whirl around and knock the whole house down. So he
lay quiet for almost an hour, scared to death. Finally,
though, the old steer backed out. "I've seen lots of
steers," Will said, "but never one that wanted salt so
bad."

Willie's cabin didn't last, however. A few mornings
later, his pony, while tied to one of the projecting logs,
was frightened by something, and jerking back, brought
the cabin down in a pile of logs. And Willie had to
swallow his pride and move back to the big house with
the "nester" and his family.

Uncle Clem had hoped that having cattle of his own
would stimulate the boy's interest and give him a sense
of responsibility. But Willie found his work dull. In
Texas and New Mexico, he had got jobs for himself
and worked on real ranches. He had ridden for miles
without seeing a fence. He had helped in rounding
up thousands of head of cattle. He had carried a bed-

roll and lived for days at a time out on the range. Taking care of the little bunch of cattle on what was left of his father's place was tame ranching for Willie, and there was hardly enough work to keep him busy.

So he didn't stay home much. He visited around with the boys in the neighborhood, and if there happened to be a rodeo anywhere about the country, he could always find one of his friends living on adjoining farms—Tommy and Gunter Lane, the Lipe boys, the Riders, the Musgroves, or the McClellans—to go with him.

At that time the whole West was being flooded with tales of South America. All the boys in the Indian Territory were talking about the Argentine; opportunities were greater there, they said; ranches were bigger, the country was freer, and there were no farmers and no fences.

Naturally, Will was excited by these stories. Uncle Clem had tried to keep him interested in the ranch, encouraging him to save his money and take on responsibility. But money meant little to Will. He handed his around to anyone who needed it and was creditor to half his acquaintances. However, he did take his father's wishes seriously enough to sign up for a twenty-year life-insurance policy which required him to meet a premium of $140 each year. But as far as responsibility was concerned, that was just what Willie didn't want.

So he went to Claremore to have a talk with his father about South America. Uncle Clem was not pleased. He wanted Willie to stay at home, but after a heated argument it seemed to him that the only solution was to let Willie go his own way. With characteristic generosity, he agreed to buy back the cattle that he had given Willie in the first place, and paid him some three thousand dollars for the herd.

CHAPTER V

SHORTLY after the Christmas holidays, Will left the Indian Territory. Packing his saddle and outfit and taking along a cowboy friend, Dick Parris, he started for the Argentine. He didn't have the faintest idea of how to reach his destination. There were no travel agencies then and nobody in the Territory could give him the information. Because South America was south, Will, reasonably enough, left for New Orleans, confident that he was headed in the right direction anyway. But there were no ships from New Orleans to the Argentine, and the boys were advised to go to New York. After a week in New Orleans, they backtracked to Galveston, Texas, boarded a small steamer, and arrived in New York to find that South America had moved off again, in a different direction, and farther away than before. They were told if they went to England, they could get a boat from Liverpool to Buenos Aires.

After a couple of weeks, sightseeing in New York, where Will said, "We never got farther up town than Fourteenth Street," Dick and Will sailed for England on the S.S. *Philadelphia,* in March of 1902. Will's first letter home, mailed from Southampton, reported his seasickness during the eight days' voyage, and how, after one hearty dinner just after coming aboard, he hadn't got out of his bunk until they reached Southampton. "We arrived Wednesday night at 10 o'clock," he said in this letter to his sister. "Our baggage was searched for tobacco and spirits; they did not find any in mine, for I don't smoke and my spirits had all left me on that boat. If I had any at all, I contributed them to the briny deep."

The Boer War was practically over then—peace negotiations had just begun, and London was already making preparations for the coronation, later postponed because of the sudden illness of Edward VII. The boys found much to see during the week or ten days they stayed in London waiting for their boat to South America. After this second crossing of the Atlantic, over a route twice as long and on a slower boat, they finally arrived in Buenos Aires the first week in May.

Once in the Argentine, little time was needed to disillusion them about opportunities for American cowboys. The country and the cattle business were not at all what they had expected. In one of Will's first letters to his father, he said:

"I have been out into the interior and have seen a little of the country, which looks like a good cattle and farming country, but it's no place to make money unless you have at least $10,000 to invest.

"The work and cattle business here is nothing like it is at home. The head men leave most of the work to peons or natives, who get about $5 a month in our money and have to live like dogs. They drive the cattle in a run, and I asked the boss if it wouldn't take too much of the fat off, and he gave me the laugh and said, 'Why, they fill right up again.' In cutting out, there are from two to three men to each animal. They would not begin to believe that a horse knew enough to cut out a cow without guiding.

"There are few Americans handling cattle here. It is all English. And as for American cowboys, I guess we are the only ones here. My saddle and all have been a big show ever since they seen it. As for roping, riding or any old thing, they can't teach the 'punchers' in America anything. As I now see things, I don't expect to make any money here, but I would not take a fortune for my trip. Here is a bit of advice for my old comrades: 'Just stay where you are, boys.' "

Traveling first class and stopping at good hotels— they had been gone from the Indian Territory almost five months—had made Will's money disappear surprisingly fast. And after their disillusioning trip into the interior, the boys had to face the fact that there wasn't much chance of a job for either of them. At this point, Dick Parris began to get homesick. Uncle Clem had always been generous with Will, and the boys probably thought he would soon be sending money. So Will bought one ticket back to the United States, and characteristically spent a good deal of his remaining cash on presents for Uncle Clem and his sisters, to send home by Dick.

Buenos Aires was a lonely place after Dick left, and each day brought Will nearer to the absolute end of his money. Though he was too proud to ask his father for help, Uncle Clem no doubt could read between the lines of his letters. A letter dated on June seventeenth:

"Dear Papa:

"I don't think there is any use of my staying here and I may start home any time. You can probably collect enough of what is owed me up there to pay my insurance, which comes due on the 10th of September. Please see that they take care of my ponies and don't let anyone use them. Papa, don't let old Comanche be touched till I come home. Have the 'bay colt' driven in town, but don't let them take my buggy or harness and don't sell them. Write and tell me all the news. I may not be here to get the letter, but then I might.

"I guess you are in the new hotel and have your fine barn and all done by now. Give all who might ask of me my best regards. Tell the boys to stay at home, for that is the best place in the land for them. You don't know how good your country is until you get away from it. You tell all those boys to stay right there. I will write more often from now on. I may see you soon though. I will close with all my love to a dear father. I am your loving son,

"Willie"

But Uncle Clem sent no money. The whole expedition had been Will's idea, and his father felt that he should work it out in his own way. But among strangers who do not even speak your language, working things out can be difficult. Will's last month in Buenos Aires was a very unhappy time.

Will knew that his family thought it extravagant of him to dispose of his cattle and start out with all the money. He knew, too, that folks back home were saying he was irresponsible and that he had let his father down. Willie was sensitive to this criticism and feeling hurt about it, as he did, made it impossible for him to come out frankly and ask his father for help.

Willie had a good time on the Fourth of July, at least. He spent it with the sailors of the U.S. battleship *Atlanta*. The *Atlanta* was there for two weeks, and during this time he almost lived on board. The sailors had been away from home two years, longer than Willie had, and he taught them all the new American coon songs. "They had a minstrel troop and tried to get me to join them," he wrote home, "and told me when I got on the rocks and wanted to go to God's country, they would make up enough to send me back."

But on the rocks was where Willie was. Finally, he was forced to leave his hotel. One night he had to sleep in the park, and early next morning, with no breakfast in sight, he wandered down to the stock pens, where he found Gauchos roping mules in a corral. The mules were wild and the Gauchos weren't very expert in their catches. Will, in his feeble Spanish, tried to tell them that he knew how to use a lasso. They couldn't, or wouldn't, understand. They pushed him away. Finally Will climbed upon the corral fence and watched his chance to get his hands on a rope. When the mules raced past, Will threw a loop and made his catch with the first throw. The Gauchos were elated, and the boss of the outfit, recognizing Will's ability, paid him the equivalent of twenty-five cents for every mule he caught.

Will was told that a boat was leaving in a few weeks for South Africa with a load of stock. Did he want a job as cattle tender? Well, not exactly. He wanted

most of all to go back home, and this boat to South
Africa would only take him farther away. But he had
no choice.

Before leaving, he wrote a letter to his father. No
doubt his conscience was hurting him a little. However
much Will and his father may have disagreed upon the
value of an education and other matters, Will was de-
voted to Clem and had great respect for him. This
letter from Buenos Aires, July 31, 1902, seems to show
a distinct effort on Will's part to reach some sort of
understanding:

"My dear father:
    "I will write you again, as I guess I will get away
from this country about the third of August, or four
more days. I have given this place a trial and I know
that it is no better or, for that matter, any other place
any better than the U.S. for a man with a small capital,
or none at all. I only wanted to see the country. Now,
as you say, Alf owes me enough to pay my insurance
this Fall and what other is owed me will pay for the
next year and I do not owe anyone a cent, I don't think.
    "I never cared for money, only for what pleasure
it was to spend it, and I am not afraid of work, and so,
as I am now, I feel better than I ever did in my life,
and am in good health, so don't you all worry about me.
    "I have spent a world of money in my time and I
am satisfied, as someone else has got the good of some
of it. It has not been all on myself and if you will
only give me credit for just spending my own, as I
think I have, I will be as happy as if I had a million.
    "All that worries me is people there all say—'Oh,
he is no account, he blows in all of his father's money,'
and all that kind of stuff, which is not so. I am more

than willing to admit that you have done everything in the world for me and tried to make something more than I am out of me (which is not your fault) but as to our financial dealings, I think I paid you all up and everyone else.

"I only write these things so we may better understand each other. I cannot help it because my nature is not like other people, and I don't want you all to think I am no good because I don't keep my money. I have less than lots of you and I daresay I enjoy life better than any of you, and that is my policy. I have always dealt honestly with everyone and think the world and all of you and all the folks, and will be among you all soon as happy as any one in the world, as then I can work and show the people that I am only spending what I make.

"Send this up to the girls, as I have not time just now to write to them, as they are shaping up the stock, getting ready to go in a few days. I will write you a long letter as soon as I land, which I guess will be about the 25 of August.

"I got your letter and the papers from you and the girls but no letters from them. I see they are all marrying off pretty fast up there. I will have to hurry home or I will be left out.

"Have you that diamond stud that I left in your desk?

"I will close hoping to hear from you all soon. Don't think about me, for I am the happiest one in the lot, and will get along all O.K. Address my mail to me at Capetown, care of the American Consul, South Africa, although we go about 600 miles around the other side of it to Port Natal I guess I will get it all right. With all my love to a loving father,

"Willie"

Ocean voyages, in his early years, were always agony
for Will. Superbly healthy on land, on shipboard he
was seasick from the time land disappeared until land
came into view again. (It was not until his trip around
the world in 1931, I believe, that Will crossed an ocean
in comfort.) The cruise on the *Kelvinside,* from Buenos
Aires to Durban, lasted twenty-five days. Will was
presently appointed night watchman on the cattle
deck—since, as he said, they couldn't fire him and he
was too sick to be good for anything else.

The *Kelvinside* wasn't just a cattle boat; it was almost, in Will's words, "a menagerie ship." "There were
500 head of cattle, 700 hard-tail mules, 400 horses, and
on a specially built deck, a flock of wooly sheep. The
ship was manned by a German crew. There was an
Irish veterinary, who spent most of his time working
over me; and the owner of the stock, a fine old gentleman."

This English subject, a Mr. Piccione, had an estate
in South Africa where he raised and trained thoroughbred horses. And he had promised Will work. At this
time, shortly after the end of the Boer War, a man had
to have either a job or a certain amount of money to
be allowed to land in British South Africa. And since
Will lacked the certain amount of money, Mr. Piccione's offer of a job was all that made it possible for
him to get into the country.

Years later Will described it this way: "I soon found
out that I couldn't wrastle with a bale of hay and a
dose of seasickness at the same time, but they couldn't
fire me, so I was appointed night watchman on the

deck where the cows were. Well, after I did get so I could eat stuff without a return ticket on it, there wasn't much of anything left to eat.

"Well, I sat around there all night trying to figure out a way to land some extra nourishment. Some of the cows had calves. So I got a rope and tied the calves off away from their mothers and late at night I would go and try to milk these old wild cows.

"They were not dairy stock and these old sneaky heffers were mighty hard to get next to. After bear fighting them around and getting kicked over till pretty near daylight, I might have a little pint cup full of milk. I would take this up to the cook, who was tickled to get fresh milk in the middle of the ocean to use in his cooking. Well, I got plenty to eat after that and had better fare than the old Englishman had."

Off the coast of Africa, the *Kelvinside* ran into rough weather, but, fortunately, was too late to be caught in the worst of it. Several ships just a day or two ahead went down with all hands. The bad weather continued and while the *Kelvinside* was unloading in Port Natal, the harbor for Durban, one of the worst storms in years wrecked many vessels in the bay. Will himself narrowly escaped being swept overboard.

Driving stock from the port to his employer's ranch up the Mooi River, Will was astonished by the natives.

"You have to see them to realize what wild looking people they are [he wrote his father]. All have rings, chains and all kinds of old scrap iron in their ears or noses. Lots of them have horns tied on their heads.

They travel at a run all the time and they are always singing. They are as crazy as snakes. We are in Zululand and they are the hardest layout in the lot."

Of his duties on the new ranch, Will wrote:

"My principal work is to care for and help feed the thoroughbred horses and to take them out for exercise gallops every day. And when I'm not doing that, I help the veterinary surgeon in the hospital, as there are always some sick or crippled horses or mules. The only time I get to use my saddle is once or twice a week on a big old horse, to drag off the dead ones. This week I've been helping the blacksmith shoe horses and have also been roaching mules and docking horses. In the center of one of the big rock barns is a place like a circus ring, and here is where I show the horses.

"Today is Sunday and it has been an unusually hard day. Two big buyers were here and we worked very hard getting all cleaned up and the horses rubbed down. Then out they came. Only two of us were allowed to show the horses. Well, this evening here is what he did to show the visitors some excitement. He took a mare that had only been ridden a time or two and made her jump this high thing which is solid as a rock. I, hearing the melee, rushed out to see, and no sooner had I appeared than he hollered out to 'Yank' (that is what I am known by) to get on and ride her over. He took me so by surprise, and before all the hands on the farm, I told him that I had never ridden over hurdles, but that I guessed I could try. Fancy being on a horse without a bridle or saddle and a solid four-foot wall in front of you. We took the hurdle all right and were kept at it until the mare gave out, but I got so I could do it pretty well. Now he is going to school several— and I am to be the steeplechase jockey."

It has often been said that Will broke horses for the British Army in South Africa. Among the interviews in some of his old scrap books, I find where Will has even been quoted as saying this. And it would have been possible; though the Boer War was over, there was still an Army of Occupation. But from his letters home and the account he gives of how he spent his time in Africa, he simply could not have crowded it in. There was, however, a remount station near his employer's ranch, and Will liked to visit the station. From American cowboys who were working there, he heard many tales of the British horsemanship.

"American and Australian horses [Will wrote after his return home] killed and crippled more soldiers than the Boers did. They told the story over there at the Remount Station, that when a company would get new horses and they would holler 'Company Mount,' in ten seconds you couldn't see anything but loose horses and Tommies coming up and digging the dirt out of their eyes. But you have to slip it to 'em for nerve, cause soon as they got their bearings they wanted to try it again.

"During the war there was one regiment of high collars from London, that was known as 'DeWet's Remounts.' After having tea and their nails manicured, they would start out with all their fancy uniforms and good horses. The Boer General DeWet would catch 'em and take their horses and part of their wardrobe and their guns away from 'em and turn 'em loose to go get remounted. And then get 'em all over again."

I remember Will telling about two English officers

from this near-by garrison who frequently rode over in the evening to call on his employer's attractive daughters. "Yank's" job was to take care of the guests' horses and walk them around—for which he customarily received a two-shilling tip. Will didn't want the money so much as he wanted an excuse to stay around the house, where he could hear the girls and their guests play the piano and sing. Instead of walking the horses, he would tie them to a convenient tree and stroll near the window to listen to the music.

Will was still interested in keeping up with all the latest songs, but these people inside the big house sang only old ones that were not much to his taste. And he told me he could hardly keep from going in and offering to teach the British some of the snappy coon songs he knew.

After two months on the Piccione estate, Will wrote his father from Durban on November 26th:

"I have been at work all the time but quit and come in here to get a pass to go to another place (as you have to get a permit to go about the country or on railway) and I lost all of my baggage, that is my saddle and outfit and in fact all but a little grip I had with me. It was lost or stolen off the train, as they don't check things here and neither are they responsible for them. I have been hanging around here in hopes they would hear of them, but I guess they were taken.

"About the time you get this you should get a postal money order for 28 pounds in English money (that is in American $140) for my next insurance. As I guess you had enough for the last out of what I was owed there. I only send this now because I have it and I don't need any money now for I go to work for a man in a day or two. I think I will be home before it is time to pay that again but by sending it now we know that it will be provided for.

"I have the job taking a bunch of mules to Lady-smith, that is 150 miles from here. I will have some of the native boys to help me—they drive a world of stock from here as this is where it is landed from other places as they are trying to restock the country after the war. It costs too much to ship them and they only have to hire one white man and a lot of natives so it is much cheaper. They often drive to Pretoria which is close to 400 miles, cattle and horses both.

"Don't look for me for a couple or three months as I could do nothing by getting there in the winter. But I expect to turn up there in April. But if I don't get home, tell Jim Rider he can rope on 'Old Comanche' next Fourth.

"I will write soon again to a loving father from your loving son,

"Willie"

CHAPTER VI

TEXAS JACK'S WILD WEST CIRCUS was playing in Ladysmith when Will arrived. Compared to American circuses, it was not much of an outfit, but the entertainment was new and strange in South Africa, and the show had been successful. Will had heard of it, of course, and having been away from home almost a year, he was eager to know if Texas Jack was an American, if he really came from Texas and if he knew any of the boys Will knew. Texas Jack was an American and he was from Texas, and at their first meeting the showman asked Will how good he was at roping and riding. Will said he wasn't much of a rider, but he could do a few tricks with a rope.

"I would like to tell you of a little money I missed making [he wrote to his father]. For five years Texas Jack has been offering fifty pounds to any one who could do a trick that he does—the Big Crinoline—where he lets out all of his rope. When he asked me what I could do, the first thing I did was that trick, which is common at home. Of course, I knew nothing of the reward until I joined them, for he gave me a job right then and there, and we cannot try after joining the show."

Will had never had any idea of going into show business, and his career found its beginning in that accidental meeting in South Africa.

"I was hired to do roping in the ring, [he said in a letter] but the man who rides the pitching horse is laid off and I have been riding the pitching horse ever since I have been with the show. He also has a lot of plays showing Western life. I take the Indian part in some and the Negro part in others. I get $20 a week and sleeping cars to sleep in, but have to pay for my meals, which are very dear—at least 75 cents a meal. There are about 40 people with the show and about 30 horses.

"We generally stay in a town two or three days and in the large ones longer. I do all the roping and am called 'The Cherokee Kid' on the program. I have learned to do quite a bit of fancy roping, and it takes fine over here where they know nothing whatever about it.

"The matinee is especially for children and is always crowded. Jack gives a medal to the little boy who throws the rope the best. I am their ideal. They see me rope in the show and follow me around to get me to show them, so they can get the medal."

Will had trouble finding good ropes in South Africa and on March 27, 1903, he sent this letter to his father:

"I am writing to ask you to send me some rope. I want about 100 feet of the best kind of hard twist rope. You can get it there. Any of the boys will show you what I used to use. Pretty small, but hard twist. I can't get a thing here that we use. Some nights I rope with old tie ropes or any old thing. Please send this at once. Send it so it will come the quickest, fastest and shortest way—no matter the cost. I am getting blooded aint I?

"I wrote to Sallie for some coon songs. If she didn't get the letter, tell her to send me a whole lot please."

Will always regarded the nine months he spent with Texas Jack as one of the most important periods of his life. He came to admire the older man's experience and skill as a showman, and it was only natural that he should be influenced in the same direction. Texas Jack liked Will, encouraged him in every way and was glad to teach him all he knew. Will kept working with his rope, improving his old tricks and experimenting with new ones. Billed as "The Cherokee Kid—the Man Who Can Lasso the Tail off a Blowfly," he began to justify his billing. Will had christened himself and with youthful pride had had cards and letterheads printed. In his scrapbook, I found one of his cards:

THE CHEROKEE KID
FANCY LASSO ARTIST AND ROUGH RIDER
TEXAS JACK'S WILD WEST CIRCUS

In writing home, Will tried to reassure his father about circus life. "It isn't a wild mob like them at home, [he said] for Jack don't drink a drop or smoke or gamble, and likes his men to be the same. He is a man about 40 years old and has traveled all over the world. He is a much finer shot than Buffalo Bill. Of course the business is not the best business, but as long as there is good money in it and it is honest, there is no objection to it. I still keep sober and don't gamble, and Jack thinks a lot of me. I'm going to learn things while I'm with him that will enable me to make my living in the world without making it by day labor."

In a later letter he wrote, "I'm getting homesick, but don't know what I'd do there more than make a living. As it is, I'm off here bothering and worrying no one, and getting along first rate."

In August of 1903 he was still with the show, still in South Africa, and still planning, or thought he was, on coming home as soon as possible. A letter he wrote at this time shows him to be a little confused about how he really felt. In closing, he said, "Write when you can to your contented son, Willie." And then, on second thought, he postscripted, "Don't anyone write until you hear from me again, as I won't be here that long." And his second thought was correct.

He had heard of the Wirth Brothers Circus in Australia, and the idea of going home that way, by pushing on around the world, appealed to him. When he left, Texas Jack gave him this letter of recommendation:

"I have the very great pleasure of recommending Mr. W. P. Rogers (The Cherokee Kid) to circus proprietors. He has performed with me during my present South African tour and I consider him to be the champion trick rough rider and lasso thrower of the world. He is sober, industrious, hard working at all times and is always to be relied upon. I shall be very pleased to give him an engagement at any time should he wish to return."

Will always saved this letter, written in dramatic script and on stationery adorned by a full-length picture of flowing-haired Texas Jack, "World's Greatest Sharpshooter." It got him his job with the Wirth Brothers Circus after he had spent twenty days of agony sailing across the Indian Ocean to New Zealand, then five days more, on the same boat, back to Australia.

The Wirths were one of the great theatrical families of Australia. George Wirth engaged Will at once, and he and his wife made him practically a foster son. They remained great friends of ours always.

Now billed as "The Cherokee Kid, the Mexican Rope Artist," Will toured Australia and then New Zealand with the Wirths.

Will had worked hard for nine months with Texas Jack on a salary of twenty dollars a week. He had saved his money carefully, guarding it in a money belt he wore around his waist, with the ever present thought of being able to buy a steamship ticket back to Indian Territory. He had been away from his family so long that he was very homesick. And he had intended to stay but a few weeks with the Wirth show and then sail home to spend Christmas with his father and sisters.

But news of his money belt leaked out and Will was invited into a game of cards. He was young, knew little about cards and gambling, and he lost every cent of his savings. As a result, he had to postpone his return home and stayed on with the Wirth Circus for almost eight months in order to make a stake again; it gave Will a lesson in gambling that he never forgot.

"Don't get excited when you look on the map and see where I am now [Will warned his father in a letter from Wellington, New Zealand]. But I want to see a bit more and then get back home—consequently, must be on the move. I will be here a few more months, and then I am heading around this old globe to see if it really is round. I will land in America on the West Coast and then come on home."

When the New Zealand tour was finished, Will left the show and started for the United States. The first leg of his journey was an overnight trip on a small coastwise steamer. Will, of course, expected his usual seasickness. "The train I was on pulled up beside the boat," he said, "and knowing that I was going to be seasick, I rushed aboard right away, and I said to myself, I will get in the bunk and maybe that will help. Well it's the paint and that smell of varnish that does it. I got a whiff of it going down, and I crawled right into my bunk (which was among a lot of other men's bunks).

"Now I was under the impression that the boat was going to pull right out. And sure enough I started in being sick; I was going strong. I thought, well I haven't long to be sick—it's a short trip and we will be in there before long—and pretty soon some fellow came in and asked another fellow, 'What's the matter with this boat, ain't it ever going to pull out?' "

Finally Will was on his way to San Francisco. He arrived there in April, 1904. He had been gone two years; he had encircled the world, traveled more than fifty thousand miles, and he wanted to be home. He said long afterward, "I started out first class. Then I traveled second class, then third class. And when I was companion to the she cows, was what might be called no class at all. It took me two years to get enough money to get back home on, and Old Glory sure looked good to me when I sighted it outside of Golden Gate."

Nineteen hundred and four was a wonderful year. Theodore Roosevelt was President; there was general prosperity; and to youngsters of my generation the World's Fair in St. Louis was the last word in progress. It was there that I met Will Rogers again.

I had come up from my home in Arkansas to visit a sister who lived in St. Louis and to take in the fair. Though I had heard vaguely that Will had returned, I had received no word from him and had no inkling of where he was or what he might be doing.

Wandering aimlessly through the Oklahoma State Building at the exposition, I heard someone near me mention the name of Will Rogers. An Indian girl was telling her companion that she had seen Will Rogers perform that afternoon at the Cummins Wild West Show on the Pike in the fairgrounds.

I sent a note to Will at once. An answer came almost immediately, inviting my sister and me to a matinee performance of his show the next day, and to dinner afterward.

Mary Quisenberry was also visiting my sister and went with us. The girls, of course, were curious about my circus friend and made no secret of the fact that they thought the occupation an undignified one for a young man with Will's advantages. Though I wanted to see Will very much, I had a wide streak of conventionality in me, and I was not particularly thrilled about Will's profession. But I hid my misgivings and tried not to hear the teasing and joking.

Finally Will entered the arena for his roping act. To my horror, he was decked out in a very tight-fitting red velvet suit, bespattered with gold braid. He looked so funny, and I was so embarrassed when my sister and Mary gave me sidelong glances and smiled at the costume, that I didn't hear the applause or find much joy in Will's expertness with the rope.

Not until later did Will tell me the story of the red velvet suit. It wasn't his regular costume for the act. Usually he wore chaps, a colored shirt and a handkerchief around his neck, but today he had wanted to look his very best. He had worn the red velvet suit for my special benefit. Because Mexican cowboys had created the first tricks with the lasso, the Wirth Brothers Circus in Australia had advertised Will as "The Mexican Rope Artist," and Mrs. George Wirth had made the velvet costume with her own hands. Will was proud of the suit—it was one of his treasured possessions—but he never wore it again.

Will had asked us to wait for him after the show. We waited and waited. Everyone had gone and my sister and Mary were on the verge of leaving me when Will finally appeared, breathless and apologetic. He explained that he had quit the Cummins Wild West Show, that this was his last performance, and that he had been chasing the manager all over the grounds, trying to get his back salary. He expected to leave the next day for Oklahoma.

Will and I, after getting away from the other two, had dinner together and toured the Midway. We bought tickets for the Irish Village, and there, among the thatched roofs, heard John McCormack, who was singing in America for the first time that summer. And we always remembered it. Years later, John McCormack and Will became good friends and his autographed picture hangs today in a special place on the walls of our ranch house in Santa Monica.

As we strolled through the carnival gaiety of the Midway, I found out what Will had been doing since his return to the United States.

Uncle Clem, of course, had wanted him to stay home and settle down to business. But Will had heard that Colonel Zach Mulhall was putting on a Wild West show at the Delmar Gardens in St. Louis.

After a short visit at home with his family, he shipped Comanche, his old roping pony, and caught a train for St. Louis. It was at this point that Uncle Clem, his patience exhausted, confided to friends that no boy who wasted his time around Wild West circuses could ever amount to anything.

But Will hadn't returned home with the idea of giving up show business, at least not yet. Texas Jack had suggested to him that his single roping act might do well on the vaudeville stage. Will wanted to try it. And when the Mulhall show closed that summer, he got his chance.

He had his tryout in a burlesque show at the old Standard Theater in St. Louis. Colonel Hopkins, a well-known theater owner, saw the roping act and liked it. He wrote a letter to J. J. Murdock, owner of a string of vaudeville theaters, and Will was given a week's engagement in one of the Murdock theaters in Chicago at thirty dollars.

Will was ignorant of vaudeville customs; he sent no photographs or publicity material on ahead. And as a result, his engagement was canceled. He arrived in Chicago to find that there were no pictures of him in the lobby of the theater and that his name was not even on the program. Disappointed, but still determined, he stayed on in Chicago and haunted all the booking offices.

A few days later he started in to see a show at the Cleveland Theater on Wabash Avenue. While buying his ticket he overheard the house manager talking over the telephone, saying that he wanted an act immediately. Will said he had an act and the manager asked how long it would take him to get ready.

"Just as long," Will said, "as it will take me to go to my hotel and get my ropes."

Will opened the show that afternoon and played there for the rest of the week. During a matinee he was on the stage doing a routine he had perfected while with Texas Jack, when a dog from a trained-animal act on the same bill came dashing out of the wings. Almost automatically Will threw his rope and caught the dog as he ran across the stage. The catch brought a big laugh and loud applause.

"It gave me a tip," Will said. "Instead of trying to keep on with a single roping act, I decided that people wanted to see me catch something." So he began at once to figure out a routine of catches he could do with a horse. A running horse had never been roped on the stage, but Will knew it could be done with the right kind of a horse, and he knew just the horse he wanted—a little pony at the Mulhall ranch in Oklahoma. Mrs.

Mulhall owned the pony and had offered to let Will have him for $100. Will didn't have the $100, and it was to earn the money to finance the new act that he had gone into the Cummins Wild West Indian Congress of Rough Riders of the World.

When I saw him, Will had been working in the Cummins show for several weeks, and now, with a railroad pass to Oklahoma in his pocket, he was going to purchase the pony for his new act.

He promised to write when we parted that evening in St. Louis and I heard from him several times. He returned to Oklahoma, bought his pony and named him Teddy for Colonel Roosevelt. He staked out a plot of ground about the size of a stage and began practicing his new act. He had worked out all of his fancy catches and expected to leave with Colonel Mulhall who was putting on a Wild West exhibition in connection with the National Horse Show in New York.

Top: Betty Blake and her six sisters, from left to right: Cora (Mrs. Will Marshall), Anna (Mrs. Lee Adamson), Waite (Mrs. Arthur Ireland), Theda ("Aunt Dick," who never married), Betty (Mrs. Will Rogers), Virginia (Mrs. Bruce Quisenberry), Zuleki (Mrs. Everett Stroud). *Bottom:* The Blake family at home in Rogers, Arkansas, left to right: Zuleki, standing back of Maxine Marshall; Grandmother Crowder, Amelia's mother (seated), Mrs. Amelia Crowder Blake, Cora and her husband, Waite, Anna and husband; Betty (seated), Theda (in front of Betty), Sandy (J. K. Blake, only brother), Bruce Quisenberry, and Virginia Quisenberry. *(Courtesy Will Rogers Memorial)*

Mrs. Will Rogers when she was Betty Blake, 1908. *(Courtesy Will Rogers Memorial)*

CHAPTER VII

Spring came and Will went East. He shipped Teddy and his old roping horse Comanche to New York with the Mulhall stock and made his New York debut in the old Madison Square Garden, April 27, 1905, with the rest of the Mulhall riders and ropers.

I still heard from him, and once he sent me a newspaper clipping of which he was very proud. During a performance in the Garden, a wild steer broke away, jumped the guard rail and headed up into the grandstand. The spectators were in a panic. Police and cowboys tried to head him off, but the frightened animal kept charging toward the crowd. Will grabbed his rope, ran up the steps and circled in behind the stampeding steer; with cool, quick judgment he threw his loops, made a safe catch and pulled the steer back into the arena. The audience rose in applause and next day Will saw his name on the front pages of all the metropolitan newspapers.

Colonel Mulhall knew that Will's real purpose in going East with him was to get started with his new vaudeville act, but since Will's roping had become a popular feature, the Colonel was annoyed when Will refused to continue with the troupe.

Knowing Will's fondness for his old roping pony, Comanche, Colonel Mulhall jokingly refused to let him take the pony out of the Garden stalls, hoping that Will would soon be back with the show. Will was hotheaded in those days. In the dead of night, he and Jim Minnick, a Texas cowboy and lifelong friend of Will's, kidnapped Comanche from the Garden stalls and hid him uptown in a side-street livery stable.

Somehow the colonel got wind of the pony's hideout, and he was determined not to let Will get the better of him in what he considered a practical joke. He sent one of his men to the livery stable and, when Comanche was brought back, shipped the pony away with the rest of the Mulhall stock before Will knew anything about it.

But nothing about horses was ever a joke to Will. Comanche was growing old and Will had a deep affection for his old pony. Not until years later, after Will and I were married, did Colonel Mulhall and Will clear up their misunderstanding. Colonel Mulhall was always very fond of Will. It had never been his intention to keep Comanche and he regretted the whole incident. The pony had not been used in the Mulhall show. Instead he had been put out on pasture in Florida, where he grew sleek, fat and happy. Will had intended shipping him back home, but Comanche never returned to Oologah. Full of honors and triumphs and remembered by hundreds of cowboys around the rodeos as the king of cow ponies, he died soon afterward in his Florida meadow.

On June 11, 1905, Will made his first appearance on a New York stage. The vaudeville agents had stared at him incredulously when, armed with a letter from Colonel Hopkins, Will told them he wanted to rope a running horse on the stage.

"It can't be done," they said flatly; there wasn't room on any stage for such an act. But Will was not easily put off and finally they sent him down to Keith's old Union Square Theater to do a "supper show."

"It was 6:30 on a hot afternoon," Will wrote of his first performance, "when the ten or twelve people that were in there laid their afternoon papers down and kidded us into a pretty good hit."

With Jim Minnick riding for his catches, Will played through the week, and readily consented when the manager suggested that he do three shows a day. Most of the principal performers did only two shows, but Will, naïve Oklahoma boy that he was, felt very proud of being asked to do the extra show. Other actors tried to make him understand that only the minor acts had to appear in the suppertime performance, but Will was feeling important now and believed these other actors were jealous.

When Jim Minnick had to leave for his ranch in Texas, Buck McKee, an Oklahoma cowboy and, according to legend, a one-time sheriff of Pawnee County, began to ride for Will. Buck stayed with the act as long as Will used a horse on the stage; the act, incidentally, was listed with booking agents as a "dumb act"—Will did no talking whatever, and at first used no special music.

A few weeks later someone suggested to Will that it might be a good thing for the act if he announced one difficult catch from the stage. Without preparing what he would say or deciding how he would say it, Will stopped the orchestra and announced the trick.

The audience started laughing. Will was embarrassed and angry. He had no idea that his Southwestern drawl was either pleasing or comic. Not meaning to say anything funny, he thought the audience was making sport of him, and he wanted to quit then and there. Will was always joking and clowning with his friends and with members of the other acts; but laughter coming from a crowd of strangers was something else again. Will didn't like it. Other performers on the program tried to tell him that it was fine, that a laugh was the best thing for his act and by all means to leave it in, but Will took his roping seriously and he was a long time getting used to being laughed at.

The act was a novelty and well received from the beginning. Soon Will was booked to play the Paradise Roof for three weeks. Hammerstein's Paradise Roof and Hammerstein's Victoria Theater were the leading vaudeville houses, and an act booked there was beginning to arrive. By this time, Will had his own special musical score—a medley of tunes, including *Pony Boy* and other Western songs. The orchestra, with the brasses bearing down for all they were worth, played loudly as Will made his entrance on Teddy. Will wore his customary chaps, colored shirt and a small hat.

Teddy was a beautiful little pony—a dark bay with black mane and tail—well reined, and very quick in starting and stopping. He wore specially made felt boots, buckled on like galoshes, to prevent slipping on the wooden stage. After Will made his spectacular entrance, he gave Teddy an affectionate slap on the rump and sent him scampering into the wings.

Will opened the act with his single trick roping specialty, which he did easily and in rhythm with the soft music of the orchestra. He used many ropes, all of different lengths and each of them with a differently weighted honda—balanced precisely for the particular trick for which it was used. Most of them were soft cotton ropes and were already there placed in neat coils just behind the footlights.

For the fancy horse catches which came later in the act, a heavier rope, stiffer and more tightly woven, was used. Teddy would stand in the wings, his ears arched, nervously waiting for his cue. When Will called "Right!" Teddy would dash out instantly with Buck in the saddle. Before Teddy and rider could reach the footlights, Will's lariat had caught the horse by all four feet. Then horse and rider would dash off the stage to wait for the next signal.

There were many catches—throwing two ropes at once, catching the man with one loop and the horse with the other; a three-rope catch, a nose catch, a figure eight, and a tail catch so difficult that Will never ceased practicing on it. Another variation was to rope Buck, and then throw a half hitch around his hands, another over his head, another around his body, and so on until he was completely tied and helpless.

The act closed with the beautiful big loop, called "the Crinoline"—the same that had won Will his job with Texas Jack. A rope of some 90 or 100 feet was used. Handing one end of the rope to an usher, Will would ask the boy to back down the aisle to the rear of the house. Standing on the edge of the stage, Will would hold up the other end of the rope so the audience could see for itself how much was used. Then, mounting Teddy center stage just back of the footlights, he would start twirling the rope in a very small loop, vertical at first. Gradually he would let out the rope as he lifted the circle over his head, spinning it out into larger and larger whirls until, in a beautiful big circle, the rope was whizzing high over the heads of the orchestra. The people in the front rows of the audience were amused and sometimes a little frightened to hear the swish of the rope that swung above their heads. The spinning loop of 100 feet was very heavy, but Will managed to keep it going until, pulling Teddy back, he let the big heavy loop fall to the floor with a bang. Then, giving a cowboy whoop, he whirled Teddy around and dashed off the stage into the wings.

The first night on the Paradise Roof was a great success and the applause at the end of the act lasted a long time. Ernest Hogan, a great Negro entertainer of the time, was playing on the bill and standing in the wings as Will took a bow and started for his dressing room. Hogan seized Will bodily and pushed him out in front of the curtain again. As Will told it: "I went fine and took a bow and started to my dressing room when Hogan grabbed me and pushed me out in front of the curtains. As I came off, he apologized and said, 'Boy, don't overlook any of them; them ain't bows. Them's curtain calls and there's darned few of them up here.'"

Will was paid $125 a week. With a salary to Buck, board for his pony and an agent's commission, there was little left. "I waited and waited," said Will in later years, "trying to muster up enough courage to ask Willie Hammerstein for a raise—and the raise I finally asked for was ten dollars."

Gradually learning the tricks of showmanship, Will bought Teddy a beautiful dark blue blanket bordered with a gold band and with the name "Will Rogers" in huge gold letters. Buck always chose a stable near the theater for the horse, and when they landed in a new city, Buck would ride Teddy until he reached the main thoroughfare. Then he would get off and Teddy, without a halter of any kind, would follow Buck down the street and up to the stage door. This always attracted attention in the streets. Small boys fell into procession, and by the time the stage door was reached, one might think the Pied Piper had come to town.

Will was too busy to get home that year for Christmas, but he kept his family supplied with clippings, and Uncle Clem, though still skeptical, was almost reconciled to the way Willie chose to spend his time. Then in the early spring of 1906, just before leaving for Europe, Will made a quick visit home. And Clem himself must have been a little impressed when he learned that Willie's act had been booked for the Winter Garden in Berlin. The Winter Garden in that heyday of the theater was the most important for variety on the continent. It was a reputation just to have played there. Will shipped Teddy over on a slow boat and managed to go home to Oklahoma for a brief visit before taking a fast liner to Europe and arrived in Berlin about the same time Buck and Teddy arrived.

It was on Will's return from this European trip that I met his family for the first time. His three sisters lived in Chelsea, Oklahoma, and one day a letter came from Maude inviting me to a house party, which she and her husband, Cap Lane, were giving in honor of Willie. Three other girls, Gazelle Lane, Ada Foreman and Mary Gulager had been invited. Mary was Will's first cousin, a very pretty girl, witty and full of fun. Cap Lane's mother and his sister Nell had come on from Paris, Texas, and also were guests.

Will's first showing in Europe had been a minor triumph, his success in Berlin bringing him two weeks' booking at London's leading music hall, the Palace. I don't think Will realized how he had caught the fancy of the English, even when Sir Alfred Butt, manager of the Palace, told him that he had been asked to appear before the exclusive Ranelagh Club. Will took Teddy, his roping pony, and went through his act, not knowing until later, when the club presented him with a beautiful silver cup, that King Edward VII had been present.

Will had become a well-established vaudeville performer in an unusually short time. It was little over a year ago that he had left to join the Mulhall show in Madison Square Garden, and this summer in Chelsea was his first long visit back to Oklahoma since then.

Chelsea was hardly a hundred miles from my home in Arkansas, but I had to take a roundabout way to get there. Leaving on a slow train at four-thirty in the morning and changing to another slow train at Monett, Missouri, I was due in Chelsea at two o'clock in the afternoon. It was a hot summer day and I had to ride the whole way in day coaches. I was completely bored and weary when the train pulled up at Vinita, twenty miles from Chelsea and still a good hour's ride on the slow train. There, to my great surprise and delight, Will walked into my coach.

His theatrical success hadn't changed him a bit. He was still bashful, and at this particular moment fate played a low trick on his gallantry. For after he had come up to Vinita on an early-morning train to meet me, it happened that the chair next to mine was occupied. Will reached over, shook hands and then found a seat for himself far ahead in the crowded coach. And that was the way we finished the journey.

Maude and her guests were at the station in Chelsea to meet me. When Will stepped down from the train carrying my two heavy bags, the girls immediately started teasing. No one had come up the road to meet them and they said, "Why all the chivalry?" After that, neither of us had any peace.

Will's sister May lived some twelve miles out of Chelsea. Sallie and Maude lived just on the outskirts of town. Both had beautiful country places, with room for the many friends who came to visit them, and they always had company. Relatives and friends were constantly dropping in for dinner. Often guests would come to stay for a few days, or for a few weeks. It was not at all unusual that three times a day their tables would be set for twenty places.

Maude's house itself had been planned for guests. Upstairs a screened-in sleeping porch extended across the back, and there were five large bedrooms, one of which was Willie's room. Years before when Maude and Cap Lane had built their new home, they had set aside a room for Will. The furniture in it was his, the pictures on the walls and the little trinkets in the room belonged to him. No matter how crowded their home might be with company, Maude never allowed anyone to use Willie's room—it was a sacred spot in the family household.

In spite of his first attentive gestures, Will was very elusive during the busy days Maude and Sallie had planned for us. We took horseback rides around the country. Parties and dinners were given. But half of the time Will wouldn't go, and if he did, he never looked in my direction or singled me out. We all went together in a crowd and came home the same way. Even on our moonlight horseback rides, we both rode up in front with the rest of the riders. He never came around where I was unless we were playing and singing at the piano. I just could not understand him.

I had a wonderful time, despite Will's apparent indifference, and grew very fond of his sisters and his friends. So far as Will himself was concerned, I was a baffled young lady when I left for home. But I had been home not more than a week, I believe, when he came by on his way to New York, with the idea that we should get married at once.

Top: Party in Claremore, summer of 1906: In front seat of wagon: Betty Blake and Ida Collins. Seated man in front unidentified. Standing in wagon: with cigar in mouth, Dick Parris (who went to South America with Will), Tom Lane, Taylor Foreman, Denny Lane. Seated in wagon: Bess Schrimsher (Will's cousin), Shasta Lane, Gazelle Lane, unidentified man, Ada Foreman, Will Rogers. *Bottom:* In his red velvet suit made by Mrs. Wirth, Will performs for group of youngsters while with the Wirth Brothers Circus in Australia, where he was billed as "The Mexican Rope Artist." *(Courtesy Will Rogers Memorial)*

Top: Betty and a well-dressed Will pose with friend at Brighton Beach, London, summer of 1914. *Bottom:* Will and Betty on tour. *(Courtesy Will Rogers Memorial)*

Top: Sightseeing in Atlantic City, 1908. *Middle left:* As the "Mexican Rope Artist" in Australia, 1903. *Middle right:* As a prospective bridegroom in New York, 1908. *Bottom:* In Goldwyn Studio, with son Jimmy, 1922.

Top: Proud parents with oldest son Bill, in New York, 1913. *Bottom:* The family, about 1916–17, in Overland car, while living on Long Island, New York and while Will was in the *Follies:* Will, Jimmy, Mary, Bill, and Betty. *(Courtesy Will Rogers Museum)*

CHAPTER VIII

Will was earning $200 a week, had a good season booked for the fall and winter, and was proud of his success in the theater. He had no intention of giving up his stage career and settling down at home. But from my point of view, show business was not a very stable occupation. All I knew about the theater and the people connected with it had been gathered from the little traveling shows that visited our town from time to time. And I simply could not see a life of trouping the country in vaudeville. Will could not understand my attitude. Our parting was a sad one, but we promised to write.

Late that winter, just before the holidays, Will was in Syracuse, New York, and in a sentimental mood. He sent me from there a little lace handkerchief. This was his Christmas gift. "I want to send you a little token," his letter said, "that I have carried with me and which I prize very highly (although not of much financial value)." He explained that he had got the handkerchief in South America, after "landing there flush," when he bought his sisters a quantity of lace and needle-work to send home by Dick Parris. Parris had smuggled this in, Will admitted, "since there is a very high duty."

"The old Indian lady I bought it from, [Will continued] gave me this handkerchief, asking me if I was married. I said 'No.' She said, 'then give it to the wife when you do marry.' I have kept it, carried it all through Africa at times when I didn't have a cent and was actually hungry, then to Australia, then back home,—and on all my travels I did intend always to do as the old woman said, but I guess there's nothing doing for me. I will just give it to you as I kinda prize it. And you might do the same. Hoping you have a Happy Christmas and Grand New Year.''

Shortly afterward in the early part of the new year (this was 1907), and acting on impulse, without preparation of any kind, Will left New York to try England with a larger act. He took along two cowboys besides Buck McKee, three ponies in addition to Teddy, and planned to stage a real Wild West show—bucking horses and everything—in the theaters of London and Berlin.

But the act was too big and perhaps poorly organized. It simply didn't click. Stranded in London, with men and horses to board, Will had to take his regular roping act, just Buck and Teddy, on a tour of the Provinces, to meet expenses and to get his troupe back to the United States. Once more on home ground and after dropping the additional men and horses, Will had no trouble getting bookings for his old act and was now able to demand $250 a week. He continued to play the circuits regularly and during this time made one brief trip home.

Will was feeling quite prosperous now. But it was difficult for him to save, since he could never resist a salesman. Those were the good old days of vaudeville, and salesmen of all kinds—furs, diamonds, anything that would tempt the actor—haunted the stage doors. Besides furs for me, Will had purchased for himself a huge diamond ring—slightly yellow—and two conspicuous diamond scarf pins. These were considered important to a rising young man in the theater, and actors believed earnestly that diamonds were a sound investment. In fact, they did mean quick money when stranded, and Will's diamond, in our early days together, was often in and out of hock. Will never wore the ring; he never wore jewelry of any kind. During the war years he decided to sell the ring and invest the money in Liberty Bonds. Diamond prices were depressed and he could find no buyer. Then one day a Mr. Brady, of Philadelphia, whom Will knew, introduced him to a man who said he had a friend—a racing man—who might be interested in the stone. Will was elated and turned the ring over at once to Mr. Brady's friend. Weeks passed and nothing happened. Will had no receipt for the ring, nor as much as an acknowledgment. I questioned him about the supposed buyer, and he seemed to know nothing whatever about him, except that he was interested in race horses. He didn't know his name, never had seen him. I was amazed, but Will saw nothing unusual in the deal.

"Don't worry," he told me, "he's all right; Brady knows a friend of his." More weeks passed and I decided that Will might at least get some much-needed worldly wisdom in exchange for his big yellow diamond. As more weeks went by, even Will had begun to wonder. But one day an envelope arrived and we learned the name of the racing man. It was written on the bottom of a check for $1,000. That was all the envelope contained. Will was not surprised. He took for granted that every man was honest, until he proved himself otherwise. And it was rarely indeed that Will was ever deliberately swindled out of anything; being easy about money, he was often overcharged. But this bothered him little, even when the fact was pointed out to him. "I would rather be the one to pay too much," he always said, "than to be the man that charged too much."

Will had a haphazard way with money that was sometimes frightening. When he was with the *Follies,* he was apt to carry in his pockets as many as eight or ten uncashed weekly pay checks, and then, to the horror of the Ziegfeld business office, deposit them in the bank at one time and almost break the company.

He never kept an account or any kind of personal business record, in spite of which he seemed always to know, as if by instinct, just what obligations had to be met and when, how much it would take to meet them and almost to a dollar what he had in the bank. When he first worked in motion pictures at a large salary, someone asked him about his personal bookkeeper. "Haven't got any bookkeeper or any bookkeeping," Will told him. "We just put a check in the bank and draw on it until it's gone."

In his early vaudeville days—along with the furs and diamonds, Will was making weekly installment payments on Long Island real estate. A well-known vaudeville team, turned salesmen, had convinced ballad singers, acrobats, dance teams and others, that a fortune awaited them at the far end of the island, on a weekly-payment basis, as soon as the transatlantic liners began docking at Montauk Point, and that was to be very soon. Long after, when we were married, we found Will's city lots in the middle of an old man's cornfield. But never were we able to locate definitely his supposed acreage near Deer Park.

Will's act was becoming very popular. His agent was able to book one vaudeville circuit after another. There were no open weeks, and when Will returned to Oklahoma again, it was because of Uncle Clem. His health had been failing for some time and a letter saying that he was in bed led Will to cancel all engagements and go home at once. Clem was ill for many weeks and during Will's time at home, he often came over to see me. He was really worried about his father, and on his visits to Rogers I found that his idea of the show business had changed. He talked of returning home to stay. He said the same old show afternoon and night was growing monotonous, and that trouping around the country was losing its interest. I felt that at last he was coming around to my way of thinking.

When Uncle Clem had completely recovered, Will left again for the East. I think we had known from the beginning that we cared for each other. His letters were now more frequent, and then one day early in November, 1908, he arrived in Rogers without any forewarning to announce flatly that he was going to take me back to New York with him.

Will had to play a few weeks' engagements in the East, and then, in early spring he was booked for a tour on the Orpheum Circuit. This would be our honeymoon, he said. I had never been East, and Will wanted me to see New York. And the prospect, afterward, of a tour to the Pacific Coast sounded very nice indeed. As for my scruples about show business, there was a most definite promise that, once this tour was finished, we would settle down in the house his father had given him in Claremore.

In two weeks we were married. The ceremony was performed at my mother's home, November 25, 1908. Will, his father and his sisters, May and Maude, were to arrive on the train at 11:30 A.M. and we were to be married immediately afterward. His sister Sallie was unable to come because her children were ill.

My mother's house was but a few blocks from the railroad station. If we left home when the train whistled, we could be at the depot by the time it arrived. That morning I remember hearing the whistle and looking through the window of my room upstairs to watch my brother drive away to meet Will and his family.

Very soon, however, I saw him driving slowly back, alone in the empty carriage, and my heart sank. He came up to my room with a woebegone look on his face, to tell me that there had been no Will and no family. I was on the verge of tears before he finally explained that the train was in two sections that day and that the wedding party was on the second section.

We had a small wedding, with just the two families

present. The ceremony was performed by Doctor
Bailey, a close friend of ours and pastor of the little
Congregational Church. I wore a blue and white silk
dress and I remember well my going-away suit of
dark blue broadcloth, ordered "special" from Marshall
Field's in Chicago, with hat and veil to match.

We drove down the muddy, deep-rutted street in a
carriage and found the whole town gathered on the station platform to bid us goodbye with rice and cheers. On
the stuffy local train—all day coaches—we settled ourselves among a group of curious passengers. But at
Monett, the division point, some fifty miles away, Will
had reserved a stateroom in the through train to St.
Louis. It was nice to be reminded then that he was
an experienced traveler and a man of the world.

Next day was Thanksgiving. We stopped off in St.
Louis, and during the afternoon went to see the Car-
lisle Indians play football. That evening Will ordered
Thanksgiving dinner served in our room at the
Planters Hotel. This was to be our real wedding celebration—champagne and everything. It was the first
champagne I had ever tasted.

Will had bought tickets for *What Every Woman
Knows,* in which the distinguished actress, Maude
Adams, was appearing. Naturally, I was delighted
with this chance to see a real New York star. The theater was packed when we arrived; it seemed to be un-
pleasantly hot and stuffy. And we were hardly more
than seated when I began to feel extremely strange—
then progressively stranger. Finally, when the brightly-
lighted stage began to tilt, I was really alarmed and

whispered to Will in a faraway voice to take me out at once.

Will quietly hustled me up the long aisle of the theater and tactfully suggested that we walk back to the hotel. We walked and walked—miles it seemed to me. I didn't understand until afterward, when Will explained that he had wondered during dinner just what sort of a girl he had married. From the way I drank champagne, he explained, he had decided champagne-drinking must be an "old Arkansas custom."

Before starting west on the Orpheum Circuit, Will had several weeks to play in and around New York City. The first week was at the Proctor's Theater in Newark, and there for the first time I watched him perform on the stage. Will had no talk in the act, except for announcements of the different tricks. And I wasn't much impressed. I must confess that I then had little interest in or curiosity about his career on the stage.

The act never ran longer than twenty minutes and Will always arrived at the theater just in time to go on. He used no makeup; Buck McKee would have the ropes laid out, and all Will had to do was slip on a dark blue flannel shirt and his leather chaps, and he was ready. Because of the horse in Will's act, he was usually last on the program. With only one matinee and one evening performance, this gave us a chance to attend the other theaters, and there was plenty of time for him to show me the sights of New York.

We saw Chinatown and the Bowery and battered our way along Wall Street at the lunch hour. We went to the Aquarium and Will pointed out the hotel down near the Battery where he and Dick Parris had stayed when they were in New York on their way to South America. To Bedloe Island and to the Statue of Liberty we went, and to the top of the Singer Building— forty-one stories high, and at that time the highest building in the world. We heard the bells of Old Trinity ring in the New Year and out the Old. Will took me to the Bronx Zoo and we had horseback rides in the arena at Durland's Riding Academy, and on nice days in Central Park. And although it made Will utterly miserable, we went many times to grand opera. I remember how Enrico Caruso laughed years later when Will told him, "The two things my wife wanted most to do on her arrival in New York were to see Grant's Tomb and hear Caruso sing."

Two very dear Arkansas friends, Mrs. W. H. (Coin) Harvey and her daughter Annette, were visiting in New York, and they took me around to the shops and gave me much-needed advice. Annette had been my best girl friend at home. I remember Mrs. Harvey's shocked expression when she discovered that Will had taken Annette and me to dinner at the Metropole Cafe. This was a rendezvous for newspapermen, gamblers, sportsmen and actors. Battling Nelson stopped at our table and Will had introduced us. Mrs. Harvey said, "Betty, what will your mother think of you meeting a prizefighter?"

Having lived always in a little town in Northwestern Arkansas, where our home had been one of the first houses built, I had really been carried into a new world

by my marriage. But it was a world in which, for all
the publicity and all the strange people met, Will and
I lived more or less alone. We were even more to ourselves when Will's Eastern engagements were filled and
we started west on his tour of the Orpheum Circuit—
which was a tour, in the full sense of the word. The
extent of my traveling had been occasional trips to
Kansas City or St. Louis, and Will was determined,
wherever he played, that I should see everything. Almost too determined, for Will was a difficult person to
keep up with. He hated to lose a moment of his life;
he wanted to do everything right now. And he nearly
ran me ragged. Occasionally I protested a little. Will
would have plans—somewhere we should go, something
we should see—for the morning. I would be feeling
lazy and suggest that we put it off till the afternoon.
But Will had an unanswerable argument against such
delay. "Do it now," he would insist. "Then we'll have
the afternoon free for something else."

But those were grand days for Will and me; we spent
all our time together—constantly on the go, taking in
the sight-seeing trips, wandering here and there, curious
about everything. If weather permitted, we would
go horseback riding in the parks of the various cities;
or on Sunday, we would take sandwiches into the
country for a picnic. It was a carefree life. We both
loved it and I soon began to wonder if the theater was
so bad after all. Outside of his brief twice-daily appearances, we really didn't have much to do with the
theater, for Will joined little in the social life of the
other troupers. After the show we usually had sand-

wiches and beer at some little restaurant or in our hotel room.

In his years of traveling, Will had always been much to himself. As a little boy on horseback, he had learned to be alone, and it had stayed with him. "I've always been a lone wolf," he used to say. "I never ran with the pack." Now that he had someone to share his life, he took great delight in telling all about himself. His life had been full and he wanted me to know all about it—the bad along with the good—every little thing as far back as he could remember. Although Will and I had been friends for a good many years, we had not been together a great deal, and actually I had known little about the boy I married.

One of our first thoughts, of course, was to save something out of Will's salary. With jewelry and Long Island real estate to pay for, and the expenses of carrying a man and a horse around, agent's commissions, railroad fare and hotel bills, there was not much left. And there were idle weeks, of course, during which Will received no salary but the expenses of the act went on just the same. But we did manage to adopt a savings plan—one that Will's sister Maude and her husband had started when they were first married. We put aside one dollar every day. Will bought a big, clumsy box with a slot in it, and we dropped a silver dollar or poked a greenback in the slot each day.

Out West most of the dollars were silver and the bank began to grow heavy. Acts were laid off for one week in order to make the long jump from St. Paul to Butte, Montana, and we arrived a few days before

Will was scheduled to open. Our first afternoon in Butte, after a fine time ice skating at an outdoor rink, we returned to the hotel late, cold and tired, to find that my trunk had been pried open. On the floor beside it, in our room, was a brand new ax, the handle broken off in the middle. Our steel box with 125 days of a-dollar-a-day was gone.

Not only our savings but many other things were taken—wedding presents, little trinkets, jewelry and presents from Will—many things that I treasured.

I was brokenhearted. Will wanted to laugh it off and tried to console me with the story of what a good sport his sister Maude had been when her house burned. They had been curing meat in the smokehouse that day and a spark had blown to the roof of the main house, which was being painted. The fresh paint caught fire and in a moment the whole place was in flames, with the painters rolling and jumping from the roof. Though Maude had lost everything, the antics of the painters were so ludicrous that she saw the funny side of it and laughed. And she always laughed afterward whenever the fire was mentioned. I listened to the story and admired Maude's fortitude, but still I couldn't laugh.

Will had promised, as I said, to give up the theater at the end of the tour and we had made glowing plans for our home in Claremore. But at the end of the tour an offer came to play the Percy Williams houses in the East at $300 a week. This was more than Will had ever been paid, and even I agreed that the offer should be accepted.

As other dates came along at the same figure, Will continued to play in the East. I was growing reconciled to show business, and our promised return to Claremore kept being postponed. Newspapers were already beginning to take notice of Will and in backstage interviews—even at that early date—he made many friends among the press. But he was not a headline act and he was eager to try out something a little more spectacular. In spite of the fact that he had failed miserably with a big act in England, he was determined to try again.

Engaging Goldie St. Clair, who had just won the woman's bucking-horse championship at Cheyenne and had been congratulated in person by President Theodore Roosevelt, he started getting a company together. There were other girls in the act; Florence LaRue—Mrs. Guy Weadick—did fancy roping, and Hazel Moran performed a graceful rope dance. There were also a trick rider and a girl who did a Cossack ride, making her entrance standing high in the stirrups and waving a sword.

It was in this big act that Will really began to talk to his audience. Standing at the side of the stage, he kept up a continual patter about the girls and the feats they were performing. The act closed with Goldie riding a bucking horse. She was young and pretty, with long blonde hair that hung down her back in a braid. The act was last on the bill, and I usually watched from the side of the wing the variety artists who occupied the first part of the program.

One night at Keith's Theater in Philadelphia when

I was standing backstage watching Will's act, Harry
Jordan, the manager, spoke to me. "Tell me, Mrs.
Rogers," he said, "why does Will carry all those horses
and people around with him? I would rather have Will
Rogers alone than that whole bunch put together."

That settled it for Will. Getting costumes and
working out a routine took a lot of time, and there were
annoyances in managing a troupe. So, taking Mr.
Jordan's advice, Will went back to the original act
with which he had started in vaudeville—just himself
and his rope. But now he talked continuously, ram-
bling on about other performers on the bill and the
different tricks he was trying to do.

"Worked that pretty good," he could confide to the
audience when things had gone smoothly, "made my
joke and the trick come out even." Or, when things
hadn't gone so well: "I've only got jokes enough for
one miss. I've either got to practice roping or learn
more jokes." It was Will's delivery, the way he said
things, that got the laughs in those days, rather than
the gags themselves. But this was a natural delivery,
simply the way Will talked, off-stage or on. I remember one bit of business, with an accompanying line,
that was sure-fire. There was a rope trick Will did
which consisted of jumping with both feet inside a
spinning loop. Not a particularly difficult trick, but
one time Will happened to miss and break the loop.
After that, however, he always managed to miss this
trick on the first try; then gathering up his rope for
another attempt, he would drawl the cheerful apology
that had automatically come to his lips on the first oc-

casion: "Well, got all my feet through but one." It always brought down the house.

There was one sad parting when Will started out with his new single turn. Teddy was shipped back to the old ranch near Oologah and put to pasture with a bunch of other horses. Once the fence broke down and the horses got away. The others were rounded up, but Teddy could not be found. Will took this as a real personal tragedy and sent instructions to his nephew, Herb McSpadden, to spare neither time nor expense in searching for the pony. Several months later the horse was found. Teddy, who had been the idol of boys in the streets, who had played in the leading vaudeville theaters of America, the music halls of Europe and before the King of England, was in the hands of an old full-blood Indian, who was working him in his cornfield, hitched to a plow. Teddy was brought home to Oologah, watched over carefully and given the best of everything. He lived to be very old.

CHAPTER IX

WILL admired Fred Stone long before meeting him. The first show he took me to see in New York after we were married was *The Red Mill,* in which Fred and his partner, Dave Montgomery, were playing a return engagement. *The Red Mill* was one of the great musicals of all time.

Fred's next show was *The Old Town,* written for him by George Ade. In the second act he introduced a rope dance which was an immediate sensation. Fred had hired an Oklahoma boy to teach him to rope and he had rehearsed the act for nearly a year.

Because of Will's success in vaudeville, every boy in his home town wanted to be a roper. Will had heard that the boy who was teaching Fred was Black Chambers, a Cherokee Indian boy of Claremore, and so he went around one night to see Chambers. It was a warm evening and Will noticed a man in shirt sleeves sitting beside the stage door. Will asked to see Fred Stone, but the doorman apparently had instructions to discourage anonymous visitors.

"Mr. Stone isn't here," he said.

"Well, just say that Will Rogers called to see Black Chambers," and Will turned to go.

The shirt-sleeved man rose and came over, grinning, "Wait a minute," he said, "I'm Fred Stone. Chambers hasn't been well and I sent him home last week."

And that's how their friendship began.

When *The Old Town* finished its New York run and went on tour, Will was playing the vaudeville circuits. Many times his bookings brought him to cities where the Montgomery and Stone musical was showing, and when this happened Will and Fred always got together. Both of them had lived eventful and adventurous lives. They were both outdoor men and always kept themselves in trim as trained athletes do. Fred was already an expert roper and he loved the twirling of the lasso as much as Will did.

While their cronies of the theater slept, dreaming of their names in electric lights, Will and Fred were up and at work. Usually they met early in the morning and practiced on the stage of the theater where Fred was playing. Will taught Fred the rope tricks that he knew and Fred taught Will his own dance routines. As a result, Will added to his act—under Fred's tutelage—an imitation of Fred's rope dance in *The Old Town*, using Fred's music, *I Am a Cowboy with Gun and Lariat*. Later he added one of George M. Cohan's characteristic steps to the tune of *A Grand Old Flag*.

Both Fred and Will had the work habit—which is just as real as any other habit. Once you have formed it you aren't comfortable in idleness. They both needed work and plenty of it to keep them happy.

Neither one ever changed. When both families were living in California and our children were grown, Fred's and Will's manners at dinner were exactly the same as they had always been. Neither could sit still long. They would get up from the table between courses and start roping. After dinner the two would continue their roping, using as a target a piece of furniture or anything in the room that happened to catch their eye. The average wife I suppose would be a little upset if she saw lassos flying through her living room but Mrs. Stone and I were used to it and we found it entertaining. Fred and Will kept up a flow of conversation—they talked better if their hands were busy—and that little barrel of ropes tucked back under the stairway at our house provided a lot of good talk and good roping.

We formed many other lifelong friendships during the old vaudeville days. Among the earliest I remember the comedienne and singer, Mable Hite, one of the top performers of her day. Our first winter in New York, just after Will and I were married, we met Mable and her husband, Mike Donlin. Will played on the same bill with them. "They were the big headliners and drawing cards," he said, "my act was put in just to make the bill read 'Ten Acts of Vaudeville.'"

They invited us, one evening, up to their beautiful apartment in New York. This was a large occasion for Will and me. As Will said "There was 'class' in vaudeville as well as in society, and for an 'act' to visit a headliner was an event." It was the first time we had ever been invited out by big-time actors. And neither of us ever forgot the kindness shown to us that night by Mike and Mable.

Will recalled it years later when Mike Donlin worked with him in one of his talking pictures, *Dr. Bull.*

"He was not of the stage originally, [Will wrote]

he was drafted from another line of recreation—Mike was the best known baseball player of his generation. He it was who really introduced so-called 'color' into our national pastime. When Mike Donlin joined the Giants away along about 1904, or thereabout, he was the Babe Ruth of his time. When Mike and Mable Hite married, it was the most popular wedding New York ever had. Mable put him on the stage in a vaudeville act, and I saw their opening at Hammerstein's Theater on a Monday afternoon. In my thirty years in all branches of show business, I never heard such a reception. It's always lingered in my memory, and when dear old Mike was playing with me in my last picture *Dr. Bull,* I used to tell him about it."

Chick Sale and his wife were early friends of ours. We first met Chick when Will and he were on the bill together at the Grand Opera House in Pittsburgh. "Chick was doing those great characters," Will said, "that have lived so long and have become classics—the old man with the horn, sitting on a stool; the preacher making the announcements; the fresh boy; then the girl reciting. They applauded and yelled then, and would do the same today."

"Those were great old days," Will would say in later years, "but darn it any old days are great old days. Even the tough ones, after they are over you can look back on them with great memories.

"I regret the loss of vaudeville. It was the greatest form of entertainment ever conceived. Nothing in the world takes the place of a good vaudeville show."

At that time, of course, vaudeville was a very important part of show business, not only in itself but as a training ground for future stars. Louise Dresser, who later played with Will in several pictures, and her husband, Jack Gardner, were a headline team and early friends of ours. I remember Winona Winters, Eddie Cantor, W. C. Fields (who then had a juggling act), DeWolfe Hopper, and the distinguished actress, Madame Bertha Kalich.

Once in Omaha, Will was on the same bill with Madame Kalich. His dressing room was just above hers. Will had bought a violin. Playing an instrument came hard for him, but he loved music and was always trying to play a tune on something. One afternoon he was scraping away on his fiddle, when a message came from below. Would he please stop playing? The noise annoyed Madame Kalich terribly. Will smiled at the maid. "Madame doesn't like that tune? Will you tell madame to pick her own tune. I can play anything she wants." His reply must have amused Madame Kalich, for she was very sweet about Will's playing after that. Later we became good friends and saw her often with her little daughter, Lillian.

It was quite by accident that gum chewing became a part of Will's early vaudeville act. He was a great baseball fan and formed firm friendships with many major-league players. They all chewed gum and he picked up the habit from them. One day he had to hurry to make the theater in time for a matinee and he happened at the moment to be chewing gum. He was still chewing it as he walked out in the stage to begin his act. When the audience started laughing, Will remembered about the gum, so he parked it on the proscenium arch and the audience roared with laughter.

Laughs didn't have to happen twice to Will. So, after that, the little wad of gum went into his act as a standard prop. I remember there was a particularly difficult rope trick he did, so difficult, in fact, that on the first try he sometimes failed to bring it off. But when this happened, and he might now and then have deliberately let it happen, Will could always delight the audience by parking his wad of gum somewhere— then making a second attempt and going through the trick with flying colors.

Eventually, of course, gum became so associated with Will's name that it was mentioned in almost everything written about him. Off-stage, however, Will was no inveterate gum chewer. It kept me busy trying to give away all the cartons of gum that were sent to him by the manufacturers. Will didn't smoke and it was difficult for him to be completely still. If not jingling coins, he was usually chewing on something. But he wasn't, I'm afraid, particularly partial to gum—the earpieces of his glasses, rubber bands, or even paper clips would do.

Will received $300 a week now for his single roping act. There were few expenses and no excess baggage to bother with. Things were simpler and we were getting ahead. I liked the carefree life of the theater and we decided to stay on, at least for a while.

During this time I was with Will constantly and some of my happiest recollections are of those years. We toured mostly through the East. Will was popular everywhere, things were going smoothly for us and we had a happy, carefree time enjoying the life of a trouper.

We managed to spend the holidays with my mother in Rogers and we always looked forward to our visits every summer with Will's father and his sisters.

Will's sister May, the youngest, had died within a few months after Will and I were married, and our visits to Chelsea were divided between Maude and Sallie. Usually we would spend two days with Sallie and two with Maude. Both women were active in the life of the community, and under their leadership everyone in town would take part in planning social activities for Will and me.

Sallie and her husband, Tom McSpadden, had a fine country place just outside of town, about a mile from Maude's. In both homes there was a sweet and intimate family life, with wonderful children—Maude had four, Sallie seven, and since their sister May's death, they had taken over the care of May's two youngest children. I can remember well our evenings spent in the living room, where the little girls would be busy at their needlework, while they listened, spellbound, to Uncle Willie talk of New York and the theatrical world. When Will came home it was always a big event for everybody, but the children idolized him—his visits gave them things to talk of for weeks afterward.

Uncle Clem's second wife had died some years before and he had moved into a big corner room over the First National Bank in Claremore. He took his meals in a hotel across the street and a loyal Negro boy cleaned up his room and ran his errands. He spent his week-ends with his daughters in Chelsea. Uncle Clem's disappointment in Willie had now changed to great pride. He carried around in his pockets the newspaper clippings we sent to him and produced these to show his friends, telling them of Willie's success in the big cities.

Uncle Clem knew every man in his section of the country and he was loved by everyone. Young people adored him. They took him into their confidence and he was the first to be told of an engagement or an approaching marriage. He was generous with his gifts to young couples and many a baby in Rogers County was named for him.

Although he was now past seventy, he continued to drive good horses. One I remember was Roger K, a high-stepping Kentucky-bred horse. Uncle Clem's days in the saddle might be over, but he could raise plenty of dust when he drove Roger K and his rubber-tired runabout. I'd hang on to my New York hat with one hand and cling to the seat with the other when Uncle Clem took me out on, as he said, "a spin around the town."

At first he could not understand Willie's making so much money. "Two hundred and fifty dollars a week," he confided to his friends in the early days of Will's career; "looks like something is wrong somewhere." But when he brought his daughters, Maude and Sallie, to Washington for a week, while Will was playing in Chase's Opera House there, he changed his mind.

Uncle Clem was a banker after all. He had seen the show a number of times that week and in a box seat with a good view of the crowd he began to count the house in a leisurely fashion—and as the figures grew, his business mind started working. Overlooking the fact that Willie was only one small act on a very extensive bill, he was very indignant when he said to his daughters at the hotel that night, "I tell you, girls, that manager sure is making a lot of money off Willie."

Uncle Clem attended every performance, and after the show he liked to stand around outside to listen to what the people had to say as they came out of the theater. Will was billed as "the Oklahoma Cowboy," and if Uncle Clem overheard anyone expressing a doubt about Will being a real cowboy, he immediately set him right. "Sure he's a real cowboy," he would say, "and from Oklahoma, too—just like it's printed on the program." Then, making his identity known, he would add, "I'll introduce you if you want to know him." When Will came out of the stage door, his father always had a crowd waiting there to meet him.

Will and I had been married three years and our first baby, Bill, was one week old when Uncle Clem died. I had just received a package from Uncle Clem—three pairs of little black wool stockings with pink-and-blue toes and heels, and a pair of tiny beaded Indian moccasins—when the message arrived. He had spent the week-end as usual with his daughters in Chelsea, and on Saturday night he died suddenly in his sleep at Maude's home. Will was terribly hard hit by the news and left immediately for Oklahoma.

It was the following spring that Will went into his first musical show, *The Wall Street Girl,* starring Blanche Ring. We rode to the opening on the subway and I remember how nervous I was and how anxious for Will's success. I took my seat well down in front, and shortly after the curtain went up I began to hear whisperings in the audience and to notice people rising abruptly and leaving the theater. This alarmed me. Then Will came on the stage and, interrupting the action of the play, announced that the ocean liner *Titanic*, on its maiden voyage, had struck an iceberg and gone down at sea with a shocking loss of life.

The play went on but rows of seats were empty, and those who remained were stunned into a numbness which made it impossible to say whether *The Wall Street Girl* was a success. Despite this unhappy opening, the show had a good New York run, and when it closed for the summer Will and I took the baby to Rogers, the beautiful little town on the edge of the Ozarks where my mother lived. We made our home with her for the next few years and during this time Will toured with *The Wall Street Girl* and played vaudeville dates in the Middle West and through the South. I remember that he was playing Dallas, Texas, the week our daughter Mary was born.

Early that summer I went to meet Will in Atlantic City. We were to spend a week there, and I packed only one small bag for the trip. I had no sooner arrived, however, than Will decided he wanted to take me to Europe. He had no definite bookings at home for that summer and it seemed a good time to go; so without any planning or much extra packing, and with but a day's stop in New York, we left for England.

This was my first trip on a boat and we traveled in

style—aboard the *Vaterland,* at that time the largest and most luxurious liner afloat. She was making the return trip after her maiden voyage. Will, the experienced traveler, was much exercised to see that I did nothing wrong. Our first night out I shall never forget. Will had assured me that we must dress for dinner. On state occasions, in those days, Will wore a tuxedo—though always with an air of suffering—and dutifully he put it on. So I took great pains in making my toilet for the evening. Long before I was ready in a little pink taffeta dress purchased during our brief pause in New York, Will was fussing and fuming for me to hurry. He didn't want to be late, he said, and have to walk into the dining room after everyone else was seated.

Finally, after much stewing on Will's part, I was ready. He hurried me to the dining room. We were met at the door by the head steward, who explained, with a knowing glance at our finery, that the dining room would not be open for another half hour. But that was not the worst for Will. We were the first ones in the dining room, of course, and later at dinner, as the tables gradually filled, it became very clear that for the worldly-wise and sophisticated, the first night out was strictly informal—they were dining just as they had come aboard.

Since Will had no theatrical bookings in London, this European jaunt was something of an adventure, but London had always been kind to Will and this was no exception. Sir Alfred Butt, who had managed the Palace Music Hall when Will had played there years before, almost immediately offered him an engagement.

This was at the Empire Theater in a musical show, *The Merry-Go-Round,* starring Nora Bayes.

Will felt glum about the offer. The Empire Theater, a tremendous music hall, was a noisy place. Sir Alfred was trying to establish it as a legitimate theater, but many of its characteristics as a music hall remained. In a large lobby just inside the entrance, there was constant activity and the hum of conversation—people were continually coming in and going out. There was a bar just off the lobby, and what we would call "hostesses," or "percentage girls," mixed with the audience—strolling up and down the series of broad steps that formed the aisle, and inviting lonely gentlemen to buy them drinks. Will thought the Empire would be too noisy, too full of distractions, and tried to convince Sir Alfred that his act would not be successful there.

Will's drawling talk was now an important part of his act, and it was intimate talk, pitched low. He had to have quiet and the full attention of his audience to get over. He was particularly afraid of the "percentage girls." He didn't think they would like him or understand what he was doing, and when they were not impressed by an act, they could easily ruin it by creating such a clamor that the performer went unheard. Will's honest efforts to talk Sir Alfred out of hiring him only made the producer more eager. He asked how much money Will wanted.

Will agreed to try it; he insisted, however, on playing the opening night without pay. If the act went over, he said, Sir Alfred could fix the amount. If it flopped, he wouldn't continue at any salary. But the girls Will had been afraid of were pleased with him.

Curious at first, and then interested, they finally quieted their escorts, stopped their strolling, and settled themselved on the aisle steps to listen to Will and watch him rope. Even the lobby emptied as it became obvious that something unusual was going on inside. To his own astonishment, Will was a huge success. Sir Alfred promptly wrote $400 on Will's weekly paycheck, a new high for Will in salary.

While Will worked on in London, I made a sightseeing trip to the Continent with Charlotte Perry, the American actress, her mother and her small daughter. We spent a week in Paris and then went on to Berlin.

After I returned to London, Will and I had a grand time sightseeing. We took in all the rubberneck bus trips and went out to the opening of the Ascot Race Track where we got a glimpse of the King and Queen as they drove in state around the track.

This was the summer of 1914 and wartalk was general. But the better informed all seemed to believe that the powers would settle their difficulties amicably. "The world has outgrown war," they said. Will was not so sure. Though Sir Alfred Butt wanted him to continue in *The Merry-Go-Round,* Will decided we had better start for home.

When we arrived in New York on another German liner, the *Imperator,* the war already was on. Kermit Roosevelt and his bride, and Alice Longworth, his sister, who later became one of Will's best friends, were fellow passengers.

The following summer, after another winter in vaudeville, we took a house at Amityville, Long Island. The friendship between Will and Fred Stone had blossomed into a friendship between two families, and we took a house just across the road from Fred Stone's summer home. We bought our first automobile—an Overland touring car. And Jimmy, our third baby, was born in July that year.

Will had vaudeville bookings in and around New York and lived at home most of the time. Fred Stone owned a boat and with Rex Beach, Fred's brother-in-law, they spent a lot of time on Great South Bay. Rex was a wonderful swimmer and diver. He was teaching Will to dive one day, when Will hit his head on the bottom and was pulled out of the water almost unconscious. For weeks afterward, Will could not rope with his right arm.

Will, of course, had to conceal his injury from theater managers. He had his bookings to protect. And it was because of this accident that in later years he was able to surprise audiences by shifting his ropes from one hand to the other. For, by hours of painful drudgery, he learned to do many different tricks with his left hand.

During our Amityville time, Will was in one show—a spectacular review, *Town Topics,* produced by Ned Wayburn in the huge Century Theater on Central Park West. But like everything else that had been tried in that endowed theater, the show closed within a few weeks and Will found himself back in vaudeville.

He was getting a comfortable salary, but he felt that he had gone about as far as he could hope to go with his type of act. Though usually more warmly received by audiences than the headline acts, he was not himself a headline act, and his salary seemed stuck at a certain figure.

Fred Stone was a great New York star and knew all the hard realities of the theater. He had come up through vaudeville and he had definite advice for Will. "Stay in New York," he urged him. "Stick it out here, even at less money, for a time. A part in a show is what you need and what you never can get while you continue to troupe the country in vaudeville."

Acting on Fred's advice, we leased a little house in Forest Hills, Long Island, twenty minutes from the city, and decided to stay there as long as Will could keep working. Although he played all the big-time vaudeville houses in and around New York, there were not enough of them to keep him busy, and we had house rent, a family to support, a stable of horses and now an automobile. When funds ran low, Will would change his name and play small suburban theaters for as little as seventy-five dollars a week, or do one and two-night stands. Anything to pay expenses and stay on in New York waiting for a part in a show.

His chance came in a Shubert musical called *Hands Up*. The show did not promise too well in rehearsal, and at the last moment Will was called in to bolster it as an added attraction for the opening night only. As is usual with musical shows, which have to be cut sharply from their rehearsal or tryout length, the opening performance was long and draggy, and when Will finally made his appearance the audience sat up and gave him such a warm welcome that he responded too generously.

When he did finish, the audience wanted still more. He came back, told a few jokes. did some tricks—perhaps he did take up more time than he was supposed

to—when suddenly, the lights went out. Will walked
off the stage in irritation, suspecting that it was a ruse
to get him to stop.

The opening night crowd with Fred Stone as a ringleader began to applaud in earnest. When the next
number was put on, they still wanted Will. In the
meantime Will had picked up his ropes and walked
back to his dressing room. The scene began to turn into
a riot. The stage manager came to Will with the ex-
planation that the turning out of the lights was an accident. But Will was hurt and humiliated and angry.
The applause roared on in the theater and the audience
refused to let the show proceed.

Finally Mr. Shubert himself came to Will's dressing
room and asked him please to go out and do something.
Will liked Mr. Shubert and gave in. The crowd yelled
with delight as, grinning sheepishly, Will ambled back
onto the stage. There were headlines in all the papers
next day, and though Will had been engaged only for
the opening night he played on in *Hands Up* for several
weeks. Later he was booked as a feature attraction and
held over for a second week at the Palace Theater, the
greatest vaudeville house in America.

Then came an engagement for a few weeks in the
Midnight Frolic, a fashionable late night show on the
roof of the New Amsterdam Theater. This was produced by Florenz Ziegfeld, Jr., who also produced the
famous *Ziegfeld Follies.* The *Frolic* audience sat at
tables; liquor and food were served; there was an orchestra and a dance floor. It was one of our first swank
night clubs. Mr. Ziegfeld liked Will's act and he played
on through the winter.

CHAPTER X

WILL had developed steadily from the serious roper of a few years ago, who had been outraged when laughter greeted his announcement of a trick. He was beginning now to feel the temper of his audiences—his monologue had taken on personality and become the expression of a viewpoint. It was no longer an assortment of wise-cracks tied together by his rope. Once the people had liked Will's roping; now they liked Will.

In his continued development, the long engagement on the Midnight Roof was an important period. It was there in the *Frolic* that the final form of his topical, ever-changing monologue took shape. And since the *Frolic* was more a night club than a theater, it was easy for Will to fall into the intimate, informal manner that became so important to him.

As a critic explained years afterward, when Will was appearing at Carnegie Hall, New York, on one of his lecture tours:

"Will Rogers always talks to us privately and confidentially. Even before he opens his mouth to speak, the barrier of the footlights is down and we are in the same room with him. If he didn't have supreme command of this informal mood, some of the things he says, the cracks he gets off at big people, all the way up to the President, would sound fresh and in poor taste. But his drawling tact always saves them from that."

With many patrons coming time and again to see
the midnight show, Will was forced to keep changing
his routine and adding material. It was not always easy
to have enough new gags prepared beforehand. So he
began to be alert for leads and ideas that cropped up
during the show; and learning to think upon his feet
before an audience, he found he could think pretty fast
that way—faster maybe than he could without an
audience. Which led him into his true vein of spon-
taneity.

Will's sense of humor was always at its best when
dealing with things of the present moment. He couldn't
tell a "funny story." "I never told a story in my life,"
he said. "What little humor I've got always pertains
to now." And that might be an event of the day or one
of the last minute; for Will was very quick to seize the
opportunities that suddenly offered themselves.

There was the time Will was speaking at a Democratic rally in northern California. The Governor was
ill, and the Lieutenant Governor was doing the honors.
The Lieutenant Governor spoke just ahead of Will and
explained that he would not try to make any jokes,
since the biggest joke in California was to be next on
the program. "He's conceited like all actors," the
Lieutenant Governor continued. "Right now I see him
whispering to his companion instead of listening to me."

Later, when he sat down, the chairman introduced
Will.

"Mr. Chairman; ladies and gentlemen," Will started
in, "I want to apologize to our Lieutenant Governor.
I was whispering to the lady next to me and I am very

sorry. The reason it created such a disturbance was that I asked her, 'Who is that man talking?' She said, 'I don't know.' So she asked the gentleman next to her, then he asked the lady next to him, and you know it had to go all the way down the aisle and over there by the door. And when they found out, it had to come all the way back. 'Why, it's the Lieutenant Governor!' they said.

"The Lieutenant Governor! Now that sounds pretty big when you say it—so that's why it made such a disturbance. And then I said to the lady, 'Oh, it's the Lieutenant Governor, is it? What does he do?' 'He don't do anything,' she said. 'What do you mean, don't do anything?' I said. 'Don't he even get up in the morning?' 'Oh, yes,' she said, 'he gets up every morning and asks if the Governor's any worse.' "

But Will didn't always have a comeback. Once Irvin S. Cobb and Will were both to speak at a dinner in New York. Will Hays introduced Will, and he did so in flowery terms. He ended his eulogy something like this: "And I want to say to you, ladies and gentlemen, that when this Oklahoma cowboy first strolled in here from the open spaces, it did not take New York long to discover that Will Rogers had something under the old ten-gallon hat besides hair!"

Will was still blushing modestly, when Irvin Cobb jumped to his feet without an introduction. "Ladies and gentlemen," he said, "I want to endorse from a full heart the glowing words that have just been spoken, and I want to add that it was high time somebody in this broad land of ours said a good word for dandruff!"

Will was still in the *Midnight Frolic* in the spring of 1916, when that year's edition of the *Ziegfeld Follies* began rehearsing. Mr. Ziegfeld had asked Will to join the cast of the *Follies*. But the salary was not good enough, we thought, and it meant leaving New York when the *Follies* went on tour. I talked Will out of taking it. We had stayed on in New York for one purpose only—to wait until some manager was willing to pay him at least $500 a week. It was not hard for Will to make his decision. He liked being at home with the children. We had a comfortable little house in Forest Hills, kept our horses in a stable near by and had many good horseback rides through the country. Altogether we were having the best time we had had up to then.

When the *Follies* opened, we felt very important, for Will had bought, for twelve dollars each, four tickets for the opening night. Our old Arkansas friends, Mr. and Mrs. Thomas W. Harvey, now of Huntington, West Virginia, were our guests for the evening.

It started out as a wonderful party. *The Follies of 1916* was one of the most extravagant and spectacular revues ever produced, but the opening night was slow. Certain scenes were long and a little dull. Will grew nervous and irritable as one top-heavy number followed another, and he was cross with me because he was not in the show. He knew he could have picked it up. He kept whispering and nudging me, all during the evening: "See, Blake, what did I tell you. This was my one big chance." Another nudge: "Boy, I wish I could have got my crack at it." And so on and on throughout the whole performance.

We left our friends and went home to Forest Hills that night pretty blue. I felt that a mistake had been made and I blamed myself. In the midst of all that glittering splendor, dull for want of contrast, Will's homey, down-to-earth act would have been a tremendous success. I knew it, and I knew, too, that I had talked him out of his greatest opportunity—an opportunity that probably would never come again. We were both very sad that night and I understood full well why Will was put out with me.

A few days later Mr. Ziegfeld telephoned Will to come into town at once. The *Follies* was sagging for want of humor. And so it was arranged that Will, with no announcement whatever, would go into the show that night. He was to continue also with his performance in the *Midnight Frolic.* Nothing was said about salary. Will was interested only in getting a "crack" at the *Follies.*

He dashed out to Forest Hills to get me, and it was, I think, the very proudest moment of our lives. When Will went on the stage that night, the audience broke into applause. Never had he gone over so well. It was a big and exciting evening and when he went upstairs to do his midnight performance in the *Frolic,* his magic stayed with him.

We had arranged to spend the night in town. After Will's last performance on the Roof, we sat in our little hotel room, and over sandwiches and beer discussed the triumphs of the evening. We waited for the morning papers, and all of them gave Will excellent notices—the best, most important he had ever received.

Will continued to play in both shows. That meant two performances each night and two matinees each week.

Many would attend the *Follies* and then go upstairs afterward, where they could eat and drink. That demanded constant new material for Will, because he couldn't use the same jokes in both shows. The papers were full of news—the war was on, though we had not yet entered it—and Will began to talk about political and national affairs. Starting with his familiar opening phrase, "Well, all I know is what I read in the papers," his remarks were as topical as the latest edition, and constantly changing. One critic described Will—and how well it fitted him—as the "columnist of the theater." Since the *Midnight Frolic* was an intimate kind of show, Will had joked with the guests who came night after night to see the performance. This eventually led to his introducing prominent personalities to the audience. The idea had caught on so well, that now he started doing the same thing downstairs in the *Follies*. Out-of-town visitors would come around to Will's dressing room during intermission. They liked to chat with him and to get a close-up view of the magnificent girls, clad in dazzling silks and satins.

"A mess of governors from various provinces have been in New York," Will said, "and my good friend, Governor Allen of Kansas, came back to see me. I stood him in the wings and he was supposed to be looking at my act—but he wasn't. He was watching what really is the 'backbone' of our show. Anyway, he heard some of my gags about our Government and all those who are elected to help misrun it. At the first of my act I roped him and dragged him out on the stage and introduced him to the audience. He made a mighty pretty speech and said he enjoyed 'Will's impertinences,' and he got a big laugh on that, and then he said I was the only man in America who was able to tell the truth about our men of affairs. When he finished, I explained to the audience why I was able to tell the truth. It is because I have never mixed up in politics. You know, the more you read about politics the more you have to admit that each party looks worse than the other. The one that is out always looks the best. My only solution would be to keep both parties out for one term and then hire my good friend, Henry Ford, to run the whole thing and pay him a commission on what he saves us. Put his factory in the Government, and instead of sending out radish seeds every spring, mail out one of those things of his."

The head ushers were always on the watch for celebrities, and notes were sent back to Will's dressing room with the location of their seats. "I have been looking for a bribe from some of our prominent men to keep their names out of my act," Will said, "but the only ones who ever speak to me are the ones I mention."

Sometimes Mr. Ziegfeld would have special friends in the house and would tell Will about them, and sometimes Will's own sharp eyes, peering out over the footlights, would pick out an old friend or modest great man. The stage, to Will, was no different from any place else he happened to be. He said whatever popped into his head at the moment and so naturally and sincerely that it was rarely misunderstood.

One night Will's rope flashed out front and caught Fred Stone, who was sitting in the center aisle about three rows back. Fred for all his natural presence of mind, was flabbergasted when Will's insistent lasso pulled him up on the stage. Will made Fred do one of his own rope routines for the audience and, leaning against the proscenium arch, he asked Fred about Mrs. Stone and each one of the children, and other personal matters, just as though they had stopped to chat on the street. The audience listened in to the two old friends visiting, and they loved it.

Another night Father Duffy, chaplain of the Fighting 69th Regiment during the war, was seated near the distinguished actress, Ruth Draper. Father Duffy loved the theater and the theater loved Father Duffy. Will spied them. "Ruth," he said, "do you know Father Duffy?" She smiled and shook her head. Then Will turned to the priest. "Father Duffy," he said, "shake hands with Ruth Draper. You two fine people ought to know each other."

Chauncey Depew, the grand old man of New York, rarely attended the theater, but on his ninetieth birthday he came to see Will. Will admired him greatly and, introducing him to the audience, started in with his good-natured ribbing about how Chauncey Depew and himself, who were both in demand as after-dinner speakers, were "barking" around town for their dinners. So the witty old man arose and made a little speech about how he'd been talking around New York and entertaining audiences for seventy years. "But I never found it necessary to use a rope," he smiled, and sat down.

For weeks Will played in both shows at the same small salary paid to him for the *Midnight Frolic,* and nothing had been said about the extra show. But Will knew Mr. Ziegfeld would want him to go on tour when the *Follies* left town. The *Follies* was known as one show that lived up to its promise of "a New York cast." Regardless of business, it had a regular schedule— spring and summer in New York, Thanksgiving in Pittsburgh, Christmas in Chicago. The show could have stayed on in New York indefinitely if Mr. Ziegfeld had been guided by the box office, but the *Follies* was an American institution—like the World Series or the Statue of Liberty—something that must be seen and talked about back home. A new edition was produced every year and the bookings and schedule always remained the same.

"A funny thing about the *Follies,* [Will wrote] people never spoke of it in comparison to any other show. It was always 'It's better than the last year's, or it's not so good as least year's.' The *Follies* always stood alone. Ziegfeld's greatest opposition was himself. If he had been new to show business every year, and that particular *Follies* was his first show, why each one would have been heralded as a masterpiece."

And through the years, what a galaxy of stars appeared under Mr. Ziegfeld's management! In Will's day, Bert Williams, perhaps the greatest Negro entertainer of all time, was in the *Follies.* "Man, I sho does love to hear you talk," he once told Will. W. C. Fields and Eddie Cantor were fellow performers and two of his best friends. There were Brandon Tynan, Andy Tombes, Fanny Brice, Ina Claire, Ann Pennington, Walter Catlett, Sam Hardy, Carl Randall, and dozens and dozens more—and the Ziegfeld show girls. Even today people say, "She is as lovely to look at as a *Follies* beauty."

We had decided in the beginning that Will would not leave New York without a salary of $500 a week. When it was time for the *Follies* to go on tour, Mr. Ziegfeld came to Will's dressing room to talk things over. Without the least hesitation, he offered Will a two-year contract—he would pay him $600 a week the first year and $750 a week the second year. He suggested that Will come to his office the next day to sign the contract. Will said, "I don't like contracts. You can trust me and I know I can trust you." Mr. Ziegfeld was not in the habit of doing that sort of thing, but he must have felt pretty sure of Will, for he called in Charley Dillingham, who happened to be standing backstage, as a witness, and the verbal agreement was made.

Will worked for Mr. Ziegfeld a long time, but there was never a written contract. And when Will left the *Follies* to make pictures in California, Mr. Ziegfeld presented him with a platinum watch, engraved, "To Will Rogers, in appreciation of a real fellow, whose word is his bond."

Mr. Ziegfeld had his own theater, the New Amsterdam on Forty-second Street, where the *Follies* always played in New York. Year in and year out Will used the same little third-floor dressing room, a dingy, uncarpeted place, with one small window that looked out on a back street. The New Amsterdam was a rather old theater, even in those days, and the accommodations for performers were far from elaborate. Will's dressing-room equipment consisted of a row of hooks along one wall, where he carelessly hung his clothes, and the regulation dresser shelf for a dressing table, and a light-bordered mirror above it. There was no other furniture except a few uncomfortable straight-backed chairs. Once, when he was not feeling well, I came in unexpectedly, and felt almost sick myself when I found that Will, with his overcoat for a blanket, had curled up on the floor to rest.

Will did have a shower in his room, however. Mr. Ziegfeld had it installed for him. Over to one side of the room two or three steps led up to a little platform on which was mounted an old tin tub. The waterpipe came out overhead, and around it all was a curtain. Though a very crude affair, it was considered quite a luxury. But it was certainly not very pretty.

Once I conspired with Mary Hope Hammond, an old Arkansas friend of mine, to fix up Will's dressing room. It was to be a surprise, of course, and we had to sneak in when Will was not there, to take all the measurements. But finally, our interior decorating complete, we felt quite pleased with ourselves. We had curtained the little window, fixed draw curtains to go over the row of hooks on which Will hung his clothes, and supplied a more tasteful curtain for the shower. The most important addition, we felt, was a couch on which Will could relax. Then we added a rug and substituted a few comfortable chairs for the rickety things that had been there before.

But what a roar went up when Will saw our handiwork. I don't really recall what happened, but I do know that the lovely couch almost immediately was sent down to the orchestra boys to furnish their lounging room under the stage. Will didn't want his dressing room "fancied up," as he called it—he liked it the way it was. He had been used to much worse in the little vaudeville theaters around the country. He liked to come in and throw his clothes around as he pleased. Will never had a dresser or valet to help him at the theater. In fact he had no assistance whatever in connection with his act.

The *Follies* traveled in its own special train, and Mr. Ziegfeld knew how to keep Will satisfied, and arranged for Will to carry two horses in the scenery car. Will's little black roping pony, Dopey, and another horse, with Charley Aldridge, a cowboy, in charge was the troupe that Will carried around with him year in and year out. Whether in Boston, Chicago or New York, Will was up early in the morning in the riding arena, practicing fancy rope catches each day with his horses.

The spring rehearsal for a new edition of the *Follies* was fascinating to watch. Will and I usually sat in some dark corner of the theater while the rehearsal was in progress on the stage. Mr. Ziegfeld sat out in front in the dimly lighted theater and gave commands as he watched every detail of costumes and movements of the beautiful girls assembled to take their places for the different routine numbers. It was interesting to watch the crude beginning—the beautiful show girls in rompers, bathing suits or shorts—then later to see the same routine mature into something of sensational and artistic beauty. Even though Mr. Ziegfeld had the best designers and artists, his eye for beauty and color far surpassed theirs. He watched every little detail of costume. Often he would change the color of a flower or a bow at the belt. I recall a dress rehearsal of the *Midnight Frolic* at which he threw out an entire set of costumes for the finale and ordered new ones. That must have cost him some ten or fifteen thousand dollars—but Mr. Ziegfeld was an artist of the theater, rather than a businessman.

The *Follies* girls worked hard and never allowed their private lives to interfere with their work in the theater. They were prompt in arriving for rehearsals and took their work seriously. With the same routine night after night, rehearsals often running into early dawn, with a call for eleven o'clock the next morning, it was a mystery to me how they could ever find time to rest or sleep. But no one complained, although it was not uncommon for girls to faint from sheer exhaustion.

Will used to tell many jokes on the *Follies* girls. It was a legend that they all married millionaires—and many of them did. "We have a hard time keeping our girls together," Will said once on tour. "Every time we get to a new town some of them marry millionaires, but in a few weeks they catch up with the show again."

During dress rehearsals, when Will's name was called, he would amble out in his street clothes and occupy the stage for the fifteen or twenty minutes allotted to his single turn. He would kid about the show, the various numbers and performers, incidents that had happened in rehearsal—anything that came into his mind. Will could always find laughs in whatever was going on around him, and in the last nerve-wracking days of putting a show together, when tempers were generally short, his good-humored impromptu gags would help a lot.

But Will never actually rehearsed. He liked to keep everything he had to say as fresh for the performers in the show as for the opening-night audience. As a result, the cast always crowded around the wings when Will's act was on. Even for the opening night audience, he would have special material; jokes that later, when the show was running smoothly, would not have been funny—just as his rehearsal gags, for the cast, the directors and the stage hands, would have been appreciated by no other audience. And Mr. Ziegfeld allowed him absolute freedom. As Will wrote years later, "I would never have been as lucky again, for no other manager in the world would have let me go my own way and do as I saw fit. He never bothered me as to what to do or say, never suggested or never cut out."

Will had great admiration and respect for Mr. Ziegfeld. Many of the actors in the *Follies* called him "Ziggy" or "Flo," but to Will he was "Mr. Ziegfeld" in speaking to or about him. The close friendship between the two men did not develop until years later, when Will had left the stage for good.

I had never met Mrs. Ziegfeld—Billie Burke—until she came out to California to live. She took a house not far away from the ranch and her daughter, Patricia,

used to ride with our children. When Mr. Ziegfeld
came West on visits, he and Will often rode together.

We saw a great deal of Mr. Ziegfeld during his last
illness. Miss Burke brought him to California when his
health failed. His death was a great shock to us all.
Will and I had seen him that afternoon, and Miss
Burke and Patricia had had dinner with him in his
room in the hospital. They stayed quite late, until
after eight o'clock. He seemed much improved and
Miss Burke left him to go to one of the studios where
she was working that night on a picture. At ten o'clock
our telephone rang. Mr. Ziegfeld had suffered a sudden
relapse. He died before any of us could get to him.

I like to remember Mr. Ziegfeld and Will as they
looked on one of their many horseback rides together.
Mr. Ziegfeld was mounted on one of Will's spirited
polo ponies, Sundown, a beautiful dapple gray. He was
a well-set-up rider and there was great style about
everything he did. I watched the two men as they rode
along side by side—Mr. Ziegfeld in a handsome pair
of light-colored, winged chaps, sitting straight and
erect, his gray hair sleek and glistening in the sun;
Will carelessly sprawled in his saddle on his old
speckled roping pony, Soapsuds, wearing his faded
blue overalls, his shaggy hair blowing awry in the wind.

There they were, the greatest producer of all time,
and the vaudevillian with his rope who had pulled the
Follies out of many a tight place. So different they
were and yet with so much in common. Each was
grateful to the other. Once they had been partners
in making theatrical history and now they were even
closer, they were friends.

At Beverly Hills home: Betty and Mary pose in front, while Bill watches Will and Jimmy toy with pieces of an erector set. *(Courtesy Will Rogers Memorial)*

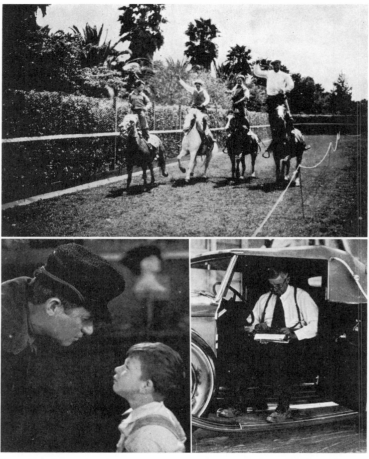

Top: Teaching the children circus stunts. *Bottom:* Two characteristic poses of Will.

Top: Will, Fred Stone, and artist Edward Borein. *Bottom:* Humorist Hughes and Secretary Rogers.

Top: Jimmy, Mary, Betty, Will, and Bill (in military academy uniform) celebrating the return from Europe and Will's appointment as "Mayor of Beverly Hills," 1926. *Bottom:* Jimmy, Bill, Mary, Will, Betty, and Jock, the dog, at Santa Monica ranch, about 1928. *(Courtesy Will Rogers Memorial)*

CHAPTER XI

WILL made his debut in motion pictures in the summer of 1918 while he was still working in the *Follies*. We had rented Fred Stone's Amityville, Long Island, home that summer while Fred and his family were away in California, where Fred had gone to make a picture for Paramount. Rex Beach, author of *Laughing Bill Hyde,* was associated with Samuel Goldwyn in making a screen version of the story, and Mrs. Beach (a sister of Mrs. Fred Stone), while lunching with us one day, said, "Will, you are the ideal man to play Bill Hyde in Rex's new picture." Will had never faced a camera and had no conviction that he would be good as a screen actor, but when Rex and Mrs. Beach insisted, an arrangement was made whereby working in the picture would not interfere with his *Follies* engagement and Will agreed to try it.

The picture was made at the old Fort Lee studio in New Jersey. Directed by Hobart Henley, it was such a financial success that after the *Follies* left New York to go on tour, Mr. Goldwyn caught up with Will in Cleveland and offered him a two-year contract to make pictures in California. His salary in the theater had been increased to $1,000 a week only a short time previously, and when Mr. Goldwyn offered $2,000 a week for the first year and $3,000 a week for the second, we were overcome by our good fortune.

We were delighted too, with the idea of moving to California, and with the prospects of at last settling

143

down in a home of our own. After the *Follies* closed in the spring, Will left for the Coast. When I joined him with the children a few weeks later, he met us at the station in Los Angeles with a grand surprise for me—a big black Cadillac sedan, and my first chauffeur.

A move for the Rogers family was always a many-sided problem. There was another baby now, and any decision that Will and I might make must necessarily give first consideration to accommodations for the children, horses and dogs.

Will had scoured the town for a house with a stable. He found one on Wilshire Boulevard, but it was close in and there were miles of paved streets to be crossed before we reached open country. Mr. Goldwyn solved our problem by offering an old building on the studio lot, which was quickly fixed up for our horses and ponies, and we settled in a comfortable house on Van Ness Avenue. The land around the Goldwyn Studio then was an enormous vacant space, securely fenced. Although Bill and Mary were very small, they rode there every afternoon in perfect freedom and safety. Jimmy, still too young to struggle with lessons, did bits in some of the first pictures, and this, of course, was great fun for Will.

Names of some of his early silent films made on the Goldwyn lot have slipped my mind, but I do remember *Jubilo,* a *Saturday Evening Post* story written by Ben Ames Williams and directed by Clarence Badger, as one of the best. It was the story of a happy-go-lucky tramp who sang *In the Land of Jubilo* as he walked along the railroad ties.

Given the usual studio treatment, the original story, much to Will's disappointment, had been considerably changed in the scenario. Though he was new to pictures, the suggestion that the title of *Jubilo* be changed to "A Poor But Honest Tramp" was too much for him—he wired a protest to Mr. Goldwyn in New York. The name *Jubilo* was retained and, instead of using the scenario, the shooting of the picture was done from the open pages of the magazine.

The technique of pictures has changed so much that most of us do not remember how enjoyable the old silent ones were. A theme song presented with titles today would seem absurd and clumsy. But the song, *In the Land of Jubilo* was a big hit and followed Will around for a long time afterward. Whenever we entered a theater or a restaurant, the orchestra would invariably strike up the tune.

In those days outdoor scenes could not be reproduced well inside the studio lot and picture companies were often forced to go long distances on location. For *Jubilo,* Will and many members of the cast were sent to New Orleans to get the correct atmosphere.

In addition to acting, Will had a hand in his scripts and wrote all the running titles that were the dialogue and description used in his silent pictures. The well-known actress, Peggy Wood, played opposite him in *Almost a Husband,* the first picture made under his new Goldwyn contract. Irene Rich was with him in *The Strange Border, Jes' Call Me Jim* and many of his other films. Will found her not only a capable and intelligent actress, but invariably good-natured and easy to work with. At that time she had the responsibility of two lovely young daughters and her devotion to them and interest in their welfare and education touched us. The Rich and Rogers family were soon fast friends. In later years, after Will had returned to Hollywood to make talking pictures, he was always delighted when Irene was cast as his leading lady.

In an article written then, in the talking picture era, Will recalled the old silent days and explained about his best camera angle. "Straight on I didn't look so good," he said, "and even sideways I wasn't so terrific, but a cross between a back and a three-quarters view, why, Brother, I was hot. The way my ear (on the side) stood out from my head was just bordering on perfect. That rear view gave you just the shot needed. In those old silent day pictures, that back right ear was a by-word from Coast to Coast."

Will kidded a great deal about his looks on the screen. He used to tell about a letter that he insisted someone had written to him, which said, "I understand you have never used a double in your pictures—now that I have seen you I wonder why you don't." Sending out autographed portraits of himself to admiring fans always struck Will as particularly preposterous. Even the idea made him feel self-conscious; he hated to do it. And in spite of constant pressure from the Goldwyn publicity department, I'm afraid Will was very remiss in his duties.

From the beginning, however, Will liked the work at the studio. Though the numerous retakes were tiresome, and he missed the warmth and friendliness of an

enthusiastic audience, he had what he had missed so
much on the stage—a chance to be out of doors and go
to bed early and get up early. There was little night
work and he often had weeks of free time between pictures. "It's the grandest show business I know anything about," he said, "and the only place where an
actor can act and at the same time sit down in front and
clap for himself."

We were living in the same house on Van Ness Avenue and he was away on location when the boys, Bill,
Jimmy and Freddie—the baby, only eighteen months
old—were all taken ill at the same time. By some
miracle, Mary escaped. At first the doctors thought
it was tonsillitis, but diphtheria developed. All three
were desperately sick, and despite the best of care, we
lost the baby.

Saddened by the baby's death, we felt a sense of relief when we moved into our new home in Beverly Hills.
We had bought this house, the first we had ever owned,
and after that, whatever our far-flung adventuring, our
permanent home was in California. Will enclosed several acres of ground with a high brick wall and added
a stable, a tanbark riding ring, a swimming pool and
two log cabins down in a corner of the garden—the
smaller cabin especially for Mary.

The larger cabin had an open fireplace and five bunks
along the walls; it became our family gathering place.
We often had meals around a barbecue grill near by and
celebrated holidays and Christmas there. Formal
Christmas Day callers could never find our hideout,
concealed by trees and shrubs. We could hear one

motorcar after another roll up to our front door and roll away again.

When Will's sister Maude came to California to visit us, she took one look at the cabin and then, reminded of some of the Oklahoma Indians made suddenly prosperous by oil, she burst out laughing.

"Willie," she said, "you're just like an old full-blood. You buy a big house, then build a little cabin at the foot of the hill and live in it."

Will fixed up a playroom and a little stage for the children in the huge basement. The theater curtain was decorated with advertisements. There were ropes to raise and lower the curtain, and all sorts of traps and equipment. After his day's work at the studio, he and the children had great fun there.

Will wanted a wall to enclose our house and grounds. At that time there was a city restriction against putting up such walls, and we had to go to considerable trouble to get permission. But our neighbors finally agreed and a brick wall some eight feet high was built around the place. It was no sooner up, however, than Will was conscience-stricken; the high bare wall looked formidable and repellent; he wanted to hide it.

Ivy, we decided, might make the bricks less grim. A hurry-up call was sent out to a greenhouse. Work began the next day, and that evening Will came home from the studio eagerly anticipating the sight of his ivy-covered walls. His disappointment and indignation, when he found nothing but little slips stuck in the ground, was boundless.

The landscape man patiently explained that they

would grow soon, but that did not suit Will. He liked to have things done as they were done on the movie lots—if a tree was needed, it was a full-grown tree that was set out; if a house was required, the four walls rose up in a few hours. And now, particularly, he wanted something done about this wall that fairly screamed of privacy. "When I want ivy," he said, "I want ivy I can see." So ivy plants with long creepers already grown were set out and draped over the bare bricks, and at a shocking cost Will had his peace of mind again.

Just as Will's contract ended, Mr. Goldwyn left the studio, which continued to operate under the Goldwyn name, however, until a few years later, when it was reorganized into Metro-Goldwyn-Mayer. This was a time of change and readjustment in the industry and we were undecided about the future. Settled in our own home, we wanted to stay in California, but although Will had several good offers from the East, there was nothing definite for him in Hollywood.

During this period many motion picture stars reasoned as Uncle Clem had reasoned, when he counted the house and said, "That manager sure is making a lot of money off Willie." Some of the biggest names in the industry had broken away from the large companies to make their pictures independently. Finally Will was bitten by the bug. Though far from a well-established star, he decided to do a little small-scale producing himself.

We plowed through innumerable books; the house was littered with manuscripts. We all helped, and every meal would be the occasion for a family story conference. Will made three pictures during this brief venture of being his own producer, *Fruits of Faith, The Roping Fool,* and *One Day in 365.* This last was the simple narrative of a day, hour by hour, with the children at home. Will wrote *The Roping Fool* himself, putting in many of his rope tricks and catches. The use of a white rope and his black pony, Dopey, made these most effective on the screen. The best tricks were shown in slow motion. Despite the fact that these were short two-reel pictures, it took considerable money to finish them—more, of course, than had been planned— and Will found it necessary to mortgage our home.

An agreement with Pathé provided that they were to refund the money invested and release the pictures, giving Will a royalty. But something went wrong, and Will wound up by having everything he owned, including his life insurance, and the Liberty Bonds bought for the children, tied up in the three little pictures. He even had to borrow money on the films themselves, leaving them at the bank as collateral.

The California outlook was gloomy indeed right then for the Rogers household. But offers continued to come from the East. In June Will returned to New York. He was gone a year, and how many cross-continental trips I made, sometimes with one or two of the three children and sometimes alone, during those fifty-two weeks! After working with the Shuberts in New York for a short time, Will went back to the *Follies,* and this time at a weekly salary of $2,500.

But Will needed more than that; he was deeply in debt. I think he worked as hard this year as he ever did in his life, and without a break or vacation of any kind. He hated to be away from the children, and he missed his favorite ponies; but when he came home the following summer to accept a new movie contract, much of his indebtedness had been paid. It was by after-dinner speaking on a commercial basis that Will made much of the extra money. He spoke from one end of New York to the other.

During his previous seasons with the *Follies,* Will had done a little after-dinner speaking, sometimes at public entertainments though usually among theatrical friends at the Lambs Club and Friars Club. But this year, in addition to the benefits and charity affairs to which he always gave his time freely, he was booked by an agent to speak before public and private entertainments of all kinds. Here are just a few of the organizations he spoke before: The Automobile Manufacturers, Chamber of Commerce, Ohio Society of New York, Corset Manufacturers, Retail Milliners, Leather and Shoe Men, Rug Manufacturers and Dealers, Wholesale Silk Stocking Manufacturers, Grand Rapids Retail Furniture Dealers, Woolen Men, Bicycle Manufacturers, Automobile Engineers, Paper Dealers, the National Association of Waste Material Dealers. At times he would be booked for as many as two or three banquets a week.

"A great many will think that it is Dispepsia that is driving me away from behind the old Banquet Table [Will wrote when leaving New York for the Coast]. But it is not. There is only one way a person can survive a year of banquets and not wind up with a Burlesque stomach—that is not to eat there at all.

"Now I tell you how I did. There is a little Chili
Joint on Broadway and 47th Street, where there is just
a counter and a few stools, but what Chili! Well, on
any night I had to go to a Banquet, I would go in
there and play about two rounds of Enchilades, and a
few encores on the Chili, and I want to tell you that I
was fortified. Not only to refuse anything that might
be offered to me at the Dinner, but I could just set
through almost any kind of a speech."

Will went on to describe the horrors of the standardized banquet food. However, even if the choicest Texas
chili had been set before him at these dinners, he would
have been too nervous to touch it. "I am always
nervous; I never saw an audience that I faced with any
confidence" was true to the end of his days.

His nervous preliminary fumbling, though it became
an accepted part of his technique, never had to be assumed. The first few minutes before any audience
were agony for Will. It was hard for him to get going,
and until he was warmed up, and had the people with
him, he couldn't be easy. To a certain degree, of course,
this is the case with many public speakers, though they
usually train themselves to hide it. But Will never
did learn to hide it; he was nervous and uncomfortable
and the fact was obvious. Often enough, as they have
told me, kind-hearted and sensitive members of the
audience would suffer too, feeling very embarrassed for
him and wondering what in the world the poor fellow
was doing up there, until Will finally hit his stride.

During this winter in New York, there was one occasion on which Will never did get going. He encountered an audience he couldn't handle. The possibility hadn't occurred to him beforehand, but it turned out that the people he was talking to simply didn't read the newspapers. And Will was lost; he flopped completely.

"I will never forget," he said, "one time I went over to Sherrys, a fashionable restaurant, after the *Follies* show, to play a charity affair for some New York society ladies. I thought I had some good material at the time. The League of Nations was in the height of its argument, Ireland and England was fussing, disarmament was a headline topic. I breezed out there rather cocky, thinking I had some sure-fire material.

"Well, you never saw jokes hit a ballroom floor and slide off like those did. Those old dowagers and those young debutantes had no more read a paper than I had Shakespeare. William Randolph Hearst was sitting with a party of friends at one of the tables. And he was laughing, but not at the jokes. He was laughing at me out there dying. He had heard these very same jokes get big laughs with an out-of-town audience at the *Follies,* and he got a kick out of the way they flopped there with that bunch.

"Then two nights later after that fiasco, I went to Sing Sing and did a show for them and I never had as well a read audience in my life. They didn't miss a thing. Ever since then I have always felt we had the wrong bunch in there."

This year in the East had added another step to

Will's career. His humorous slant on world and national affairs was winning attention, and things he said in the theater about political situations or people in the limelight were being constantly quoted. He had many requests for articles and occasionally, just for the fun of it, he wrote for the newspapers. Even before we had left New York for our California sojourn, comments he had made in the *Follies* were published in two small volumes—*The Peace Conference,* and *Prohibition.* In California he wrote similar comments for a series that was flashed on the screen like a news weekly, under the heading *Illiterate Digest.* This had gone over very well for a short time and he received $500 a week for it. At the same time he tried out a comic strip. An artist was sent out from New York to draw the strips and Will tried to furnish the "speakers." They struggled with it for some time, but Will was never enthusiastic about it, and as far as I know, it was never used. Now in New York, his friend, Rube Goldberg, the great cartoonist, urged Will to try out a weekly article. The first one appeared in the New York *Times* in November 1922. Soon the articles were taken over by the McNaught Syndicate and became a regular Sunday feature in newspapers all over the country.

Will's writings developed as his work on the stage had—it was just a question of finding some natural way of expressing himself, of presenting his particular slant on things unencumbered by any form or style.

Here are typical excerpts from some of his first weekly articles. All except the last were written while Will was playing in the *Follies,* and making an after-dinner speech every other night, during his stay in New York.

"As I go to press there is just about to be wound up in Paris what is called an Economic Conference, which at this early day and date looks like it will be awful lucky if it don't wind up in an awful nice war.

"England wants to settle one way with Germany, and France has a different plan. Now, as Germany owes both of them, there is no reason why each couldn't settle in their own way. But no, that's too easy. Nations don't do things that way. If they did, there would be no Diplomats, and Diplomats are nothing but high class Lawyers (some ain't even high class).

"Germany made some sort of a proposal that there would be no more wars for a Century. It was turned down by England and France. You see they been fighting every forty years and its awful hard to go against custom in those old countries."

—January 14, 1923

"Now this Farm Loan Bill is going to be one of the best things to bankrupt the Farmers I know of, outside of running a Threshing Machine. That used to be the surest indication of becoming poverty stricken.

"Well, as I say, that, and borrowing money on what's called 'easy terms,' is a one way ticket to the Poor House. Show me ten men that mortgage their land to get money and I will have to get a search warrant to find one that gets the land back again. Instead of passing Bills to make borrowing easy, if Congress had passed a Bill that no person could borrow a cent of money from any other person, they would have gone down in history as committing the greatest bit of Legislation in the World.

"I was raised on a Cattle Ranch and I never saw or heard of a Ranchman going broke—only the ones who had borrowed money. You can't break a man that don't borrow; he may not have anything, but Boy! he can look the World in the face and say, 'I don't owe you Birds a nickle'."

—March 18, 1923

"We can always depend on Judge Gary for a weekly laugh in his speeches. But last week he had the prize wheeze of his career. He had his accomplices make an investigation of the Steel Industry, and they turned in a report that it was much more beneficial to a man to work 12 hours a day than 8. They made this report so alluring that it is apt to make people who read it decide to stay the extra 4 hours on their jobs, just through the health and enjoyment they get out of it. I never knew Steel work was so easy till I read that report. But here is the kick. Judge Gary got up to read this report before the stockholders. He read for one hour in favor of a 12 hour day. Then he was so exhausted they had to carry him out."

—June 10, 1923

"Well, all I read in the papers now is about some fellow named Edward Bok, offering 100 thousand dollars for someone to suggest a plan where they stop wars. . . . There ain't nobody on earth, I don't care how smart they are, ever going to make me believe they will ever stop wars. We are not as smart as the Generations ahead of us and they tried to stop them and haven't been able to. In fact, every war has been preceded by a Peace Conference. That's what always starts the next war.

"The only way to do is just stay out of them as long as you can, and the best way to stay out of them for quite a while, instead of teaching a boy to run an automobile, teach him to fly, because the Nation in the next war that ain't up in the air, is just going to get something dropped on its Bean."

—July 22, 1923

These weekly articles brought a request for another book. Will compiled the best for a volume published in 1924, with the same title he had used on his screen comments—*Illiterate Digest.* The book was well received by the public and by book reviewers.

"His droll comments on men and events have become so popular that he finds himself—probably to his surprise—a national figure," said *The Nation,* adding: "It is just as well for Mr. Rogers that his caustic observations are wrapped in humor. If they were delivered without the funny tags, his audience would set the dogs on him."

And then in the *Saturday Review of Literature:* "Somebody once gave him a license of free speech (or perhaps he took it without asking); but, at any rate, in the past few years he has probably turned over more heavy stones and thrown hot sunlight underneath than any man in the United States."

Will's time now was divided between New York and our home in California, and during this period he made a series of two-reel comedies at the Hal Roach Studios in Culver City. These were all silent pictures, of course, and broad comedy, to put it mildly. Among the best were *The Cake Eater* and *Two Wagons, Both Covered.* The latter, directed by Rob Wagner, was a satire on Jimmy Cruze's great spectacle, *The Covered*

Wagon. It was Will's original idea and he assisted in writing the script.

During his association with Hal Roach a warm friendship developed between the two men, and it was Will who introduced Hal to polo. Eventually the producer became an outstanding player.

Years before, during the first summer we spent at Amityville, Long Island, Will had played his first polo. He had a string of some five or six roping ponies, and someone asked him, "Will, why don't you play polo? Anyone who can ride can play it."

Will found out that there was more to it than that. "The people that think riding a horse is all there is to to polo," he once wrote, "are the same people who think that anybody that can walk makes a good golfer, or anybody who looks good in a bathing suit would make a good swimmer."

It was his old friend, Jim Minnick—the same Jim who had helped him kidnap Comanche from the Mulhall show—who taught Will the game. Jim was now in New Jersey training and selling polo ponies. He knew nearly all the better players and was a good mallet man himself.

Will used to chaff Jim about gathering up all the old buggy horses in Oklahoma and Texas and foisting them on Eastern millionaires as polo mounts, though the truth was that Jim was a wizard both as a trainer and a judge of horseflesh. The real source of Will's kidding was an ingenious scheme that Jim worked of shipping his stock at a low freight rate. By loading a bed and a stove in his horsecar, throwing in a few old tools and an old buggy, and riding there himself, he automatically made the car an "emigrant car" in railroad tariff classifications, and eligible for the low rates the railroads had set years before to induce farmers to migrate West. But Jim went East.

Fred Stone took up polo at about the same time; he, like Will, already had horses, and there was a polo field on his Amityville place. Though Will's mounts were only roping ponies, he made a good showing on them. Ed Borein, the cowboy artist, Leo Carillo, Vernon Castle, Jim Minnick, Fred Stone and, occasionally, Frank Tinney made up the usual Sunday team. "The people who watched us play our Sunday games," Will once said, "soon learned that in a spill, if the falling rider hit on his feet, it was Fred Stone. If he hit on his head, it was me. We were both equally safe."

I remember one practice game on an improvised field near Massapequa. Arriving late, I found the players in a huddle on the sideline bending over someone. Everyone looked at me apprehensively, and I soon found out why. In a scramble for the ball, Leo Carrillo had cracked Will on the head with his mallet and knocked him out. They were trying to bring him to and get him cleaned up before I arrived.

"They call it a gentleman's game," Will said, "for the same reason that they call a tall man 'Shorty.' "

A few years later, when England sent Vernon Castle back to America to train Canadian and American fliers in Texas, he passed through New York and came to the *Midnight Frolic* with Irene Castle, his wife. Will spotted them at once, of course, and stopped the show to shake hands. "Here is one tango bird who made good," he told the audience. "We played polo together on Long Island and one day Fred Stone and I got him on a bucking horse. I guess that's where he got his first idea of aviation."

After we had moved to California, Will had more time for polo. As he became more familiar with the game he felt the need of better mounts, and it was through his friend Fred Post, the well-known polo player on Long Island, that he bought his first string of polo ponies. He taught all three children the game, and he was delighted when first Bill, then Mary and Jim played. The four made up a family team until "Mary went social on us."

As a member of the teams of the Midwick Country Club, the Riviera and Uplifters Clubs, Will played in many polo tournaments. Writing about one at Coronado Beach he said:

"We were playing the Eleventh Cavalry from Monterey. Things were going along pretty good until along about the third chukker. I was on a new pony that suddenly reared up and fell back on me. There he was lying right across my intermission. My head was out on one side and my feet on the other. That was all you could see. Next day in another game I'm on my horse, coming lickety-split down the field, when for no reason at all the horse crossed his front legs and starts turning somersaults. They picked me up just south of Santa Barbara. The crowd all said, 'Oh, that's Will Rogers; he just does that for laughs.'"

Will was back in New York again and working in the *Follies* when the Prince of Wales came to America in 1924 to attend the international polo matches. Jokes about the prince falling off his horse were sure-fire, and Will used many of them, but he was not kidding the prince—Will had suffered too many bad spills himself. He was kidding the people who seemed to think such falls were funny.

"England is all worked up over the Prince's numerous falls," he said, "but up to now no one has manifested much interest in any of mine—only for laughing purposes. In my falls I am not fortunate enough to spill any royal blood, but it's my blood and it's all I got. No matter how common our blood is we hate to lose it." Will asked: "Are the Prince and I supposed to fall with the horses or are we supposed to stay up in the air until the horse gets up and comes back under us?"

Will met the Prince of Wales one night at a dinner given by the Polo Association. This big affair, at the Piping Rock Country Club, was in honor of the Prince, and he had asked particularly that Will be invited.

"I stumbled over the feet of 10 of the heads of the Oldest Families of New York trying to arrive at the Speakers' Table [Will said describing the event]. Well, this little Prince guy seemed to enjoy it immensely. You know, when you are telling a joke on a man, the audience may listen to you but they will look at the person you are telling it on, and if he reacts pleasantly to it, it goes with them. Well, the Prince even worked it up to such an extent that he grabbed me by the coat tails and whispered suggestions in my ear. I never do over fifteen or twenty minutes and out there I did fifty.

"After the dinner, the Prince went to a dance, which lasted until 6 o'clock, but he was out at the polo field before 12 all dressed to play. He beat me, of course. But that is about the poorest recommendation a polo player can have. His side beat us 8 to 5. I couldn't discover anything wrong with his riding and I had a good chance to see it, as he was always in front of me."

CHAPTER XII

DURING Will's career I think he met and spoke before almost every foreign dignitary who visited our shores, and he was usually at his best on these occasions. But he was very nervous when he played for the first time before a President of the United States. It was in Baltimore, back in 1916, at an all-star benefit performance given by members of the Friars Club. Will was not a headliner in those days and he was proud of being asked to join the cast. But at the last minute, when he heard that President and Mrs. Wilson were motoring over from Washington to see the show, he had a severe attack of stage fright. This was just before we entered the war and Will's act was made up of jokes about our lack of preparedness and about the President's barrage of diplomatic notes and protests. But making these jokes on the roof of the New Amsterdam Theater and making them with the President in the house were two different things, and the nearer the time came the more nervous Will grew. He walked out of the stage door and up and down outside while waiting for his call.

In writing about it years later, after Mr. Wilson's death, Will said, "George Cohan, Willie Collier and other members of the cast, knowing how I felt, would pat me on the back and tell me, 'Why, he's just a human being; go on out and do your stuff.'

"Finally a warden knocked on my dressing-room

door and said, 'You die in five more minutes for kidding your country.' They just literally shoved me out on the stage.

"When I got out there, my first remark was, 'I'm kinder nervous here tonight.' Now, that is not an especially bright remark, and I don't hope to go down in history on the strength of it, but it was so apparent to the audience that I was speaking the truth, that they all laughed heartily at it.

"Now, Pershing was in Mexico at the time and there was a lot in the papers for and against the invasion. I said, 'I see where Villa raided Columbus, New Mexico. We had a man on guard that night at the post. But to show you how crooked this Villa is, he sneaked up on the opposite side. We chased him over the line five miles, but run into a lot of government red tape and had to come back.'

"Everybody in the house, before they would laugh, looked at the President to see how he was going to take it. Well, he started laughing and they all followed suit.

"Then I pulled the one which, I am proud to say, he afterwards repeated to various friends as the best one told on him during the war. I said, 'President Wilson is getting along fine now to what he was a few months ago. Do you realize, people, that at one time in our negotiations with Germany, he was five notes behind?'

"Well, due to his being a good fellow and setting a real example, I had the proudest and most successful night I ever had on the stage. He come back at intermission and chatted and shook hands with all of us."

After this Baltimore meeting, President Wilson never failed to be present in his box when the *Follies* played Washington.

Before we entered the war, our lack of preparedness was a great source of complaint, and Will's gag about the typewriter being a Wilson machine gun was popular with the *Follies* audience. Later, when the nation became involved, there was even more complaint about the state of our Army. Heywood Broun, then a dramatic critic, interviewed Will and demanded to know why the Wilson "machine gun" gag had disappeared from his monologue. Mr. Broun said that he knew one man who, disliking President Wilson's policies, had crossed the continent and bought tickets to the *Follies* at speculator's prices just to hear that gag. Will pointed to the war headlines in a newspaper on his dressing table.

"You can't kid a man when he's in all that trouble," he said.

Will knew when to temper his jibes. And though United States Presidents usually came in for a good bit of his ribbing, it was seldom that he was misunderstood or that anyone took offense. "You can always kid a big man," he once said. "I generally hit the fellow on top because it's not fair to hit a man when he's down." Will always felt that everyone knew it was all in fun, and the last thing he wanted to do was to offend, hurt or embarrass anyone. Occasionally, however, things were resented or misunderstood, and complications followed.

Early in the Harding Administration, Will was sent

on tour with a musical show called *The Ziegfeld Frolic.*
The show's cleverest skit was a burlesque on the recent
Washington Conference for the Limitation of Arma-
ments. Will had written the sketch himself, and in it
he played Secretary of State Hughes, beard and all.
Brandon Tynan, a distinguished actor, played Lord
Balfour, the English delegate. The sketch was very
funny, a combination of slapstick and utter nonsense
played with great dignity and aplomb. Audiences
everywhere liked it. Will called it "The Disagreement
Conference," and the sketch was especially appreciated
when the show played in Washington. Will had never
appeared before a more distinguished audience. On
the opening night the house glittered with the gold
braid of the various Embassy staffs; several Cabinet
members were present, including Secretary of State
Hughes; and there were many Senators and Congress-
men, all having the time of their lives. The Washington Conference had been considered a big achievement
of the Harding Administration; and the Democrats,
particularly, were delighted with Will's kidding.

When the show first opened in Washington, Nicholas
Longworth had taken Will in to see the President,
though Will had met him before. Mr. Harding was
friendly and congenial, and Will was naturally pleased
when the President expressed the hope that he would
be able to see the show. Not the slightest hint was
dropped during their conversation that the President
objected to any of Will's jokes. But the next day a
White House secretary came to Will's dressing room
and asked him not to make so many remarks about

President Harding's golf; the newspapers, the emissary said, had been overdoing it. Will was surprised, but he agreed, of course, and not only eliminated a golf joke or two from the Conference skit, but rearranged his monologue.

It was reported that during our stay in Washington, Will was refused an invitation to a White House reception. This was utterly untrue. Will was busy in the theater and unable to go but I attended with Senator and Mrs. Rob L. Owens, and Mr. and Mrs. Longworth. It was my first White House reception, and also my first meeting with Vice-President and Mrs. Coolidge. President Harding impressed me, even in the perfunctory greeting and handshake customary at these receptions, as a charming, warm and friendly man.

Then one night the newspapermen told Will that President and Mrs. Harding planned to attend the theater that night. This is an event in Washington. And it was taken for granted, by everybody, that the President and his party would come to the *Frolic;* the only other show in town was a road company on tour for the second season which was playing across the street. We were all excited, but just before the curtain went up, we found that the President had gone to the other show. It was almost impossible for those on the inside to consider the President's choice as anything but a deliberate sign of disapproval.

Will was disappointed and a little peeved. And during one of his curtain call speeches, he indirectly gave expression to his feelings. "I have cracked quite a few jokes on public men here," he told the audience, "both Republicans and Democrats. I hope I have not given offense. In fact, I don't believe any big man will take offense.

"I recall when Colonel Theodore Roosevelt was a Bull Moose candidate, that I took several flings at Teddy. Later, when I was invited up on the platform to hear him speak, I remarked on greeting Mr. Roosevelt, 'Well, I hope you are not going to put me in jail.' Roosevelt laughed heartily and said, 'Don't be afraid you will hurt my feelings. When you can use my name to advantage, go the limit.'

"I remember, too, that when Mr. Wilson was President during the late war, I cracked some rather rough jokes at his expense at the theater, when he and his family occupied a box. And Mr. Wilson laughed long and heartily. After all, it is the test of a big man whether he can stand the gaff."

At the time, Will's talk went over the heads of most of the audience. But the newspaper men understood and the next day there was a terrific how-do-you-do. It was meat for the Democratic papers, and Will, who made a point of never taking sides politically, was amazed at what he had gotten himself into. He was sorry, too, that he had lost his temper, and always felt afterward that the President's advisers, rather than Mr. Harding himself, had been responsible.

Will liked President Harding. "The most human of any of our late Presidents," he wrote long afterward. "There was more of the real 'Every Day Man' in him. If he had a weakness, it was in trusting his friends, and the man that don't do that, then there is something the matter with him. Betrayed by friendship is not a bad memorial to leave."

Shortly after the Harding misunderstanding, Will explained in a weekly article: "It was reported that President Harding couldn't stand the jokes about the Administration. Why, he had a great sense of humor. The first time I met him, Will Hays introduced me to him in the White House, and he repeated to me a lot of jokes that I had told on him way before.

"I said to him, 'Now, Mr. President, I don't want you to think that I am hard on you all. You know I told some pretty tough ones on the Democrats when they were in—in fact, I think I told funnier ones on the Democrats, as they were doing funnier things.'

"I explained to him that it would not be fair to the Democrats to kid them while they were down, but that the minute they got their heads above water, I would take a whack at them.

"No, I don't think I ever hurt any man's feelings by my little gags. I know I never willfully did it. I may not have always said just what they would have liked me to say, but they knew it was meant in good nature and in fun."

The most unfortunate of these misunderstandings came in 1927, when Will made his first broadcast from our home in Beverly Hills. It was the most elaborate radio program put on up to that time. Fred Stone broadcast from Chicago, Al Jolson from New Orleans, Paul Whiteman from New York and Will from Los Angeles—all four corners of the United States for the first time on the air. Technicians spent days installing apparatus in our basement and hooking up telephone and telegraph wires. Graham McNamee made a special trip to the Coast to act as Will's announcer. In introducing Will, he said specifically that the broadcast was coming from the Rogers home in Beverly Hills.

Will talked about various things as usual, and then said, "I want to introduce a friend of mine who is here and wishes to speak to you." Tightening his lips and imitating President Coolidge's rather high-pitched voice, he continued, "Farmers, I am proud to report that the country as a whole is prosperous. I don't mean by that that the whole country is prosperous, but as a hole it is prosperous. That is, it is prosperous for a hole. A hole is not supposed to be prosperous and you are certainly in a hole. There is not a whole lot of doubt about that."

President Coolidge had just returned from a trip to the Northwest to pacify the farmers. Will was good at mimicry, and some people listening in said they thought it was the President talking. Will was terribly upset. It was hard for him to believe that anyone could be so stupid as to connect President Coolidge with the silly joke. Will and the Coolidges had always been good friends. He had visited them often at the White House, and he immediately sent the President a note.

The President answered in his own hand, "I thought the matter of rather small consequence myself, though the office was informed from several sources that I had been on the air." He added that he knew it had all been in fun and closed, "I hope you will not give the affair another troubled thought."

Will visited the Coolidges many times after that, and when Mr. Coolidge returned to private life, Will wrote: "Mr. Coolidge, I have told many jokes about you, and this don't mean I am going to quit, for we love jokes about those we like."

I was inclined to worry over Will's informality in talking about public men. I was afraid he would go too far and that someone would take offense, and I thought he should be more careful.

I spoke to Father Duffy about this when he was dining with us one night in New York. At the time I was disturbed over a controversy that had arisen in the papers in regard to a political speech Will had made at the Town Hall for Ogden Mills, then a Republican candidate for Congress. Theodore Roosevelt, Jr., had asked Will to speak.

Will had no interest in the campaign, but he was very fond of the Roosevelt boys. Their friendship went back to 1905, when he had done his rope tricks for them in the White House. To him, "a Roosevelt hint was a Roosevelt command," and he agreed to make his first stump speech. He began by saying, "I have spoken in all kinds of joints, from one of Mrs. Vanderbilt's parties on Fifth Avenue to Sing Sing in Ossining, but this is my first crack at a political speech and I hope it flops. I don't want to go over and then have to go into politics, because up to now I have always tried to live honest.

"A great many think I was sent here by Mr. Mills' opponent, but this is not the case. I don't know his opponent. But he must be a 'scoundrel.' From what

I have read of politics, every opponent is. He must also be a 'tool of the interests.'

"Mr. Mills should be elected, because he's the only candidate who owns his own silk hat," Will said. "He is the only candidate for Congress who can go into a Fifth Avenue home without delivering something."

Since Mr. Mills was a very wealthy man, Will's chaffing did not make a hit with the Republican audience, but Democratic papers were delighted and printed many excerpts from the speech.

I was upset and confided to Father Duffy that I was sorry Will had said what he had, and that I thought he should be a little more tactful in the future.

"Leave that boy alone," Father Duffy told me. "He knows what he's doing. He's doing a good job, and don't you try to change him."

I had the same advice a few years later from another wise and understanding man. We were living in California then. The children had been ill. Dr. William A. Edwards was their physician and was in the house one night when Will came home from the studio. He was going to a dinner given in honor of the Mayor of Los Angeles and I had hopefully laid out a clean shirt and a freshly pressed suit on his bed.

But Will had a rule. He dressed only once a day. After his bath in the morning, he put on a clean shirt, and that bath and that shirt had to last him through the evening, no matter what came up. But tonight was the Mayor's dinner and I felt it was worth a struggle.

"What's wrong with this suit?" Will protested, brushing the lapels of his coat and straightening his tie and collar. "This shirt's clean. I just put it on this morning." I kept arguing for the freshly pressed suit. Finally Will said, "Blake, I wish you'd let me alone," and very quickly he slammed the door and was gone.

Doctor Edwards had heard it all, and he said to me, "Now, young lady, you leave Will the way he is. We like him that way. We don't want him dressed up like the rest of us."

So eventually I stopped trying to make Will tidy in his dress and careful about what he said. It was impossible, too, in spite of the ever increasing demands upon his time, to convince Will that he should plan ahead. His was a casual day-to-day existence. He hated to be tied down to prearranged plans and would not make an engagement two weeks ahead if he could possibly help it. He didn't know where he would be in two weeks' time and preferred not to think about it. If he wanted to do something, he wanted to do it immediately.

As a result living with Will had its explosive qualities. I was not made of the same kind of stuff and there were times when this life of the moment troubled me. During the early years of our marriage I would worry about things that had to be done, our obligations, our home and the future. But though I never acquired Will's ability to consider the day at hand as quite sufficient in itself, our life together must have changed me more than I was ever able to change him.

Clothes were never a problem to Will. Nor was luggage a problem when he traveled; he wore the suit he had on, packed a couple of clean shirts in the little bag and was ready to leave on a moment's notice. Once he flew to New York, intending to return the next day. But there he learned from Winfield Sheehan that his next picture would not be ready to start for a few weeks. And the Naval Disarmament Conference was about to convene in London. "When I was a little boy out in the old Indian Territory," Will explained, "I remember seeing a sheriff disarm some men one time and it always fascinated me. But I had never seen it since. So when I arrived in New York and they told me they were going to disarm whole nations over in London next week, I grabbed the first boat."

Will had landed in New York in the morning and by midafternoon he was telephoning me in California that he was going to the Conference for a few days. He had no steamship reservation and no passport, and the liner sailed at midnight, but Mr. Sheehan had promised to take care of both.

Will had only the suit he was wearing, and since he was crossing on one of the larger British ships, he needed a second and a darker suit for dinner. It now was sundown and the stores were closed, but touring by taxicab he found a cut-rate shop on Broadway that still was doing business. While one clerk scurried for shirts, socks and ties, the other fitted Will with the only blue serge suit in the shop even close to Will's size. It was double-breasted and cost $19.85. The pants were too long and the store's tailor had gone home, but there was a little cleaning-and-pressing stand down the street, and the shopkeeper sent the trousers there to be shortened.

On his arrival in London, Will was invited to dinner at the American Embassy by General Dawes, then our Ambassador. Will protested that he had no formal clothes, and told the General about his last-minute shopping expedition. That was just the sort of thing to appeal to the General and he insisted that Will wear the suit to dinner and tell the story again to his guests.

And so the story of Will's $19.85 suit served him on a whole round of formal parties. The suit even was inspected and approved by the Prince of Wales; and later Will's London friends jokingly accused him of having set the fashion for the double-breasted dinner jacket—an idea that finally was picked up and used in a "believe-it-or-not" column.

Will's interests widened and his sympathies deepened, but the essential man beneath remained always the same—Will never changed. His travels took him all over the world, and he became almost a world citizen. But in the hotel registers of Washington, New York, London, California or Mexico, he signed "Will Rogers, Claremore, Oklahoma." and he always thought of himself that way.

Attending hundreds of banquets both here and abroad, Will sampled the wares of the world's most celebrated chefs. But his taste in food remained simple, as did his tastes in everything else. He liked what they had in Oklahoma.

"About all I do when I go back to Oklahoma [he once wrote] is just shake hands and eat. We always have such good things at my sister's in Chelsea. Beans,

and what beans—kinder soupy navy beans cooked with
plenty of real fat meat. And then the Ham. Tom
McSpadden, my Brother-in-law, is the prize ham curer
of any I ever saw. Smokes 'em with the old hickory
log fire, then he salts 'em away. And you know the
cooking has got a lot to do with it. Sister Sallie does
all this herself when I get home.

"Then the cream gravy. You know an awful lot
of folks don't know much about gravy. Ham gravy
is just about the last word in gravys. Of course good
beefsteak gravy is good. And say, let me tell you
something. All this eating raw, bloody, rare meat, like
they order in big hotels—that's just city people—that
ain't old western folks. Ranch cooks and farm women
fry steak thin and hard and you can get some awful
good gravy by putting the milk in the skillet after
you fry a lot of good beefsteak.

"Now then comes the corn bread. Not the corn
bread like you mean. I mean corn pone, made with
nothing but meal, and hot water and salt. My old
Daddy always had that at every meal. Light-bread
or loaves like you all eat, he called that 'wasp nest.'
Beans, cornbread, country ham, and gravy! Then for
desert? Don't have room for any desert. Had any
more room, would eat some more beans."

I recall a party given years ago by old friends in
Claremore for "Uncle Clem's boy"—a banquet at the
Elks Club. His sisters Sallie and Maude were there.
So were his cousins, Mary, Johnnie and Christian Gul-
ager, of Tahlequah, and Dr. Jesse Bushyhead whom
Will loved like a brother. Will's eyes filled with tears
when he saw all the old schoolmates and playmates who
had gathered to honor him. It was a glorious dinner—

just what Will liked—every bit of it cooked by the
ladies of the Pocahontas Club, an organization whose
members were of Cherokee ancestry.

J. Foreman McClellan, a boyhood friend, was toast-
master, and Will's cousin, Clue Gulager, of Muskogee,
made an address of welcome. Will, usually so free
with words, was speechless for several moments when
he was called upon. But later we all had a grand time
and Will had more fun than he had had in years. There
were quadrilles and square dances, with Will calling
the figures. He danced with his cousin Bunt Robert-
son, and Bess Lewis, and there was an Indian war
dance, with Will in the lead, that shook the roof.

When we were on our way back to New York, Will
asked me, "What can I do for Claremore? I want
to do something." And then somehow he began thinking about Dr. Jesse Bushyhead, the busiest physician
in the county, a man who would go anywhere at any
time to relieve suffering. We remembered his ambition
to specialize in the treatment of children, and that he
had not been able to leave his family and practice to
do the necessary postgraduate work and study.

On our arrival in New York, Will sent for Jesse.
It was arranged for him to take the medical course he
had so long hoped for, without financial loss to his
family. For many years that community gift has been
paying dividends in healthy children.

Will once wrote a letter about children that I have
never seen reprinted. It must have been addressed to
some child welfare organization, but I have forgotten
the occasion. It was funny, but also it was pointed.

"I am mighty glad [Will wrote] that so many people in America are taking up the children work. I used to think there might be some chance of getting our Government interested in it, but that was hoping too much. Being a Ranchman and a Farmer and also a child owner, I have often wished when one of my children got sick I could wire or call up some Government expert and have him come look after them. Like I can do if one of my cows or Pigs gets some disease.

"If your fertilizer is not agreeing with your land the Government will send a specialist, but if the food is not agreeing with Baby, why we have to find out the matter ourselves, and lots of times Parents mean well but they don't know much.

"So I am glad that you people are interested in children. Course they are a lot of trouble but we just don't seem to be smart enough to find something that would be less trouble that would replace them. It's not a bad idea whoever thought of doing something for the children. If it works out and you improve them, I will send you mine."

Will was not always the humorist, and one of his most memorable articles was written upon the occasion of the death of his sister Maude. During the time that she was gravely ill, he was asked to speak before a group of Methodist ministers in New York. He had never faced an audience with so little preparation. After a few jokes, he "floundered around from one subject to another." The minister who introduced him had mentioned that Will had been raised a Methodist.

So Will started on that and finally spoke of something he hadn't intended to speak of, his sister and her illness. "Out of a large family of which I am the youngest," he said, "I have two sisters living. And I could not speak of any church without bringing in the work these two sisters have done in the little town where they both live. It's Chelsea, Oklahoma, which means nothing in your life, but it has meant a lot to people who have lived in association with them.

"They started in this little Western town some thirty-five years ago. They helped build the Methodist church, the first church there. They have helped every church, they have helped every movement that they knew was for the best upbuilding of their community. They have each raised a large family of boys and girls, who are today a credit to their community. They have carried on the same as thousands of women have carried on in every small and big town in the world. They don't think they are doing good out of the ordinary. They don't want credit. They do good simply because they don't know any other thing to do."

When Will finished, the clergymen rose in a body and offered a silent prayer for Maude's recovery.

At the very time Will spoke, I was on my way to the railroad station to go to Maude's bedside, where he later joined me. His own words tell the rest: "Today, as I write this, I am out in Oklahoma among my people, my Cherokee people, who don't expect a laugh for everything I say.

"That silent prayer that those three hundred ministers uttered didn't save my sister. She has passed away. But she had lived such a life that it was a privilege to pass away. Death didn't scare her. It was only an episode in her life. If you live right, death is a joke to you, so far as fear is concerned.

"And on the day that I am supposed to write a humorous article, I am back home at the funeral of my sister. I can't be funny. I don't want to be funny. Even Mr. Ziegfeld don't want me to be funny. I told him I wanted to go. He said, 'I would hate you if you didn't.' I told W. C. Fields, the principal comedian of the show. He said, 'Go on. I will do something to fill in.' Brandon Tynan, my friend of years, said, 'Go home where you want to be and where you ought to be.'

"I have just today witnessed a funeral that, for real sorrow and real affection, I don't think will ever be surpassed anywhere. They came in every mode of conveyance, on foot, in buggies, horseback, wagons, cars and trains, and there wasn't a soul that came that she hadn't helped or favored at one time or another . . .

"Some uninformed newspapers printed: 'Mrs. C. L. Lane, sister of the famous comedian, Will Rogers.' It's the other way around. I am the brother of Mrs. C. L. Lane, the friend of humanity. And I want to tell you that, as I saw all those people who were there to pay tribute to her memory, it was the proudest moment of my life that I was her brother.

"And all the honors that I could ever in my wildest dreams hope to reach would never equal the honor paid on a little Western prairie hilltop, among her people, to Maude Lane.

"If they love me like that at my finish, my life will not have been in vain."

Top: Everybody, including horses and cows, was welcome at the Rogers ranch. One calf was not only too tame to use for roping but too friendly to stay outside. The family watches as Jimmy wrestles "Sarah," the family pet. *Bottom:* Fred Stone, long-time friend, flew out to California to see Will and landed at the polo field on the ranch, about 1928. From left to right: Johnny Campion (Stone's pilot), Mary, Fred Stone, Jimmy, Will, Mary, and Bill. *(Courtesy Will Rogers Memorial)*

Will kisses Betty good-bye as he prepares to leave on a round-trip flight
to New York with a mail pilot. *(Courtesy Will Rogers Memorial)*

Top: Will's first radio broadcast, 1922, Pittsburgh Post Radio Station, KDKA, with Betty seated at piano. *Bottom:* Will, Betty, and Fred Stone. *(Courtesy Will Rogers Memorial)*

Betty. *(Photo by John W. Wiefert, courtesy Will Rogers Memorial)*

CHAPTER XIII

THE 1920's were fast, full years for the Rogers family. Will had gone from the *Follies* to California for the silent pictures, then back to the theater again. He had written for newspapers and magazines and his books were among the best-sellers. He did a series of weekly radio programs, and he went on lecture tours that carried him from one end of the country to the other. And when sound came to Hollywood, we returned to California and he made pictures again.

But of all the things Will did in these years, I think he got the greatest satisfaction from his work on the lecture platform. Will liked an audience that he could see and hear and feel. It stimulated him, gave him inspiration. His best ideas seemed to come to him when he was on his feet, warmed up, and feeling the mood of the people before him.

He was never quite happy with radio, although he was one of a very few on the air who submitted to no censorship. "It's made to order for a singer," he said, "and a person making a straight-forward speech, or a talk, explaining something. But to have to line up there and try to get some laughs, I want to tell you its the toughest job I ever tackled." Since much of his talk was extemporaneous, Will needed an immediate audience to play to. The microphone, or for that matter the motion-picture camera, was a poor substitute.

"They have a time getting me stopped on this radio

thing," he would explain over the air, "so I got an alarm clock here, and when it goes off, brother, I quit— even if I'm right in the middle of reciting 'Gunga Din' or 'The Declaration of Independence.' I wouldn't need this alarm clock if I hadn't been so dumb about this broadcasting. You see, everybody reads everything they do over the radio and I'm going to learn it, but the trouble with me is I don't read very well and I hate to go to the trouble of writing this out. If I ever saw in print what I do say sometimes, I would be ashamed to say it."

Will always insisted on an audience in the studio, but even so, it wasn't quite the same. He had to talk into the microphone and he couldn't tell whether the people listening in were getting it or not. But after the broadcast to countless people that he could neither see nor hear, Will usually stayed on and talked for awhile to the audience of a hundred or so there in the studio. Often he was more entertaining then for the next half hour, than he had just been in the fifteen-minute broadcast, for which he had received around $7,000.

Besides giving him large immediate audiences and putting no time limit on his talks, the lecture tour had another charm for Will. He was always going some-where. Every night he was in a different place, with fresh local material available. Each town had a per-sonality; there were new people to meet and like, a different group of old friends to look up, historic land-marks to see for the first time. "I never hit a town," he said, "that don't have something that is unique or unusual." An indefatigable sightseer, Will was like a small boy wanting to see everything and wanting to do everything.

Lecturing in Montana one year, Will found a good pilot with his own plane; and hiring him for a week, did all his traveling by air: "Would stay all night in the town I had just played, get a good night's rest, then take my time about getting out in the morning, and leave just whenever I wanted to. Fly over the beautiful mountain tops, and in two or three hours catch up with the train that had left the night before. Then when we get to the next town and the committee would come and want to take me for a drive to see their town, I could tell them all about it. Fly over a town and you get more of an idea of it than you could get in a week from driving around."

It was in 1925 that Charles Wagner, the well-known concert manager, introduced Will in what he called "an effort to humanize the concert business." It was quite a jump from the *Ziegfeld Follies,* on Broadway, to a concert tour to be sold to women's clubs and society groups all over the country, and to play before audiences accustomed to view their entertainment as culture. At first Will was dubious about his ability to fill the big auditoriums, and dubious, too, about his ability to talk for an entire evening. But the tour appealed to him. "I'm getting tired of talking to Broadway," he told his New York audience. "I want to get away and talk to America."

"I am out to see how America is living," he wrote later. "I mean the ones that don't go to New York and support the Ticket Speculators, and then come back home and brag on what everything cost 'em. I am meeting the 'regular Bird'—the one that lives in his town; stays in his town; is proud of his town—he offers no apology for not having seen last year's *Follies,* or any other years'. I wanted to find out what he was thinking about—what he was reading about."

At first Will carried along a talented male quartet, the De Reszke Singers—John Hardesty, Floyd Townsley, Howard Kellog and Erwyn Mutch. They were American-born pupils of Jean De Reszke; Mary Garden had heard them sing at De Reszke's villa in Nice and had cabled Mr. Wagner, who was also her manager, that they would be a sensation in America. The famous quartet toured with Will through the East and Southwest, but as constantly packed houses proved Will's success as a concert lecturer, he was soon giving the whole evening's entertainment alone. It was on the lecture platform, talking to America, that Will made some of his most often repeated comments.

"I don't make jokes," he said. "I just watch the Government and report the facts and I have never found it necessary to exaggerate." He philosophized on the state of the nation: "More people should work for their dinner instead of dressing for it." He considered our diplomats: "The United States never lost a war or won a conference." And: "There is one thing a nation can't accuse us of—that is secret diplomacy. Our foreign dealings are an open book—generally a checkbook." He kidded business: "Two-thirds of the people promote while one-third provide." He offered solace to agriculture: "The greatest need of the farmers today is a third mortgage." He analyzed world affairs: "At the London Naval Disarmament Conference, we stood through one speech, sat through eight, slept through twelve, and in three solid hours of conference, not a rowboat was sunk." In such comments, Will gave the audience his slant on national and international events, comments that made headlines in the Twenties and later—some of which are still making headlines today.

On his first tour Will lectured 151 nights, from September to mid-April. The following season he played more. He went through the South, then back to the Eastern states; covered the Middle West and toured up and down the Pacific Coast. "When I left New York a while ago," Will wrote in a weekly article, "I told you that I was tired of rewriting something I had already seen written. Well, when I write of Texas now, I know about it. I have been all through the State. Half of my entire act while in Texas consisted of local things in Texas. I talked with every Editor in each town; all the writers on the papers; Hotel Managers, Ranchmen, Farmers, Politicians, Head Waiters, Barbers, Newsboys, Bootblacks. Everybody I met I would try to get their angle."

Will played towns he hadn't been in since the old vaudeville days. He lectured in theaters, school auditoriums, concert and lodge halls—even churches. "If your town's got a railroad and a hall, we'll be there sooner or later," he promised.

He enjoyed his audiences as much as they enjoyed

him. "You're doing fine," he would tell them when a few hesitant chuckles had led to a roar of laughter from the crowd. "We'll get out early tonight. It takes twice as long to get out when you have to explain the jokes."

Of all his jokes, he liked best the ones that rang true to everybody. He liked to see the people nod their heads and nudge one another, as much as to say, "He's right about that. He hit the nail on the head that time."

In a new town Will would go first to the newspaper offices to pick up bits of local gossip and information on the problems of that city and to gather facts on the ins and outs of the political situation. He made notes of the things he wanted to remember, but once out on the stage he never referred to them; he relied on the inspiration of the moment and seemed to have an uncanny knowledge of when to spring an unexpected remark. This was the reason he could appear on the platform so seemingly unprepared.

His whole performance on these lecture tours was quite informal and his audience could not help smiling at him and with him. He would wander casually around the stage, lean against the piano or even sit down for awhile; and when, as sometimes happened, he had to use a microphone in the larger auditoriums, he was acutely embarrassed by this restriction on his movements. Once when his voice hadn't carried well over a microphone, he was so upset that after the lecture he refunded the price of the show.

Will had a wonderful sense of timing and never hurried into the middle of a laugh. As one critic described it: "Will Rogers makes a statement, then another, then a third. All together they make perfectly good sense, and are often funny, so that your mouth widens toward a smile. Then, after the briefest pause, comes a sudden final thrust of wit which explodes the whole business as if it were gunpowder."

His programs grew longer and longer; his audiences wouldn't let him stop talking. Sometimes, exhausted, he would sit down on the edge of the stage with his feet dangling in the orchestra pit, and finally, after a few intimate remarks he would say, "I'm tired. Now, you folks go on out of here and go home—if you've got a home." Or: "You folks go home. I'm tired of messing with you."

Will was very busy on these tours. He not only had his weekly articles to do, but before leaving New York, the Syndicate had persuaded him to try out a short daily column called "The Worst Story I Heard Today." It was simply some joke or "wise-crack," old or new, attributed to a well-known person, or to one of Will's close friends, and decorated with a few personal touches.

It was fairly easy for a time to find stories apropos or utterly absurd. I prowled from one book store to another collecting old joke books, and then we would search through them for material. People were amused to find their names attached to some ancient story or to a joke of which they had never heard. But of course we both got awfully tired of it. Will never liked it; the formula was quite rigid—it simply wasn't the sort of thing that could hold his interest. And after a short time, he gave it up. But the Syndicate had contracted to supply their newspapers, and so for a short while after he stopped doing it, the feature was continued under Will's name.

When Will finished his first lecture tour in the spring of 1926, he was asked by George Horace Lorimer to do a series of articles from abroad for the *Saturday Evening Post*. These appeared as "Letters of a Self-made Diplomat to His President," and later were published in book form.

Early that spring, Will and our eldest son, Bill, sailed for England. (I was to follow later, when the school term was over, with Mary and Jim.) Their boat was still in mid-ocean when the English general strike was called, and though most of the passengers bound for England decided to disembark instead at Cherbourg, Will was determined to go on to London. And he was always glad that he saw the English during this crisis; their calmness, as well as the co-operative way in which everyone turned out, impressed him very much.

"It looked like the greatest country in the world [he reported]. You never saw such combined strength; everybody wanted to help run street cars and trucks and do any kind of work, skilled and all. There is one thing about the English—they won't fix anything 'till it's just about totally ruined. You couldn't get an Englishman to fix anything at the start. No, they like to sit and watch it grow worse. If nothing was growing worse, they wouldn't have anything to debate and argue about. Then, when it just looks like the

whole thing has gone up salt creek, why the English
jump in and rescue it."

France was also having her troubles.

"That changing of Ministers every few hours has
been the prize Government Circus trick of Europe [he
said]. You see you can't get anywhere with any kind
of financial government in France, for the Frenchman
won't pay his taxes. There is only just one little bunch
over there that pay taxes for the whole Country. The
minute a Premier or Cabinet Minister gets up and
says: 'We will have to add one millionth part of one
percent on to the taxes,' they throw him out.

"And, Oh Boy, how they are hating us! If somebody
gets a bad cold, it is laid to the grasping nature of
Money-loving America. Mellon just arrived over here
and was met by Editorials such as: 'Uncle Andy Shy-
lock,' 'What! is he coming after more,' and dozens
of others like that. So we seem to be in pretty Dutch
with all the Natives that we were so rude as to lend
money to. It's the old Gag, (and Nations are not different from individuals) you loan a man money and
you lose his friendship."

With London as a base, Will covered most of Europe
in flying trips to gather first-hand material for his
Post articles. In Rome he had an interview with Mussolini; he saw the Preliminary Conference on Disarmament at Geneva; he met the King of Spain; was entertained by Ambassador Schurman in Berlin; and made
his first trip into Russia. And little love as Will found
for Americans in his travels, he found still less between the nations of Europe themselves.

"Talk about us being in bad [he wrote]. Say, we haven't started to get in bad. Some of these nations have been hating each other for generations, while they are only just starting in hating us. When it comes to being in wrong in Europe, we are only an Amateur.

"France and England think just as much of each other as two rival bands of Chicago Bootleggers. Gloating over our unpopularity is the only thing they have ever agreed on perfectly. Italy went to bat on the side of France in the last Series, but that was just because Austria was on the opposite side. A Frenchman and an Italian love each other just about like Minneapolis and St. Paul. Russia hates everybody so bad, it would take her a week to pick out the one she hates most.

"Germany, the winner of the last war, is about the only one that is not looking for trouble. When the Allies took their Army and Navy away from them, shortsighted Statesmen didn't know it, but they did them the greatest favor that was ever done a Nation. It didn't leave them a thing to do but go to work."

Going over on the same boat with Will had been the American delegation to the Preliminary Conference on Disarmament at Geneva. Talking with the delegates, Will had decided that they were going to the conference, "with about the same hopes for success that I would tackle Hamlet in tights." But he went to Geneva to have a look at the conference in action, and stayed, as he said, "till they were throwing inkstands at each other."

For Switzerland, however, the seat of the conference—"they just sit around and remain Neutral during these wars, and then collect from both sides. It's the only country where both sides can go and have a drink during that particular war"—Will had nothing but admiration. "The most independent country in the world," he said. "They have neither imports nor exports. Its sole commodities are Conferences and Neutrality. When Nations get ready to make peace or war (and they generally don't know which they are making), why they always go to Switzerland. It's kinder like Atlantic City is for bathing suit contests. It has a corner on all Conferences. It has had fewer wars and has been the starting place of more of them than any nation that ever lived."

Will's interview with Mussolini, conducted partly in English and partly through an interpreter, went off very well. But Will had not been above a bit of undercover kidding. "He asked me in a very confidential way," Will reported, "and in very good English—because I bet he asks this of everybody—'What has impressed you most in Italy?' Well I knew that everybody had always told him it was the 'Marvelous improvement that had taken place in the last three years.'

"But I told him that it was two things. One was the amount of automobiles meeting and neither one ever knowing which side the other was going to pass him on, and yet nobody ever got hit; and the other thing was the amount of bicycles ridden, and I never saw anyone ever fixing a puncture. Well, this answer kinder set him back for a minute. He laughed, but you could tell that he was disappointed. I was the only one that had not noticed the 'marvelous improvement in the last three years.' "

Coming out of Italy, Will paid a visit to the French Riviera. It was the off-season; he and Bill had a hotel practically to themselves; and they spent a day at Monte Carlo.

"There is some pretty good ideas about the place [Will wrote]. For instance, you don't have any taxes to pay. The Casino takes care of everything. When I said: 'Why, how can they afford to do that?' the party I said that to laughed. I didn't know what he was laughing at then. I do now.

"They also won't let a fellow from the old home town go in and wager. Now that right there struck me as being a very fine trait in the Government of Monaco. They practically say to their own flesh and blood: 'Stand back till we trim these Suckers. If we need any extra for Yachts or Palaces, we will let you home town folks know, but we won't want to call on you till we absolutely have to.'

"They have the prettiest chips to play with. I wanted some to bring home, so late at night when I was leaving the Casino, I cashed another Money Order—went over and bought thirty dollars worth of all denominations. Then I walked right by the tables rattling them and walked right on out. I showed 'em here was a Guy who wouldn't even go to the trouble of cashing in. I haven't found out yet who the joke is on. Anyway, the old prince of Monaco has a great business. It works while he sleeps."

Early in June, Mary, Jim and I met Bill and his father in London. The two of them had had a fine time sightseeing on the Continent, and now that the whole family was together, Will took special delight in driving the children around the countryside. He took care that no point of interest was overlooked. Will was a confirmed and enthusiastic tour-conductor; when you saw sights with him, you missed little.

He made one picture here in London, *Tip Toes,* in which he appeared with Dorothy Gish and Nelson Keith. Produced by British National Pictures, Ltd., it was directed by Herbert Wilcox. "Every time you finish a scene, they bring you a cup of tea," Will complained, "and what makes me sore at myself, is, I am beginning to like the stuff."

It was during the latter part of our summer in London that Will sent a casual cable to the New York *Times,* an accidental and unplanned incident, out of which grew the daily paragraph or so of comment that was eventually featured in some five hundred newspapers and became the best-known thing he did.

We had lunched one day with Lord and Lady Astor at Cliveden. Lady Astor was leaving soon for America. And on July twenty-ninth Will cabled Adolph Ochs: "Nancy Astor, which is the nom de plume of Lady Astor, is arriving on your side about now. Please ask my friend Jimmy Walker to have New York take good care of her. She is the only one over here who don't throw rocks at American tourists. Yours, Will Rogers."

The *Times* printed the cable in a box on the front page of its second section and cabled an immediate request for more. One, a few days later, was: "England's House of Parliament, or Commons (I have seen it and prefer to call it Commons) closed today to give some of the lady members a chance to try and swim the English Channel. I wanted to have my wife try it, but the Channel is all booked up for the next month."

During the remainder of our stay in Europe, Will continued to send these short wires. He had no thought of continuing them, but soon after our return to New York, the *Times*—responding to requests from readers—asked Will to go on with them. Many editors, too, were interested in the feature; Will's friend Larry Winship, editor of the Boston *Globe,* was one of the most ardent boosters for the column—as, also, was Mr. Ochs of the New York *Times.* These were the first two papers in which it regularly appeared.

Will himself had enjoyed doing the wires and was glad to continue. When he really got into the swing of the thing, these daily pieces became his favorite medium. In later years his schedule was often overcrowded, and he would have been glad to drop the weekly articles; but doing a daily wire, though it might sometimes be difficult, was never drudgery.

So from October 15, 1926, on, Will sent in his wire every day, six days a week, no matter where he was or what he was doing. There are few sections of the globe from which it was not filed. Always carrying a portable typewriter with him, he wrote the column on motion-picture sets, in trains and airplanes, in theater dressing rooms and in steamship cabins, and the diary of his last trip is to be found in the cheerful dailies he sent back from Alaska.

The McNaught Syndicate soon began to handle the daily as a regular feature. I have forgotten just what

Will received for it in the beginning, but toward the last he was getting $2500 a week for his daily and weekly articles combined. Other syndicates offered him more, but he liked the McNaught people. They had treated him fairly and he stayed on with them.

That summer in London, Will went into the *Cochran Revue,* a musical show, for four weeks. Americans were never more unpopular in Europe than in 1926. But Charles Cochran was very anxious about the success of his new show. Will was fond of his old friend and when Charles asked him to help out, Will didn't refuse. He did his usual stunt and spoke frankly about the war debts, French finance and the British general strike, as well as about America's big problem, prohibition. The English were not accustomed to such forthright discussion of national problems and there were many odd comments in the English papers. For the most part they were favorable, but occasionally one found fault with Will. Under the blunt heading Go Home, Will Rogers, *Everybody's Weekly* had this to say:

"Naturally, we of the audience assumed we would see this quaint Yankee in some of his inimitable drollery. Nothing of the sort. To the amazement and, I may truthfully say, consternation of the bulk of the audience, we were compelled to listen to a diatribe which mainly consisted of gratuitous insults aimed at Great Britain, France and Belgium.

"It seems incredible that a man like Cochran, whose sympathies should be with this country and with France because he has earned much bread and butter from each, should let his platform be used for foolish American propaganda of this sort. . . . His [Will's] remarks on the present European crisis are insulting, insolent, presumptuous and in the worst of bad taste."

From another paper:

"Will Rogers, the American humorist, has been filling a special engagement with the Cochran Revue. He is neither diplomatic as regards England nor patriotic as regards America. It is certainly a bad example to state publicly that prohibition in the U.S.A. is a total failure. He said, 'In England you can drink all the time, except at two prescribed periods, while in America you can drink all the time everywhere.' On the other hand his reference on a London stage to the Boston Tea Party was definitely bad taste and his fling at English coffee entirely uncalled for."

Other London papers, however, carried more favorable comments.

"It was strange, after the skilled dancing of Leonide Massine and Vera Nemchinova, to find oneself being thoroughly entertained by a rambling discourse on current politics. 'You haven't got anybody over here quite like me,' Will Rogers truthfully tells us. He says he hasn't come here to cement good feelings between England and America, but in saying so he is one of the cleverest unofficial ambassadors who have come to our shores. His object is to get even with the European lecturers who have visited the United States. He succeeds in revealing unsuspected humor in the fall of the franc, the Anglo-American debt problem, the coal strike, and so on. No mean feat. All those who think these matters are serious should hear him."

It was such fun sitting out in front watching the reaction of the audience while Will was talking. Sometimes it was a bit slow, but his ribbing was almost always accepted good-naturedly. Several times I noticed groups of Americans sitting up stiffly, as if fearful that their countryman was going too far.

But in spite of all this Will had a grand time in the Cochran show and the general impression was that he had helped enormously in putting the show over. One London paper said:

"Refusing a check that would have amounted to probably $16,000 or more is what Will Rogers did in England last week, and that gracious act was after saving a show from a flop and recouping C. B. Cochran, producer of the show, to the amount of $60,000 by appearing in the production.

"Rogers worked four weeks. . . . The first night saw practically a sellout, and after that he was a sensation, the show doing an enormous business and pulling back a loss and making a profit for the producer. When Will Rogers finished his four weeks' engagement, the London representative of the William Morris office handed Rogers a blank check signed by Cochran, with instructions to fill in the amount. Rogers tore up the check, with the statement that Cochran had proved himself such a great guy, had given Rogers such enormous publicity, and that he had enjoyed the engagement to such a great extent that he felt the producer owed him nothing."

Will and I stayed on in London, but the children began to tire of England; Bill went home alone, and Mary and Jim were sent to Switzerland.

One of the most entertaining things arranged for Will that summer was a stag dinner in the Pinafore Room of the Savoy Hotel. We saved a clipping of the event which said:

"Never before have so many wits sat around a table. Epigrams, jokes, jests, satire and a volley of witticism and repartee ought to have taken the shine off the silver and the bubbles out of the champagne, which, fortunately, they didn't. These were the guests who were invited to meet Mr. Rogers, and the list shows, it might be added, who are considered to be the wittiest, smartest, funniest men in England today. They included:

"George Bernard Shaw, G. K. Chesterton, Sir James Barrie, Lord Dewar, of whisky fame, Lord Derby, Sir Harry Lauder, Sir Thomas Lipton and Michael Arlen—who came over especially from Paris."

Will thought Lord Dewar the best after-dinner speaker he had ever heard, and of George Bernard Shaw he said: "We've got a great deal in common. Both of us know the world is wrong, but we don't know what's the matter with it." After the dinner Will went with Sir James Barrie to his house, where in the early dawn they leaned out of a top window to look at sleeping London. Barrie pointed out the roof of Shaw's house, as they both laughed again at the memory of Shaw's famous greeting to Will, "Why, they told me you were an Indian—I don't see any feathers."

In writing of his visit to Barrie's home, Will said:

"He has the funniest looking fireplace. You kinda get back in it like you was crawling in under a shed—

and the fire is not back in a regular place, it is just built against the wall, and he has a cook stove in it and a pot for brewing tea. He is one great little Scotchman, so quiet and soft spoken you are afraid you will scare him away if you speak. And I expect I would if I had said much. But for once in my life I happened to know enough to keep my mouth shut."

Going to Dublin to play a benefit for the families of the victims of the terrible theater fire at Dromcolliher, Will fell in love with Ireland, which he never had seen until then. We met Eamon De Valera, and President Cosgrave entertained us at his home in the country.

"It's so peaceful and quiet here in Dublin [Will cabled to the New York *Times*] that it is almost disappointing. Even the Irish are beginning to get used to it and like it. They have a representative at the Peace Conference. I've been in twenty countries, and the funny part about it is there is more to see here than in all the others put together. They don't owe us and they don't hate us."

When we returned to London, Will insisted on flying the Channel to Amsterdam. It was to be my first flight, and I was in a real panic. With a sinking heart, I thought of Mary and Jim waiting for us in Switzerland. It seemed folly for both of us to take what I felt to be a frightful risk. I prayed for rain or fog— anything to which I might cling as a legitimate excuse— but, perversely for London, the day dawned bright and clear. With the ground falling away under me, I reached over to hold on to Will. He laughed and said, "Woman, don't hold on to me. I couldn't be of any help to you."

Will had been little less frightened himself when he made his first flight. Many contradictory stories have been told about this incident. The facts are that it happened in Atlantic City in 1915 while Will was filling a vaudeville engagement there. A Glenn Curtiss flying boat was moored just off the Boardwalk; passengers were taken out pick-a-back by an attendant who waded through the water. The price was five dollars a flight. Will wanted to go up when he first saw the plane, but day after day as we stood watching the passengers being carried out to the plane his courage would fail him. On the last day of his engagement he bought a five-dollar ticket, on the theory that, having spent the money, he would not back out.

He was carried out while I watched, and when he landed he was still scared, but vastly excited, and so pleased that he had a picture made of himself in the plane and took delight in exhibiting it.

It was in Europe this year, however, that Will did his first extensive flying. For in Europe there were regular passenger lines long before such service was established in this country. Already, before our flight across the Channel, he had traveled by air from Paris to Rome, from Berlin to Moscow, and twice from London to Berlin. Back home a little later, he was one of the first to make a transcontinental round-trip flight. He flew in mail planes by special permission. The trip took eighty-two hours and Will was forced down only once—in the back yard of a surprised Dutch farmer at Bellefonte, Pennsylvania.

Will had a few minor accidents. On one flying trip east to the Republican Convention in 1928, he had two crackups within a few hours. Landing at Las Vegas, New Mexico, his plane broke a wheel and turned over. At Cheyenne, Wyoming, a few hours later, he was spilled again.

Will was a valiant defender of flying as a safe mode of travel and he made light of these mishaps. When he had an accident not so trivial, he managed to conceal it entirely from the newspapers and he concealed it because he thought it would be bad publicity for the airplane.

Will was on his way to attend a dinner given by Henry Ford for Thomas A. Edison. Arriving in Chicago, he found the plane on the regular Detroit run had been grounded because of bad weather. Impatient, he found a good pilot with a private plane, who was willing to make the trip.

The plane fought a head wind and finally arrived over Detroit. But the pilot then decided that he did not want to attempt a landing at the unlighted field. He passed a note back to Will in the rear of the little two-seater, saying that they would have to return to Chicago. And just a few miles from the home field, the plane ran out of gasoline. Another note was passed back to Will. They were going down and he was to brace himself for a crash landing.

The pilot dropped emergency flares to try to find an empty spot, and started down. Will told me later that as they went down into the city, with lights twinkling everywhere, he was sure they would hit something. He didn't see how they could help it, in all those lights, and he thought it would be the finish. But guided by his flares, the pilot proceeded to make an amazing landing on a vacant lot. And Will was so relieved that they had touched solid ground without crashing that he immediately heaved a sigh and relaxed. At that moment the plane turned over.

The pilot was unhurt. But Will, limp with thankfulness, was battered against the sides of the plane. The pilot saw a taxicab near by, hustled Will into it and told the driver to take him to the airport. Will was conscious and physically able to take care of himself, but mentally he was in a daze. When the taxicab driver asked him where he was going, he didn't know who he was. The only thing that came definitely through the haze was Chicago. So he said he was going to Chicago.

"Well, buddy," said the driver, "you're in Chicago now."

Will stayed in Chicago over night at the Sherman Hotel, where his friend Frank Bering took him in charge. A doctor strapped him up to cure his aches, and he went on next day to the dinner in Detroit. He had telephoned to reassure me about the accident, in case the news got out. But it didn't.

After Mr. Edison's party Will took a train to New York, and the doctor there insisted upon X-raying him. It was found that every one of his ribs had been fractured in the accident.

Will came home with several yards of adhesive tape bound around him. And being laced up like this made him very uncomfortable. He complained bitterly that he couldn't even ride a horse. He wanted to get rid of the tape. Our chauffeur, John Marcin, had broken a rib one time and he knew just the thing to use instead— an old inner tube, split and then wrapped around the torso. After the first X-ray and taping Will had refused to see a doctor again, and John's suggestion appealed to him as a great idea. So for the next few weeks Will started out every morning with the chauffeur's split inner tube wound around him. He found it more comfortable, particularly late in the day. For when he came home from the studio in the evening the inner tube had always sagged from its position and lay in a loose fat roll around his waist.

But our flight that day across the English Channel was a perfect trip; long before we made our smooth landing I had forgotten all my terror. After that we flew as often as possible. Whenever we were going any place Will's first question was whether we could fly. The magnificent airports humming with planes coming and leaving on regular schedules for all parts of Europe were a revelation to us. Will, always keenly interested in aviation, was fascinated by this development, so far ahead of anything we had in our country, and, although he was not much of a crusader, he came home resolved to do all that he could toward calling attention to our backwardness at that time in commercial aviation.

We stayed a few days in Holland and then flew to Berlin. Arrangements had been made with an independent motion picture company, and a cameraman was with us who took a series of short pictures, later released under the title *Strolling Through Europe with Will Rogers*.

We went on to Switzerland, and gathered up the children, who were in the best of health and spirits, and with Jock, the little Sealyham dog which Lord Dewar had given them, we sailed for home on the *Leviathan*. There were many interesting passengers aboard. Among them were Charles Evans Hughes, returning from The Hague, and Mrs. Hughes.

Will had never met the dignified and seemingly formidable Mr. Hughes, and frankly was a little nervous at the prospect of meeting him. For Will, of course, had told many jokes on Mr. Hughes, and had impersonated the then Secretary of State in his burlesque sketch on the Washington Disarmament Conference. "When I was first introduced," Will said, "I didn't know whether to hold out my hand to shake, or to cover up and protect myself."

The meeting took place at a shipboard conference to arrange a benefit for victims of the Florida hurricane, news of which had arrived just as the boat was sailing. And Mr. Hughes was not at all what Will had expected. "The Secretary has been so thoroughly humanized that he has almost gotten common," Will said. They became very good friends and spent pleasant hours arguing good-naturedly about many things— among them the problem of our Marines in Nicaragua, which was a sore spot with Will. Later at the benefit— which exceeded all expectations: $40,000 was raised—

everyone was amused to find Hughes billed as a humorist and Will as a diplomat.

We arrived in New York in September 1926, and after a few days there Will started out over the country on his second concert tour. He came home to California for the Christmas holidays, however, and on this occasion received a stirring welcome.

CHAPTER XIV

ON HIS lecture tours Will had often been invited to speak before State Legislatures, and he had been given the figurative keys to many cities. Now that he was returning to Beverly Hills for the holidays his friends decided that he should be one prophet to be honored in his own country. Since Beverly Hills (under the law) had no Mayor, they would make one.

The children and I had been with Will in New York. We all returned together and were met at the Santa Fé station by a delegation that included Stanley Anderson, Silsby M. Spaulding, Norman Pabst, Fred Lewis, Douglas Fairbanks, Bill Hart, Rob Wagner, Chief Blair and his corps of motorcycle police, most of the film stars, the Chamber of Commerce, groups of citizens and two brass bands. Displaying boxlike placards, such as "The Hon. Will Rogers, Mayor of Beverly Hills," "The Kiddies' Pal," and "The Dogs' Best Friend," the parade in open cars moved out Wilshire Boulevard and on to Beverly Hills. Not even the onset of California's rainy season could dampen the enthusiasm of the welcoming crowd, although I do seem to recall that before we reached our destination, the Mayor's family abandoned an open car in favor of drier accommodations.

On a raised platform in the park opposite the Beverly Hills Hotel, Sil Spaulding, Will's old friend and president of the city board of trustees, made a wonderful speech and presented Will with an elegant illuminated scroll that stood five feet high. The scroll, inscribed in red and gold lettering, had been made at the Douglas Fairbanks studio and was a beautiful job of craftsmanship. Sil had written the flowery tribute signed by the members of the Board, which conferred on Will the position of Mayor.

"They say I'll be a comedy Mayor," Will said in his speech of acceptance. "Well, I won't be the only one. I never saw a Mayor yet that wasn't comical. As to my administration, I won't say I'll be exactly honest, but I'll agree to split 50-50 with you and give the town an even break. I'm for the common people, and as Beverly Hills has no common people, I'll be sure to make good."

Will was photographed with his police force and his fire department, and I recall that when he found they had no recreation facilities, he furnished gymnasium equipment and paid for the establishment of a handball court. "I'm the only Mayor that never made a mistake," Will explained later during his administration. "I never made a decision."

After the holidays, Will went back East to finish his lecture engagements. He was speaking in Richmond, Virginia, in April when the Mississippi River flood of 1927 began to reach the proportions of a catastrophe.

"There's hundreds of thousands of people being driven from their homes—homes that won't be there when they come back," he wrote. "These poor people have never harmed a soul or broke a law. Yet Mrs.

Snyder's picture has occupied more space in some of the papers than the whole state of Mississippi fighting for its life. There are ten reporters and photographers at the trial to one at the flood."

He wired Mr. Ziegfeld that he would come to New York and put on a Sunday-night benefit for the flood sufferers if Mr. Ziegfeld would donate the theater. When it was announced that Will was giving the program alone, his friend John McCormack offered to help. The Ziegfeld Theater was packed, and some tickets sold for as much as twenty-five dollars. John McCormack sang several numbers and Will was delighted with the large receipts at the box office, which were turned over to the Red Cross.

"Some Western people who don't know," Will said, "are always saying Easterners have no heart; everything is for themselves and the dough. Say, don't tell me that! Geography don't change human nature. If you are right, people are for you whether it's in Africa or Siberia."

A great deal has been said and written about Will's generosity. He took his responsibilities seriously. I think few people know that during the whole time this country was at war he contributed one hundred dollars every week from his pay check to the Red Cross; and at that time his salary was not spectacularly large. "I pray to God this terrible war will be over in less than a year," Will wrote in a letter to Mr. William Fox, head of the Red Cross committee, "but if not, I hereby pledge myself to continue my subscription of $100 a week for the duration of the war."

And many years later I remember a series of radio programs Will had agreed to do, and how I had counted on using the check he would receive to cut down our indebtedness to a certain Los Angeles bank. But when Will was paid he promptly gave one-half the amount to the Red Cross and the other to the Salvation Army.

Will was as generous with his time as with his money. I don't think that any actor of his generation played more benefits than he did; certainly no one played them with more grace and honest enthusiasm. He was deeply disturbed by human suffering; it was almost as though he felt he had been lucky beyond his deserts and should pay up the score as best he could.

And needing funds to be generous with, Will seldom refused, when opportunities came by which he could make extra money. Early in his career a chewing-gum manufacturer offered him $30,000 for the use of his name and some comment on the product. Will was criticized for agreeing to this, and he wasn't very happy himself when the enormous posters with his picture appeared everywhere. He also wrote ads for Bull Durham—explaining in each, however, that he didn't smoke. And during most of his years in the Ziegfeld *Follies* Will was booked with an agent to make talks at clubs and various entertainments both public and private.

Out of this last arrangement grew a story that upset him as much as anything that I can remember in his whole life. It began in California and was repeated later, with a change of name, in the East. The story was that Will had been asked to the Doheny's for dinner, had made a talk there, and later sent Mr. Doheny a bill for $1000, saying that, as his wife had not been invited, he took it for granted that he had been there in his professional capacity. This story, of course, has been told in different forms about many entertainers, and, so far as Will is concerned, was utterly untrue.

Will had been working constantly since his return from Europe in the fall of 1926. Besides the speaking engagements he had his weekly articles and daily telegrams to send to the newspapers. The schedule was a strain, and after he had finished his tour early in the following summer he came home with an illness that led to a sudden operation.

In Bluefield, West Virginia, near the end of his tour, and then again a few weeks later when he visited his sister Sallie in Chelsea, Oklahoma, and the family's old ranch on the Verdigris River, Will suffered from what he insisted were mere attacks of stomach-ache. But on the train coming back to California, the pain was worse, and when, after a few days at home, there was no improvement, Will finally let me call in Dr. P. G. White, our family physician, for an examination. After a consultation with his associate, Dr. Clarence Moore, Doctor White said it was gallstones and advised an immediate operation.

In his book *Ether and Me,* Will described the experience:

"You know, in the operating room they have a little balcony where you can go and see operations. That must be loads of fun for people with a wonderfully well developed sense of humor. Well, I looked up, and there was nobody up there. That kind of hurt my pride.

I thought, 'This is the poorest business I ever did in my life.'

"Before I went in I didn't know what might happen to me, so I said, 'Well, I've got a lot of laughs in my lifetime and I want to pass out with one.' So I thought all night of a good joke; and just before they operated, I was going to pull this joke and then they would all laugh hilariously and say, 'Well, old Will wasn't so bad at that.'

"So I got ready to pull the joke, and there was one fellow standing behind me—he's the fellow you can't see, that's going to knock you out; he's the fellow that's got a jar of ether in his hand—well, I was all ready to set the world laughing uproariously when this old boy just gently slipped that nozzle right over my mouth and nose both.

"I wanted to tell him, 'Just a minute!' And I started to reach up and snatch it off, and a couple of men who had enlisted as interns, but who in reality were wrestlers on vacation, had me by each hand. Out I went, and from that day to this I have never been able to think of that joke. It was the best one I ever had.

"I don't know what they operated on me for, but they certainly took out that joke."

Will's first anxious thought when he was ordered to the hospital had been of his promise to speak that night at a banquet. The proceeds of this affair at the Biltmore Hotel, for which tickets had already been sold at fifty dollars a plate, were to be used for a new athletic field at Occidental College. Weeks ahead Will had promised to help, and he hated to let the sponsors down. He had never disappointed an audience before—when Will said he would come, he always did. It was a rule on which he prided himself.

But this time there was nothing else to do. With Will in a hospital bed, his operation scheduled for the next morning, I had to find someone to take his place as the principal speaker. It wasn't an easy job, on such short notice, but at last I thought of our good friend William S. Hart. Bill Hart is the sort who always comes through in an emergency—he agreed to speak and we attended the banquet together.

When Bill finished his talk, Dr. Remsen Bird, President of Occidental, asked me if I would say a few words and explain to the audience why it was impossible for Will to come. He had warned me beforehand, but I had firmly refused to think of it through the dinner. Having never spoken before a crowd in my life, I knew that any attempt to plan a speech would simply make things worse. When I stood up I saw a sweet-faced little woman sitting directly in front of the speakers' table. She was sorry about Will's illness and she was sorry for me; so I talked to her and for the moment forgot I was facing a crowd. With this task done, Bill and I went back to the hospital.

Most people never knew how grave Will's illness was. He never gave them a hint of it. He did not miss a day with his newspaper article. Friday morning he dictated his daily to me just before he went to the operating table. Since his wire did not appear in the Sunday paper, he was able to skip Saturday. But on Sunday, so sick he was hardly able to speak, he called me to his bedside and dictated his Monday daily wire. After the dateline, "CALIFORNIA HOSPITAL, LOS ANGELES, June 19," it was just six words: "Relax—lie perfectly still, just relax."

Despite the operation, Will's body continued to absorb poison and he ran a high temperature. The situation was so serious that his sister Sallie came out at once from Oklahoma and stayed with him until he was well on his way to recovery.

"I wouldn't have minded the whole thing so much," Will said, "but they wouldn't let me have any chili, or chili con carne as you amateur eaters call it. But I got the next best thing that I wanted and that was some cornbread. Not this old yellow kind made with eggs, but real corn dodger, or corn pone, made with meal, hot water and salt. But I had to have my sister Sallie, from Chelsea, Oklahoma, show 'em how it should be made. She even had to send back to get the meal—they don't know what corn meal is out here. I mean corn meal!"

When Will was able to work again, he made *The Texas Steer,* his last silent picture, for Sam Rork, an independent producer. It was directed by Richard Wallace, and Douglas Fairbanks, Jr., played the juvenile role. Will portrayed the part of a Texas rancher who is elected to Congress, and many of the political scenes for the picture were shot in Washington, D. C.

A short time before the company had left for the capital, the California Legislature passed a law providing that in a city of the sixth class, such as Beverly Hills, the president of the board of trustees was constitutionally the Mayor. In commenting on the loss of his political office, Will said, "There is only one thing that makes me sore about the whole thing. My Lord, if I had known that I was ruling in a city of the sixth class,

I would never have taken the thing in the first place. I should sue them for lowering my standards. Sixth class—why, that's the lowest class there is, I reckon. Why, I will be years living that down."

Now, in Washington, the National Press Club was determined to keep Will in office. The club staged a big public reception at Washington auditorium in Will's honor, and most of Washington's notables were present. Senator Ashurst made the opening address; General Pershing was there, and I sat in a box with Mr. and Mrs. Herbert Hoover. Mr. Hoover was then Secretary of Commerce under President Coolidge. Louis Ludlow, president of the club, presented Will with a parchment scroll and in introducing him explained that the club had liked Will's administration— "despite the fact that we have not always approved his foreign policy. Mr. Rogers' assertion that he did not visit Queen Marie of Rumania when he was in Europe because he could not find her country struck some of us as a grave diplomatic error.

"Nevertheless," Mr. Ludlow continued, "since Mr. Rogers is in the status, as he has carefully explained, of 'a good man—looking for something better,' we have decided to appoint him congressman-at-large for the United States of America; his duties being to roam over the country, pry into the state of the Union, check up on prohibition enforcement and report at regular intervals to the National Press Club.

"We are happy to state to Mr. Rogers tonight that this new office upon which he is about to enter is not without its material rewards and that it automatically carries with it a suspended salary of one dollar per annum."

"It was an awful good speech," Will said, "but while the speech was good, it was the poorest appointment I ever got."

Late in 1927, after *The Texas Steer* was finished, Will made his first trip into Mexico. He was there as the guest of Dwight Morrow, our newly appointed Ambassador, and was invited to accompany the Ambassador and President Calles on an inspection tour of the country. "If you want to know a man," Will often said, "travel on some extended trip with him." And this was the beginning of the very great regard Will always felt for Mr. Morrow.

The car in which President Calles traveled was guarded front and rear by carloads of soldiers. On the second afternoon of the trip Will strolled off through the train, stopping so long to chat with the soldiers that he was late for dinner. A member of the President's entourage suggested politely that it was not customary to keep the President waiting.

"I'm sorry," Will said to the interpreter. "You tell President Calles that I've been in Mexico only a few days and I have found out that it's better down here to stand in right with the soldiers than with the President."

Will and President Calles became friends almost at once. During the ten-day trip of inspection their companionship was very close. President Calles played the guitar and Will and Ambassador Morrow both loved to sing close harmony. Calles was a man of tremendous courage and Will admired him for it. Once on a ranch where they were being entertained the President went into the bull ring and did all the bullfighters' tricks—the only difference was that he had no weapons.

"He tried to get me to go in," Will wrote, "but the bull was still armed. So I stayed in the grandstand."

Traveling through troublesome provinces the President of course was surrounded by guards and soldiers, and after Will arrived home he told me of the time Calles eluded his bodyguard, got off the train by himself, and rode with Will and Ambassador Morrow to an hacienda where they were to be entertained. The lack of a protective escort didn't bother the President at all, but Will said he and Mr. Morrow were really worried.

General Escobar took him to his first bullfight.

"The general got a great kick out of it [Will wrote]. Any time the bull was near the horses, I would bury my head on my arms and look down at the floor. We were sitting in the front row and there was a big concrete balustrade where our elbows were resting. The general would tell me when to look up. Finally it got to be the laugh of everyone there. My friend President Calles and his party were around the circle almost facing us, and Calles started kidding me about not looking up. They had pictures in the Mexico papers next day of 'American humorist enjoying Mexican bullfight,' and all you could see was the top of my hat buried in a couple of folded arms on the railing, and General Escobar laughing and pointing at me.

"I could stand part of it, for there is some very clever things done in the ring, but when it comes to the horses, I sure couldn't go that."

General Cruz, who was chief of police of Mexico City, and members of "La Asociacion Nacional de Charros," gave a *jaripeo* in Will's honor, followed by a big banquet. In a telegram Will sent home he said, "They gave me so many maguey ropes I had to send some by freight. General Obregon gave me a fine knife or sword or something and my grip is full of fine spurs and bits. They play good polo down here too; I played with the Secretary of War, General Amaro. They wanted me to run for President, but I didn't have a steel vest. They are great people if they like you."

While Will was in Mexico Mr. Morrow gave a dinner for him and President Calles attended. It was the first time, I am told, that a Mexican President had ever dined at the American Embassy. Dwight Morrow was greatly loved in Mexico. Will was on another trip there in 1931 when the news came of Morrow's death. "I heard that in the heart of Mexico," he wrote, "and from the heart of Mexico. Morrow was a great little fellow. He used to say, 'Will, I don't know anything about Diplomacy, but these people are our neighbors, and we have to live by each other, so their problems can't be any different from those of any other Neighbors.' And that's how he solved everything—he brought it down from what at first looked like something big, and reduced it to its natural size—then he sat down across a table and talked it over with the other side. He fixed it so nothing was a 'Big Problem.' I don't know when I had ever come to like and admire a man more than I did him."

CHAPTER XV

1928 was a Presidential year, and early in January Will was back in Washington to attend the Jackson Day Dinner, the big pre-Convention meeting of the Democrats. The Democratic party was, in a way, Will's favorite, but he didn't take sides. He couldn't take sides and still maintain the privileged position he enjoyed. He was born a Democrat and always called himself a Democrat—as he sometimes said, because "it's funnier to be a Democrat." But he could see little difference between the two parties. "One side is in and wants to stay in," he said, "the other side is out and wants in. They are both good if things are going good, and both terrible if things are bad."

Will had friends in both parties. Joe Robinson, Pat Harrison, and Bob LaFollette were special friends, as was Senator Borah—of whom Will once wrote, referring to him as a statesman, "A statesman is a man that can do what the politicians would like to do, but can't, because he is afraid of not being elected." Charley Curtis and General Dawes were men he often spoke and wrote about. Pat Hurley, Secretary of War under Herbert Hoover, was an Oklahoma boy and a friend of long standing. Robert L. Owen and Senator Gore were from Oklahoma, too, and both had known Will's father. Will had a warm affection for Jesse Jones of Texas, one of the first men he looked for whenever he visited the capital. And to Alice Longworth, Will said, he always went for his political information.

Washington became almost as familiar to Will as his own home town. John Nance Garner's office was his headquarters, and he used to drop around to the Vice-President's apartment in the early morning, knowing that the Garners would be sitting down to an old-fashioned breakfast. Members of the Senate and House were always cordial to Will, and he found a warm greeting when he dropped in at the Senate Gallery or at the Capitol restaurant for lunch.

Will won the personal friendship of most of the Presidents of his time. During the Administrations of Calvin Coolidge and Herbert Hoover, as well as that of Franklin Roosevelt, he was a welcome visitor at the White House. He took delight in the Yankee dryness of President Coolidge, "one of the wisest little birds that was ever in there," he said, and for Grace Coolidge he had a special liking and respect. He always admired Herbert Hoover, not only during his term in office but long before. "America's physician," Will had said of him, "when our country gets sick and hungry we call in Hoover." And he liked President Roosevelt's bold action in the crisis of 1933—"I never was one of those predictors," Will wrote that March, "but we are off to somewhere."

Will's friendship with many of the prominent men he joked about started long before he became a public figure. They liked him for himself. Back in the *Midnight Frolic* his monologue for a time was made up largely of quips about the Ford Peace Ship, yet Henry Ford and Will became the best of friends. Among Will's most prized possessions were two notes written

in the hand of Colonel Theodore Roosevelt, and sent
to him during the old vaudeville days when, with jokes
about Colonel Roosevelt, Will was making his first
attempts in the vein of personalities and national
affairs.

Politics had always fascinated Will. As far back as
1916 when Woodrow Wilson was President, he had
begun to specialize in political comment. But what he
had to say in those days was said chiefly in monologues
from the stage. It was not until 1922, during the Harding Administration, that Will began doing a regular
weekly newspaper article.

These articles attracted considerable attention, and
the next election year the syndicate that handled them
proposed that Will report both national conventions in
a series of daily dispatches. These conventions held in
the summer of 1924 were the first Will had attended.
And a paragraph he wrote then, after observing how
the convention buildings were literally lined with flags,
seems to express fairly well the attitude that he con-
sistently held toward his specialty. "I could never understand," he wrote, "the exact connection between the
flag and a bunch of politicians. Why a political speaker's platform should be draped in flags, any more than
a factory where men work, or an office building, is
beyond me."

Over a period of twelve years, Will never missed a
National Convention. His excuse for going was, of
course, business—he was paid to cover them for the
newspapers—and he would insist that they were terrible ordeals, simply "thousands of people in a hot,

stuffy hall away up to the early morning hours, listening to 'The man I am about to nominate has the statesmanship of a Jefferson, the courage of a Jackson and the homely common sense of an Abraham Lincoln.' "
But nothing could have kept him away from one.

"Of all the Trades and Deals and Under Cover happenings that go on during one of those conventions!" Will said. "And you meet some great folks. Governors, ex-governors, senators, ex-senators, all the names you have become accustomed to in the past, and maybe haven't heard of in a long time—why, you find 'em at these conventions. If they can't get on the delegation, they come as mere spectators. It's the Fourth of July celebration of national politics. It's a clambake of big politicians."

At the Republican Convention of 1924, in Cleveland, Will found that a fellow newspaper correspondent, writing for the same syndicate, was William Jennings Bryan. Bryan was no longer the great Convention-dominating figure he had been in the old days, but Will remembered. "Bryan's speeches," he said, "have been the only thing to look forward to at a Democratic Convention for years. He has sent more Presidential Candidates home without a Reception Committee meeting them than any orator living. He could take a batch of words and scramble them together and leaven them properly with a hunk of Oratory and knock the White House doorknob right out of a Candidate's hand."

Mr. Bryan asked Will to lunch one day, and that, so far as Will was concerned, was the high spot of the Convention. They sat together in the press stand, comparing professional notes, and Will remarked: "When he said he wrote serious and I said I wrote humorously, I thought afterwards we both may be wrong." But they agreed to co-operate on that basis. If Bryan happened to think of anything funny, he would give it to Will; if Will thought of anything serious, he would pass it on to Bryan. After the keynote speech, Bryan turned to Will and observed, "The speaker suffered from a premature climax." Will thought he would have to give Bryan a couple of very good serious reflections to make up for that.

A brief and orderly affair, the Convention itself was a disappointment to Will. "Coolidge," he said, "could have been nominated by post card." And after a few days in Cleveland, he left to join the cast of the *Follies*. The Ziegfeld show had a week's tryout at Atlantic City, and opened in New York late in June just as the Democrats were gathering for their meeting in Madison Square Garden.

The Democratic National Convention that year was one of the longest on record; it ran for almost three weeks. Before it was over, Will complained: "What a bone-headed move I made by signing up with the papers to write this Convention for so much for the whole thing. I have spent more in taxi fares and lead pencils than I have been paid." Women delegates, he insisted, "had started out with bobbed hair and can now sit on it."

But the Democrats had looked great at first. New York was full of enthusiastic delegates; there were bands and there were parades. "The Convention can adjourn right now," Will said, "which is 6 o'clock in the evening before it is billed to start, and it will have been a better convention than the Republicans had."

Will was fond of the Democrats; they were usually more entertaining than the business-like Republicans; besides they allowed hot dogs to be sold at their conventions. But on the opening day at Madison Square Garden, when Pat Harrison, the keynote speaker, mentioned Woodrow Wilson, it seemed to Will that the high-spirited Democrats went too far. "I am not up on political etiquette," he said, "but it struck me as rather strange, after paying tribute to a wonderful man, that the delegates should rise up and start shouting and singing, 'Hail, Hail, the Gang's All Here, What the Hell Do we Care.'

"Even my old Side-Kick Bryan was prancing around the hall shouting. Now, he has been brought up different. He knew, even if those other delegates didn't, that that was no way to pay tribute to a martyred President. As poor as the Republican Convention was, I will give them credit, they didn't sing 'Hail, Hail, the Gang's All Here' when the speaker mentioned Lincoln."

After the first long week of nominations, Will wrote: "I wish you could have been here and heard what great men we have in this Country. We started out with 16 men for President. Here is what each one of them was—'The only Man who can carry the Democratic Party to a Glorious Victory in November. Whose every act has been an inspiration to his fellow men. Not only loved in his Home State but in every State.' We have had six continuous days of 'The Man I am about to name to you.' And you could never tell until one got through who he was going to name. They all kept the names until the last word. It was safer. One guy from Montana, Maloney, was the hit of the Convention. He forgot his speech and didn't say anything. They applauded for five minutes."

The two chief candidates for the Democratic nomination that year were William McAdoo and Al Smith. But John W. Davis, a dark horse, was finally chosen by the deadlocked Convention. Some days before, Will had accepted an invitation to call on Mr. Davis. While they were talking—the candidate, of course, had the Convention tuned in on the radio—the tide had begun to turn in Mr. Davis' favor. Will told of the visit in his dispatch of the next day and predicted that Davis would be nominated. "Just in thirty minutes," he said, "I witnessed a political dark horse turning white, and I was the only human being that was there to witness it. Outside of the time Bryan asked me to have luncheon with him, it was the biggest thrill I ever got."

Six days later Mr. Davis became the Democratic candidate; Charles Bryan, younger brother of William Jennings, was chosen as his running mate. Will's personal telegram of congratulation amused the candidate and was often quoted: "Congratulations on your nomination. Understand you are to be associated with one of the Bryan boys. For the Lord's sake pick the right one."

Of the Presidential candidate's wife, Will had written in one of his weekly articles: "If Mrs. J. W.

Davis gets into the White House, it will have a mistress no titled European visitor can embarrass by doing the right thing first. She will never tip her Soup plate even if she can't get it all." Will's innocent line led to an exchange of articles with Percy Hammond, the late New York dramatic critic, who took occasion to reprove Will on his ignorance.

"For Years I have been tipping my Soup plate," wrote Mr. Hammond, "but never until Mr. Rogers instructed me, did I know that I was performing a social error. Consultation with the polished and urbane head waiters of the Middle West, where I spent my boyhood, taught me, I believe to eat soup. . . . It is proper to tip one's plate, provided, (and here is the subtlety that escapes Mr. Rogers) provided that one tips one's plate from and not toward. Mr. Rogers might well observe the modesty in such matters that adorns Mr. Tom Mix, his fellow ex-cowman. Mr. Mix, telling of a dinner given in his honor at the Hotel Astor, said, 'I et for two hours and didn't recognize a thing I et except an olive.' "

Percy Hammond was a well-known literary figure, famous as wit and critic. But Will maintained and energetically defended his "soup plate position." New York was delighted with his reply.

"Percy, [Will wrote] you say you learned to eat Soup from a Head Waiter. Well, I admit my ignorance; I never saw a head waiter eat Soup. Down in Oklahoma where I come from, we won't let a head waiter eat at our Table, even if we had a head waiter, which we haven't. If I remember right, I think it was my Mother taught me what little she knew of how I should eat, because if we had had to wait until we sent and got a head waiter to show us, we would have all starved to death.

"And as for your saying that anything of subtlety would escape me, that I also admit. But as for me being too Dumb to get the idea of 'the Soup plate being tipped away and not toward one,' that's not Etiquette, Percy; that's just Self Protection. As bad as you plate tippers want all you can get, you don't want it in your lap.

When the 1924 election was over, "the result," Will said, "was just as big a surprise as the announcement that Xmas was coming in December." But in the after-effects of the Republican landslide, with Coolidge safely returned to the White House, Will found a great deal at which to be surprised.

"Wall street," he wrote, "never had such a two weeks in the history of that ancient and honorable Institution as she is going through now. People would wire in, 'Buy me some stocks.' The Brokers would answer, 'What kind?' The buyers would wire back, 'Any kind; the Republicans are in, ain't they all supposed to go up?'"

Will observed that wheat had gone up, but without doing the farmer any good. "He had sold his wheat early because he had to get something to eat. It was just like someone telling you the big price they got for your house after you had been foreclosed out of it on a Mortgage." "Steak on the Plate went up," Will summarized. "Steak on the Hoof went down. Prosperity remained with them that had."

To Will's amazement: "Even Moving Picture Companies' stock went up, figuring I guess that Pictures will be funnier with Charley Dawes as Vice President than they would have been with Charley Bryan. I didn't know that Gloria Swanson could look better in her Pictures if there was only about 35 Democrats in the Senate, than she could if there were 40. But the stocks showed that such was the case, because there is absolutely no sentiment in business."

Will was sorry there was no Ziegfeld stock on the Exchange; he was curious to see if the public expected Coolidge to make the girls handsomer, and his jokes funnier. "But while our *Follies'* stocks were not listed," he wrote, "I knew that prosperity had struck Wall Street long before the Papers announced the fact, as I could tell by the class of fur coats our girls were showing up in, I never saw in all my years with the show a better or more expensive line of coats. Only one Seal has shown up so far. All the rest have been Minks and Sables. That's the best financial barometer in the World."

Will finished his piece on the "country's return to Wall Street" in a serious mood. "What makes these things worth so much more on November the 5th than they were on November the 3rd?" he wanted to know. "You mean to tell me that in a country that was run really on the level, 200 of their National commodities could jump their value millions of Dollars in two days? Where is this sudden demand coming from all at once? I am supposed to be a Comedian, but I don't have to use any of my humor to get a laugh out of that."

This edition of the *Follies,* in which Will was playing during the 1924 campaign, ran a long time in New York. It was late in 1925 before the show finally closed. Then Will deserted Broadway in favor of talking to America from the lecture platform. And he was glad to get away. He hadn't been too eager to go into the *Follies* that year in the first place; but Mr. Ziegfeld had coaxed until finally Will agreed to join the show for the New York run. It was understood that when the *Follies* went on tour, presumably in a few months, Will would be released. And he was impatient and annoyed when the New York run went on and on. Holding Will to his verbal promise, Mr. Ziegfeld kept the show there for over a year—something that had never happened before, and which never did again.

The whole family lived together in Forest Hills during this time, and the children were put in school there; but when the *Follies* closed and Will was released, we moved back to California. Except for an unfortunate accident, this might have been Will's last season on Broadway. (Though he played New York on his lecture tours, it was simply a one-night stand like any other town.) But in 1928, during the Smith-Hoover campaign, Will was once more—and for the last time—appearing in a Broadway show. This was *Three Cheers.* Will's joining the cast, to pinch-hit for his friend Fred Stone, had been a hasty, last-minute arrangement.

CHAPTER XVI

WE WERE at home for the summer and Will was planning another concert tour for the fall of 1928 when Fred Stone had an accident while piloting his own plane. Only a few weeks before, Fred had flown his own plane out to California to see Will, and had been a visitor at the Santa Monica Ranch, where we were living. "Not really a ranch," as Will said, "but we call it that. It sounds big and don't really do any harm."

Perhaps I should explain that Mary's bathroom was responsible for our move to the ranch. We had decided the year before that Mary, whose room was next to ours with a community bath between, should have a bathroom of her own. So an architect was called in to do a little remodeling on our Beverly Hills home. But when termites were discovered, the architect began to shake his head sadly. He would salvage what he could, he said. The plans for remodeling grew more and more extensive, until finally, in disgust, Will ordered the whole house torn down. Then we moved out to the ranch—where, as a matter of fact, Will had wanted to live all along.

On his recent visit Fred had been enthusiastic about his new show, *Three Cheers*. And at the time of his accident, which proved to be serious, rehearsals were well under way. The opening date was already set, the company had been looking forward to a long run in New York, and Charley Dillingham, the producer, was desperate.

Although Will had never played a character part running through an entire musical show, he understood the situation and it was the most natural thing in the world for him to drop his own plans for the season and wire Fred at once that he would try to take his place if it was agreeable to all concerned. Everyone, and particularly Fred, was delighted.

Will rehearsed with the cast a scant two weeks. "Rehearsing," he said. "Think of it! Twenty-three years on the stage and never rehearsed before. I feel like a kid at his first school entertainment." And on the opening night he hadn't learned his lines very well. He read most of them from the script, which he carried around in his pocket on the stage. One critic wrote: "Acting just a little bit like grandma taking part in a children's charade, the one and only Rogers appeared, as far as program print and outrageous costumes could make him, as King Pompanola of Itza. He had a crown and red leggings, and Fred Stone's part in his pocket. . . . He played hooky from the show now and then to come out in whatever was handy around the dressing room, and spring his old-time gags. He imitated Jack Dempsey's acting and Mr. Belasco; took a straw vote and tried to teach Dorothy Stone to dance."

There was no question of Will's being able to play the part as it had been written for Fred Stone, and when he sang Fred's songs, it was after remarking, "When I sing, I feel that is as far as any man has ever gone for a friend."

Dorothy Stone, who always danced with her father, was very patient in teaching Will their dance routines, and as Will and Fred were about the same size, he was able to wear all of Fred's costumes.

Reviewers mentioned the fact that Fred, in spite of his smash-up, also seemed to be one of the performers. One of them wrote, "Nearly everything that happened when Dorothy Stone and Will Rogers were in front of the footlights was by way of being a natural and pleasant reminder of Fred. One felt all the time that Will Rogers had the best of reasons for giving everything that was in him, and he gave and gave until our ribs hurt."

Three Cheers was an immediate success; it stayed in New York for the year. "I am afraid Will Rogers disorganized the show," one reviewer said, "but so far as I am concerned, he can continue to disorganize shows for the rest of his and my life." Will never did learn his lines thoroughly and he took many liberties with the script. But several years later, in the Pacific Coast production of Eugene O'Neill's *Ah, Wilderness!* Will did, for once in his life, play a part as it was written. This was the only time he ever played a character part in a legitimate drama and the only show in which he ad-libbed not once.

Colonel Charles Lindbergh came to the opening of *Three Cheers* and naturally attracted great attention. There was whispering and a craning of necks when he took his seat down front. Colonel Lindbergh's companion, knowing Will's habit of mentioning prominent people in the audience, offered to make a rather substantial bet that Will would introduce the Colonel from the stage. Smiling, Lindbergh took the bet.

Of course Will knew that Colonel Lindbergh was there. They had been together that afternoon and I suspect that Will, without the box office's knowledge, had arranged for seats. But Will generally used good judgment in situations of this kind, and later, when Lindbergh came around to the dressing room, he was beaming when he told us about winning the bet.

Will had met Colonel Lindbergh for the first time in San Diego soon after his transatlantic flight. We were guests of the city, which was staging a celebration in Lindbergh's honor. At the huge banquet we sat at the speaker's table, not far from the flier. After all the others had showered praise upon Lindbergh, Will was introduced.

"Colonel," he said, "they're all telling you what an inspiration you are to our boys—what a great thing you offer them. Well, that's a lot of applesauce, because if all our boys followed you, they would be in the Atlantic Ocean. I've got two boys, and I don't want them trying any of the stunts you are trying to do."

Apparently the Colonel had never heard Will speak before, and he did not understand what Will was up to. He blushed a little and looked uncomfortable.

"You've done all the wonderful things they say you've done," Will went on, "but engines will improve and things will get better and your time will be beaten. But you have one record I think will remain unsurpassed right on down through the ages—you are the only man who ever took a ham sandwich to Paris."

Then Colonel Lindbergh laughed as heartily as the rest. The next day he offered to fly us back to Los Angeles. Just before we took off someone whispered to him that a huge reception was awaiting his arrival at the Los Angeles Airport, and he told us that he would land at the new proposed Mines Field to avoid it. Will sat up in the cockpit with him. It was a smooth, short flight, but there were no runways at the new field and we had a very bumpy landing. Lindbergh was terribly embarrassed about it and was full of apologies, much to Will's amusement.

Will liked the boy at once and from the beginning there was an understanding between the two that developed into a close and lasting friendship. Later he told about their flight together:

"Lindbergh said he was going to land at a field where there was no hangar—nothing to show which way the wind was blowing. 'How can you tell how to land when you don't know which way the wind is blowing?' I said to him. And he says, 'Why, didn't you see the way those clothes were blowing on that line a while ago?' I hadn't even noticed the clothes, so I said, 'Well, suppose it wasn't Monday, what would you do then? I guess we'd have to fly around till they washed, is that it?' Say, listen, I wasn't kidding this boy. He come right back at me. He said, 'I wouldn't fly over such a dirty country.'"

Will admired the younger man, his high ideals and his frank and honest outlook on things generally. Though Will seldom betrayed an annoyance at life's occasional irritations, he was really indignant at the in-

considerate and often rude treatment Lindbergh received from crowds. To Will, the public's vagaries
were all in a day's work and play, but they were just
not in Colonel Lindbergh's game.

Will gave vent to his feelings:

"There is a hundred and twenty million people in
America all ready to tell Lindbergh what to do. The
first thing we want to get into our heads is that this boy
is not the usual type hero. He is all the others rolled
into one and then multiplied by ten, and his case should
be treated in a more dignified way."

Three Cheers closed early in the summer of 1929,
and returning to Hollywood, Will found everybody
talking. "I haven't had a chance to say a word since
I got home," he said, "just for people practising on
me to show they can talk. You meet an actor or girl,
and where in the old days they would have just nodded
and passed by, now they stop and start chattering.
Weather, politics, Babe Ruth, anything to practise
talking."

Will was soon making talking pictures himself. He
signed with William Fox. Contracts were always a
source of annoyance to Will—he could never understand why a man's word was not sufficient—and when
he was presented with a ponderous document by Winfield Sheehan, a personal friend and vice-president of
the company, he groaned at the thought of struggling
through it. Merely turning the pages of the contract
over, he wrote on the back, "I haven't read this thing,
but if Winnie Sheehan says it's all right, that's good

enough for me." Then he signed his name. After that—
and Will was still with the studio at the time of his
accident in Alaska—his contracts with Fox consisted
merely of an exchange of letters.

At first Will found the talkies rather troublesome.
He was accustomed to saying things his own way. A
system was finally worked out, however, which permitted him to use his own style as long as he followed
the action of the play and did not omit the cues necessary for the other actors. And eventually talking pictures became more to Will's liking than the silent ones.

The first talking picture selected for Will was *They
Had to See Paris*. Written by Homer Croy and directed by Frank Borzage, it was without doubt one of
the best pictures Will ever made. Irene Rich played
opposite him, Owen Davis, Jr., was the juvenile lead
and there was an excellent supporting cast.

Winfield Sheehan continued to select good stories
for him, and Will was soon established in the front
rank of motion-picture stars—by 1933, in fact, he was
the highest paid of the year. Henry King directed
State Fair; Dave Butler, *A Connecticut Yankee;*
Jimmy Cruze, *David Harum,* and George Marshall,
In Old Kentucky. Will's last picture was *Steamboat
Round the Bend,* directed by Jack Ford. In it Will
and Irvin S. Cobb were cast as rival steamboat captains,
and many of the scenes were taken on the Sacramento
River. Irvin and Will had known each other for many
years, and I believe Will never had a happier time than
on this last picture, sitting around and swapping yarns
with his old friend.

"One of the pleasant things connected with working in the movies [Will wrote] is that you are all the time running into actors and friends from the stage, folks you haven't seen maybe in years, but that you used to play on the same bill with. We lay around under the shade here when not 'Shooting' and talk old time vaudeville. Or I might roll over under the shade of the next tree and talk 'Calf Roping' to some boys that had made the Cheyenne or Pendleton contests away back when rodeos were really wild. Picture making is a 'Nutty' business, but it's fascinating."

In another article written on the set, Will explained for his readers one of the major mysteries:

"You can't fool audiences nowadays [he said]. They like to take your picture apart, and the more things you can put in there that they can take apart, why the more talk it creates.

"You see we take scenes where we go in one door and come out on the other side with another suit on. Or maybe with our hat in our hand, where it was on our head before. Well we know that, but we do it to see if the audience is paying attention. Now if they don't notice, and we don't get letters about it, why we know that they were asleep, or that they didn't go to the picture at all. But if we get letters, why that tickles us to death. We know that they are right with us. That they have seen the picture, and that they are awake, and following the story every minute. It shows that we have their interest."

Will was very happy at the Fox Studio; they were most considerate—always notifying him early in the morning if he would not be needed during the day. He could never adjust himself, however, to the ornate Spanish bungalow the studio had insisted on building for him as a dressing room. There was a large reception room with an open fireplace; one room which was to be used as an office; a dressing room with many mirrors, huge closets, a couch and a shower bath. Will treated the place with great disrespect, flinging a shirt over the light fixtures on the wall of the reception room, a shoe or a boot in the corner of the office, and draping a discarded collar and tie on the shade of the desk lamp.

Instead of the comfortable couch in his dressing room, Will preferred to use his car for relaxation in the long spells of waiting between shots. He would park it out on the lot wherever they happened to be shooting, and he would open the typewriter he always carried and do his daily wire or work on the weekly article. Or he would curl up in the seat or stretch out on the running board to rest and read the papers.

Will now wore glasses for reading, and always wore them down on the end of his nose, but his eyes had never been tested or prescribed for. The spectacles he used—and with complete satisfaction, for he never had a headache or a symptom of eye strain—came to Will in the way that most things came to Will. One day in the Lambs Club in New York, Tommy Meighan, the actor, saw Will reading a newspaper and holding it at arm's length away from his eyes. "Here, Will, for the Lord's sake, take my glasses," Meighan said.

Will calmly put them on, and later walked out of the club with the glasses in his pocket. And he wore Tommy's spectacles for the rest of his life. But, of

course, not the same pair. I afterward got the Meighan
prescription and used to order them by the dozen. Will
was very hard on glasses. Those he used were tortoise-
shell rimmed, and Will was in the habit of chewing on
the ear pieces. I must have many pairs even now, with
one or both ear pieces chewed down until they could
no longer be worn.

Besides the ornate dressing-room bungalow, there
was another thing about picture work that Will could
never adjust himself to—the Hollywood première. He
always kidded them, and only once, I believe, did he
attend one. This was when he acted as Master of Cere-
monies for the opening at Grauman's Chinese Theater
of *Grand Hotel,* starring Greta Garbo. At least I'm
quite sure that Will never again agreed to officiate at
such a function. Perhaps he was never asked again.

For he used a gag there that aroused a higher degree of indignation than had his radio imitation, long
before, of President Coolidge. This was another imitation; but nobody was fooled. Everybody knew it
wasn't Greta Garbo. The only misunderstanding was
that the Hollywood audience—composed, according to
Will, of "what the film fan reporters would call the
'Aristocracy of Filmdom' "—took Will quite seriously
when he announced that Miss Garbo had consented,
for once, to make a personal appearance. Will's Garbo,
after the film had been shown, was dear old Wally
Beery in skirts. "Sounds kinder funny, don't it?" Will
said. "Well it wasn't. He looked like her, but not
enough to satisfy that crowd."

Will was a long time being forgiven. And after this

fiasco he thought even less of the Hollywood première than he had before. The premières of his own pictures he avoided, as a rule, by simply leaving town.

"I was sitting around home after finishing an 'Audible,' [he wrote, after making *They Had to See Paris*] and as it was to appear with a sort of Ballyhoo opening, charging those poor people $5, I just couldn't be a party to such brigandage. First night audiences pay their money to look at each other. If they get stuck they can't blame me—it will be because they don't look good to each other. So I figured I better kinder take to the woods until the effects blew over. Well, then the thought came, where will I go. Now just off-hand, that is more of a problem than you would think. Here I was with some time on my hands and wanting to get out of town. But nowhere in particular to go. In fact I could go wherever I wanted, but where?

"Just think, going somewhere. Didn't have to go at any certain time; didn't have to make some Town to lecture the people out of anything on any certain night; didn't have to make a Show at eight o'clock in New York. I just didn't have to do nothing. Well of course my mind turned to planes. So I called 'em up and told 'em to reserve me a seat the following morning. They told me we left for Kansas City at five o'clock. Well that's pretty early to be woke up and shoved on an airplane and it's still dark—but I made it.

"And the plane was full, ten or twelve people. There were some boys and girls on there going back to their homes, who had made a ten thousand mile trip as the Guests of the Western Air Express Co. They had won a Song Title Contest, in their respective cities all over the country. I had always wondered what kind of people it was that answered puzzles and entered all newspaper contests. It was a kind of a mania that I couldn't hardly see what would drive 'em to it. But do you know they were an awful normal bunch. Old ones, young ones, school boys and men with good jobs. All had answered some ad and sent in a title for a song. You would have been surprised what a rational crowd it was—awful normal.

"I got off in Wichita at eight o'clock that same evening. Stayed there all night, then from there down to Tulsa, Oklahoma. Was met by my sister Sallie and driven to her home in Chelsea.

"Well for the next few days I did nothing but just visit around with all my folks and old Cronies, made no dates, just get in the car and go see 'em. The family couldn't get over the idea that there was not some place I had to rush to make a lecture date every night.

"I received a wire from my wife from California saying the picture had opened and I could come home; that's all the wire said. Left Tulsa in a fast single motored Lockheed Vega, with Oklahoma's favorite Pilot, Robert Cantwell; stopped at Fort Reno, a beautiful old Fort that I had always wanted to see. They were having a big Polo tournament there, among the best Army teams and best civilian ones in the Middle West.

"Next stop was an old friend's ranch away out in western Texas, where if it hadn't been for the planes, I would never have been able to spare the time to make the trip. Another old cowpuncher Cronie loaded me in his car and he and I drove from Amarillo, Texas, to Cimmaron, New Mexico. We was half of one night and up at five o'clock and drove most of that day. Could have made it in a plane in three hours. But did enjoy looking at all the ranches. Cattle was never fatter, and grass was never better.

"All this time I was just going where I wanted to,

and doing what I wanted to. Had nowhere to go, or no particular time to get there. Finally I says I better go home, cause I got to make another picture. So into Raton, New Mexico, by car, then by train down to Albuquerque, where I could catch one of the transcontinental air lines into Los Angeles. Left Albuquerque at eleven o'clock in the morning, landed at Los Angeles at four-thirty. So I finished ten days of just 'bumming.' Course it was high class 'bumming,' but it was 'bumming' none the less."

CHAPTER XVII

WILL never lost his enthusiasm for traveling. From early boyhood to his last years, it seemed almost necessary for him every once in awhile to be going somewhere. The South American jaunt, made in his early twenties, which stretched out into a trip around the world, was reported in his letters home to Uncle Clem. Now in his daily newspaper wires he described his travels all over the country and abroad.

Never satisfied with second-hand information, Will wanted to find out for himself what was going on. He wanted to be there, where the thing was happening, and talk with people on the spot. And in spite of the heavy schedule of work that he undertook, he usually managed without confusion or excitement to catch a plane and go.

"I got one little old soft red grip," Will wrote, "that if I just tell it when I am leaving it will pack itself. A few white shirts with the collars attached, and a little batch of underwear and sox that you can replenish at any store anywhere. All I take is my typewriter and the little red bag, one extra suit in it. It's always packed the same, no matter if I'm going to New York or to Singapore."

The record of even one year of Will's daily wires shows the astonishing amount of country he covered. In January 1931, the second winter of the depression, the condition of farmers through the South and Middle-

West, after the drouth of the year before in which entire crops had been lost, was very serious. Early that month occurred the dramatic incident at England, Arkansas, when five hundred farmers came into town and demanded food for their families.

"Those birds woke up America," Will wrote from California. "I don't want to discourage Mr. Mellon and his carefully balanced budget, but you let this country get hungry and they are going to eat, no matter what happens to budgets, income taxes or Wall Street values."

January twelfth, a week later, Will was flying east. After stopping in Claremore, he went on to Washington, where he talked with President Hoover. "He sincerely feels, with almost emotion," Will reported, "that it would set a bad precedent for the government to appropriate money for the Red Cross." For Congress was already debating the question of federal appropriations for food—of which Will said: "I don't think we have anybody in Washington that don't want to feed 'em, but they all want to feed 'em their way."

In the debating Congress Will saw little hope for immediate relief of "the fellow who is hungry now." Flying from Washington to Arkansas, he inspected for himself some of the districts about which reports were the worst—including the little town of England. And he wrote of the work being done by the Red Cross: "In just two counties I visited today, they are feeding five thousand families, with an average of six to the family. You don't know what hard times are until you go into some of these homes. This is not a plea, it's just a report, but it's the worst need I ever saw."

Will had already offered his services to the Red Cross, and late in January, from Austin, Texas, he started on one of his most memorable charity tours. Traveling in a Navy plane, piloted by Frank Hawks, he gave performances in several cities a day, sometimes assisted by the Revelers Quartet and sometimes by local talent. Will paid all the expenses and added a personal check to each city's contribution. In Fort Worth they collected $18,000, in Tulsa $30,000; approximately $250,000 was raised during the twenty furious days in which they covered Texas, Oklahoma and Arkansas.

"Talk about one-night stands," Will wrote during the tour, "some days we play half a dozen. In case I am called at any hour of the night, I simply roll over on my pillow and start in."

Amon Carter, publisher of the Fort Worth *Star-Telegram* and a warm friend of Will's, told me how Will gave two performances in Fort Worth, and between them made an appearance before some four or five hundred people at the Women's Club. Already that day Will had given a morning show in Wichita Falls. When he arrived in Fort Worth at noon, Amon said, "A negro porter at the Fort Worth Club in my apartment, where Will and Frank Hawks were stopping, remarked, 'Mr. Rogers, I sho' do wish there was some way us colored folks could hear you.'" So at Will's insistence Amon arranged for an early show at Mt. Gilead Baptist Church at 6:30 where Will was introduced by a blind colored preacher—one of the finest introductions he had ever received, he said. Altogether that day Will raised $25,000.

The middle of February, Will had to dash back to California to begin work on a new picture, *Young as You Feel,* based on George Ade's old play, *Father and the Boys.* But when that was finished early in April— finishing a picture usually meant a trip—Will was off again. For a long time he had wanted to see Central America and the islands, and now there was regular air service over the whole route. Guatemala, San Salvador, Costa Rica, Honduras, Nicaragua, Venezuela— the names had fascinated Will ever since he was a boy. He was eager to start. But the studio, afraid retakes would be necessary on the picture, held him back a few days.

Leaving when he had first planned, Will would have been in Managua, Nicaragua, the day after the tragic earthquake of 1931. As it was, he flew in eight days later. Even then the town was a shambles. Will himself gave $5,000 to the Red Cross for relief, and in his first wire from Managua he appealed to America for further aid: "Sitting here in a Marine tent writing this and am going to sleep here. The Doctor is coming around to shoot me for Typhoid. . . . Naturally, what they need is money. The Red Cross is feeding about eight thousand now. Goodness knows, you generous folks have been asked till you are ragged, but honest, if you saw it you would give again."

After Managua, Will continued south, stopping in Costa Rica and then in Panama. Senator Brookhart had just been to Panama, and he had been somewhat critical. "He was shocked," Will wrote, "and said the people down here were 'just wallowing in sin.' He was going to introduce a bill in Congress to remove the canal to go between Cedar Rapids and Des Moines. Well, I will say this for the folks down here, they are not wallowing in the canal." Will spent several days in Panama City, but insisted that he couldn't find the canal or even anybody who knew where it was.

He boarded another Pan American Airways plane, going along the Caribbean seacoast of Colombia and Venezuela. From Port of Spain, Trinidad, he turned back north over the West Indies. And he had a day in the Virgin Islands, where he found the inhabitants still indignant about President Hoover's recent visit and his reference to "an effective poorhouse."

"Did you ever see a community mad?" said Will. "No you haven't, you only think you have. You haven't seen a community mad at all until you see the Virgin Islands." Will tried to square things by explaining that the islanders should never have stopped manufacturing their famous rum just because of America's prohibition; nobody else was taking it seriously, he told them. Furthermore, seeing no bread lines and no Red Cross relief, he said they didn't look near as poor as some parts of the United States. "I asked where most of the people were and they said 'Out at the Golf Course.' That was the only evidence of poverty I saw."

At San Juan, Porto Rico, Will stopped again to visit with his old friend Colonel Theodore Roosevelt, Jr., and his family, at the Governor's mansion. And flying on over San Domingo, Haiti, and Cuba, he arrived in Miami the nineteenth of April. He had been gone from California two weeks, been in fifteen different countries and covered eight thousand miles. "Must be American territory," said his wire from Miami. "I don't see any Marines."

Will spent another week fulfilling various commitments in the East. He had promised to speak before the D.A.R. convention in Washington, and also at the banquet of the Newspaper Publishers Association in New York. Then he went to Lakewood, New Jersey, to spend a day with Arthur Brisbane, afterward returning to Washington for the annual Gridiron Dinner. Coming back the southern route, he stopped at Atlanta and at Fort Worth. Will made all these trips by plane; as he said: "It's getting so there is nowhere in this country you want to go between two real towns where they haven't got a good reliable air line. The bird flying us into Ft. Worth now from Atlanta, Herb Kindred, has had twelve thousand hours and no accident. A man couldn't walk that far without getting hurt."

Little more than a week after Will's return to our Santa Monica ranch, we started out together on an automobile trip to Carlsbad, New Mexico. Neither of us had previously seen the magnificent caverns there—though Will, many years before when he had run away from Kemper Military Academy to work on the ranches of Texas and New Mexico, had been through that part of the state; he remembered that then the town had been called "Eddy" instead of Carlsbad. The day we arrived for our trip down to the caves—"the Grand Canyon with a roof over it," Will described them—a shaft had just been cut through for the elevators which were to be installed later, and Will was as delighted as a small boy with the chance to be the first customer to make the seven-hundred-foot descent in a bucket.

For the next six months, Will spent most of his time in California. Twice in this period, however, he flew back to Oklahoma; one time to join in the welcoming celebration for Wiley Post and Harold Gatty, who had just completed their round-the-world flight.

In September, with most of his picture work done for the year, Will left with his artist friend, Ed Borein, for a trip to the great Hearst Babicora ranch in old Mexico. Across the border he was not sure when he would find the next telegraph office. So at El Paso he filed two or three extra wires—one of the few occasions on which he ever wrote his daily column ahead of time. His first wire from the interior said: "First news of the outside world I've seen was a Mexican sitting under a Mesquite bush reading in the Saturday Evening Post about Coolidge not running. His refusals are getting longer every year."

Will liked Mexico and the Mexican people. "They move just about fast enough to suit me," he said. And a few weeks later he went there again; this time to Mexico City—flying with Hal Roach, Eric Pedley and Captain Dickson in Mr. Roach's private plane. On his way back, Will stopped at the King Ranch, Kingville, Texas, owned by our friends the Klebergs—the largest ranch in the United States.

Will always enjoyed visiting with this wonderful family, and in his next weekly article he was enthusiastic about the roping and the horsemanship he had seen. "And they got good beans," he wrote. "That's what makes a good Cow outfit, is good beans. Just give me some beans and I will follow you off." From Kingville, he flew to Uvalde to spend a day with Jack Garner, and then home.

Less than two weeks later he started on a trip around the world. One reason for the trip at this time was the Chinese-Japanese clash in Manchuria, which had, by November, developed into open warfare. Once again he wanted to see—for himself and at first hand—what it was all about. Will later wrote: "After drinking at least two barrels of tea and wanting to be fair, here is about how Manchuria looked to me. China owns the Lot; Japan owns the House that's on it. Now who should have the policeman?"

Will sailed from Seattle November twenty-first pleased to find that his old friend Floyd Gibbons was a fellow passenger on the *Empress of Russia*. The war correspondent had come fully prepared for the Manchuria winter with a huge, and according to Will, "evil-smelling" fur coat—a fabulous garment of which Floyd was very proud, and which he said had come from Tibet. "He nursed this Dog Bed all the way across the Pacific," Will wrote, "wearing it into even the dining room on the boat. And in the Men's bar it was a continual source of another round."

In Tokio Will was amazed by the bicycles. "Millions of 'em. Did you ever see a Kimona on a Bicycle? And carry stuff? Say they will move your grand piano any day and do it on a bicycle. A person riding along over here on one without anything is just practically dead heading in empty. They have always got a billiard table, or a stove or bed, or a couple of mattresses on the wheel."

Will and Floyd Gibbons traveled together in Japan and flew to Korea. The Korean men, Will said, "have funnier hats than the Princess Eugenia kind the ladies are wearing back home." He described it as "a sort of old black cab driver's derby, but made of screen netting like the thing we used to keep over cheese in the Claremore grocery store." But what most amused Will in Korea, was the scene on landing when Floyd discovered that he had left his treasured fur coat back in Tokio. "He was inconsolable," Will said. "He was for not going on to Manchuria. He wanted even Russia to win the war."

Flying to Dairen alone—"Gibbons quit me and took the locomotive"—Will went on to Mukden, "where all your war news comes from." About twenty newspaper correspondents were in Mukden, several of them Americans, of course, and Will gave them all the news he had from home, some of which, probably, had come from me—and at cable tolls of a dollar and twenty-five cents a word. For on trips like this, Will was continually cabling home about things he particularly wanted to know. Just then, I recall, he was greatly interested in whether or not his friend Jack Garner had been made Speaker of the House.

Such details were not to be found in English-language papers abroad. "I was out here a month," Will complained, "before I found out that Notre Dame had lost a Game. Imagine newspapers being printed

in any language and not having that in. Now that I
have heard it, I can't find out how it happened, so that
makes me madder than ever. Darn it, I miss my paper.
I used to sit a long time over breakfast and read my
papers and just think. Over here I sit, but that's all."

Traveling on north to Harbin, Will decided that the
Siberian countryside resembled Oklahoma. "And the
farmers," he added, "are just as bad off." From Harbin, he wired: "It's 32 below. Horses wearing snow-
shoes. I got on a fur hat that looks like Daniel Boone,
and what do you thing I found? A war? A Revolution?
No! *Abie's Irish Rose!* Played by Russians and Chinese combined."

Coming back through Mukden, Will planned to go
by rail from there to Peiping. But when the newspaper
men in Mukden told how busy the bandits were just
then on that particular section of railroad, Will changed
his mind. "I figured my jokes wouldn't go so good out
in this snow, waiting for Claremore, Oklahoma to ran-
som me out," he said, "so I am taking roundance on
'em with a boat."

After Peiping, however, the line was safe, and from
there Will went on to Shanghai by train. In good
weather he would have flown, but there was a big
snowstorm then, and no chance of a plane for several
days.

Will said the only thing that you couldn't get in the
Orient, besides a satisfactory morning paper, was a
pillow. "One with feather in it," he specified. "These
out here are stuffed with rice, which wouldn't be so bad
if they had cooked it first." Outside of that, you could

find all the standard American equipment. Even some of the American peculiarities: "Chinese have planted a new big crop of soya beans, and they haven't sold the last two years' crop. Don't that sound exactly like the wheat and cotton farmers?"

Will arrived in Shanghai at a time of political crisis. One of his wires reported how he had had appointments with three different government officials, and how they were each removed just before he got to them. "China is the only country in the world strong enough to have withstood fifty years of misgovernment in a row," Will said. "What the foreigners haven't gobbled up, their own educated ones have. And it keeps right on being China."

Will spent a lonely Christmas in Shanghai, the only one he ever spent away from us. And he left the next day, deciding that he had been in China too long—"If I had only stayed a couple of days, I would have had a better idea of China. The more folks you talk to and the more you see, the less you know."

By boat he went to Hongkong, then Singapore. It was at Singapore that Will, as he used to explain, talked himself out of a visit to the Sultan of Johore. Will was spending only a day in Singapore, and it had been planned that after speaking before the Rotary Club in the afternoon, he would be driven out to the Sultan's estate. A great horseman and polo player, the Sultan of Johore's stable was famous all over the East, and Will was eager to meet him. But once started talking before a good audience, Will was notoriously hard to stop. This time he talked on and on, until finally it was too late to make the drive. "One case in history," Will said, "where a long-winded speaker suffered in the long run more than his listeners."

The next year, however, on one of his annual trips to England, the Sultan came via United States and California, and when he visited us at the ranch in Santa Monica, Will was delighted with the Sultan's gift—a souvenir of one of his hunting expeditions—the mounted skin of a large tiger and the skin of a very rare black leopard.

By boat from Singapore, Will continued up the other side of the Malay Peninsula to Penang. But he was soon flying again. In Allahabad, India, he reported that he had been forced down with a broken piston; then from Karachi he wired: "Twelve hundred miles flight today across the heart of India. Tomorrow Persia." Then Cairo, Athens, Rome and Paris.

I met Will in London, and together we flew back to France. We had planned to go to Berlin—Will wanted to "see the country there has been so much talk about saving," and had made tentative arrangements for an interview in Munich with Adolf Hitler. But bad flying weather kept us in Paris. Anyway, the newspaper men assured Will that Hitler wouldn't last. "He is only a flash in the pan," they said. "Before you get your interview published he will be through."

Then it was time to go to the Disarmament Conference opening in Geneva. We were there for three days, and Will said as he left: "The conference is off to a flying start. There is nothing to prevent their succeeding now but human nature." We sailed for

America and arrived in New York on the ninth of
February, 1932.

Will, of course, had to have a few days in Washington. Also, he flew to Cleveland and Chicago. Then
a visit to Oklahoma, which he almost never failed to
make when traveling either way across the country.
It was two weeks after we landed in New York before
he was back home on the Santa Monica ranch.

CHAPTER XVIII

As EAGER as Will was to start out on a trip, he was just as enthusiastic about getting back home. His interest in returning to the ranch was like that of a child with an ever-new toy. The very first thing he would go to the stable, saddle a horse and either go to the polo field for a work-out or head for the trails back in the hills. When the children came in he took delight in telling of his adventures, and often enough gave a glowing description of some new pony he had bought.

I remember his telling us one time about a fine roping horse he had purchased. A few days later Soapsuds arrived, and Will was quite indignant when we all laughed at the speckled old pony. Will was quick to defend him; it was what a horse could do, not how he looked, that appealed to Will. Soapsuds was a flaky roan, what the Mexicans call a *sabino*. Will always loved the old pony. From the time the horse arrived on the ranch until the day Will left for Alaska, I think I am safe in saying that there was not a single day when he was at home that Will did not ride or rope on Soapsuds. Trained by the Gardner boys of Western Texas, who had roped on him for years around the rodeos, Soapsuds, though nearly twenty years old, can still hold his own in a calf-roping contest.

From his early youth, Will could never resist a roping horse. During his lifetime he had so many good ones it is impossible to name them all. He had good polo ponies too; not the best, of course, but few players could ride him off the ball. Both of our boys—Bill and Jim—played polo. Jim, our youngest boy, became pretty fair at the game and had several good ponies of his own. It is customary for each man to have at least five or six mounts for an afternoon's play, and with three polo players in the family our stables and corrals were full. But of all Will's string of ponies there were a few of course that stood out as favorites. And how often arguments arose between Will and the boys over who would ride a certain horse; usually one of the boys would win the argument and Dad was forced to take what was left.

Bootlegger, originally trained for roping, was an unusual polo mount, and became one of Will's best known ponies. An Osage Indian boy, Alvin Carter of Pawhuska, Oklahoma, had raised the pony, and brought him East one year for the rodeo at Madison Square Garden. When Will saw Bootlegger perform in the arena he immediately wanted him. Finally, after much bickering, Bootlegger was bought and sent out to our home on Long Island.

Will was working in the *Follies* that year, and played polo at the Meadow Brook Club, Westbury, Long Island. Bootlegger soon caught on to the game, and though he was smaller than the usual polo mount, his speed and quickness in turning and stopping more than made up for his lack of weight. He was always a great favorite with the people who came to see the games. For mallet freedom it is customary to roach a polo pony's mane and have its tail either cropped or tied up when playing, but Bootlegger was so handsome that Will couldn't think of doing this. Many people have asked me about Bootlegger—they remember the black little pony and what a beautiful sight he was, with his long mane and tail standing out stiff in the wind, as he and Will came flying down the field.

Many of Will's horses are long remembered. Comanche, who had been trained for steer roping, came first of course. That was back in the old Indian Territory days; they roped full-grown steers in the rodeos then, not calves as they do now. Jim Hopkins, a Texas cowboy, broke the record on Comanche at a big contest held in Fort Worth, Texas, back in 1900. I do not remember his time, but I do know that the record held for many years. Will himself was just a boy then, but with Comanche he was able to go in and compete with older and more experienced hands.

Will recalled those early days in an article he wrote on one of his trips to Oklahoma. He was paying a visit to Claremore, and on the Fourth of July went to a near-by town for the rodeo.

"I was just thinking when I was looking at this show, [he wrote] that it was at a little Fourth of July celebration at Claremore, on July Fourth, 1899, (Boy, that's 33 years ago) they had a steer roping and I went into it. Well, as I look back on it now I know that that had quite an influence on my little career, for I kinder got to running around to rodeos, and the first thing I knew I was fit for nothing but show business.

"I had an awful good little horse that really put me in the business. A little Dun (yellow) pony, called 'Comanche.' He put you up so close to a steer that you didn't rope him, you just reached over and put a 'Hackimore' on him. Some of the old-timers mentioned Comanche there the other day.

"This calf roping has all come in the last years after they ruled out steer roping in most states. And here is something you might not know. A steer roping horse, and a calf roping horse is not the same animal. When you rope a steer, after you catch 'em, you throw your slack rope over his rear axle and then run your horse on by (having him roped by the head), the rope going over behind the steer jerking all four feet out from under him. Then while you tie him, the horse is supposed to keep pulling and dragging the steer as he attempts to get up. Now, in calf roping, the minute you catch your calf, the horse stops. You jump off and go throw the calf yourself. The horse is supposed to keep the rope tight, but his head is toward the calf, and he does it by backing up instead of pulling away like with a steer. Of course, you can in rare instances have a horse that will work both ways, but most ropers have two different horses, and say they mean about 50 or 60 per cent of the game—the horses do."

Dopey and Chapel, I believe, were the most intelligent ponies Will ever owned. Chapel was used as a stunt horse for dangerous riding in the old silent pictures. He would do anything Will wanted him to, going up and down almost perpendicular slopes, and making any kind of a jump, without the slightest hesitation. He came to be known all over the movie lot as a pony who was wonderfully human in understanding.

Dopey was a family institution, and in a class by himself. And almost from the day Will brought him home to Long Island he was a family pet. He would come in the house, go up the stairway; he never balked at anything Will or the children wanted. And when Will came out to California in 1919 to go into moving pictures, Dopey and Dodo, another pet pony that belonged to Mary, came with us, occupying the best palace horse car by express.

"Outside of a pony I had in the Indian Territory when I was a boy (he was called Comanche and put me in the exhibition roping business), why along pretty near next to him in affection was Dopey [Will wrote]. Dopey belonged to the family. Our children learned to ride on him, and during his lifetime he never did a wrong thing to throw one off, or did a wrong thing after they had fallen off. He couldn't pick 'em up, but he would stand there and look at 'em with a disgusted look for being so clumsy.

"I first saw Dopey at a town in Connecticut—I think it was Westport. I liked him, and he came home with me, and I think he liked me. And the whole family liked him, and he lived with us all these years, up to a few days ago. He came to our house in Amityville, Long Island, just across the road from Fred Stone's, the same time Jim, our youngest, did. Jim was a baby boy, and Dopey was a little round bodied, coal black pony, with glass eyes, the gentlest and greatest pony for grown-ups or children anyone ever saw.

"Dopey has been on pasture now for four or five years; hasn't had a bridle on him; fat as a pig. When nineteen years of you and your children's life is linked so closely with a horse, you can sorter imagine our feelings. We still have quite a few old favorites left, but Dopey was different. He was one of the family— he helped raise our children—he taught them to ride. He never hurt one in his life. He did everything right. That's a reputation that no human can die with."

Horses look much alike to many people, but they are no more alike than human beings are alike. Some are nervous and excitable, others lazy and easy going. Will had all kinds. Perhaps his best roping horse, before Soapsuds came, was Cowboy, a nervous, high-strung pony. Cowboy was finicky about his head, and fussy. If you were just riding along on him, he would keep you in a continual state of irritation with his head tossing, fidgeting, and shying at this and that. But in the arena, or the roping corral, Cowboy became a different animal. He was all business and efficiency when running down a calf.

Cowboy had once belonged to a great roper, Fay Adams, and had helped his owner win many championships. Will never entered these contests himself. But one time in Santa Barbara, during the Fiesta, Will was persuaded to give an exhibition. So it was announced to the packed grandstand that Will Rogers, on the famous pony Cowboy, would rope a calf.

When the gate of the chute was opened and the little calf ran out, Cowboy was after him like the wind; but Will missed his catch. His loop was too big and the calf leaped clear through. Will didn't like it very well when the crowd laughed. He started in to build his loop again and signaled the hazer to run another calf out of the chute. This time he made a beautiful catch and Cowboy stood like a statue while Will stepped off and ran down the rope to his calf. He grabbed the calf, slapped it over on its back, took the piggin' string from between his teeth, looped the two front feet, crossed a hind one and made his tie. Then he threw up his hands. Cowboy released the rope as the calf started to get up, his performance was perfect, and Will was happy for the rest of the day.

Sports in which horses played a major part were Will's favorites, but he liked all outdoor games. He was an ardent football fan, knew each season's change of rules, and could talk the college game on even terms with Bill and Jim—Knute Rockne, the great Notre Dame coach, was one of his dearest friends. Baseball he liked even better, I think. "Football is great," he said, "but baseball is a profession; it's an art that you don't learn in any four years, just from September to December." In New York in the early days I spent half my time in subway jams, running around with him to games. He knew all the players and had many warm friends among them. He recited batting and fielding averages with glib accuracy, and was always on hand, if he possibly could make it, for the World Series.

Riding, roping and polo playing kept Will in good physical condition, but that was never his idea. Will was no health or exercise enthusiast. The things he did he did for fun. Chester Byers, the champion roper, once wrote a book on roping in which he took pains to extol it as a healthful exercise. Chester was from Oklahoma and in the old days he used to hang around to watch the ropers practice. Finding him interested and eager to learn (he was only a little boy then), Will and the other cowboys had made him ropes and taught him a few tricks. Then they had forgotten all about him. But Chester had kept at it, eventually winning the national championship.

"Chester told me that he wanted to show where rope spinning was healthful and beneficial [Will wrote in the introduction to Chester Byers' book]. Well maybe it is, I don't know; I have tried it a good deal and there were lots of days I didn't feel so good, and after I would go out and miss a while, I wouldn't feel any better. Course every man to his own feelings—what might make me feel good would make you feel rotten— chances are it would. If Byers wants to tell the world what's the matter with them, why he's got as much right as anybody. Maybe the world needs rope spinning—I don't know—I know it needs something. It takes both hands to rope—so you certainly can't be drinking and do it.

"When I first met Chester, he was just starting it. He wouldn't weigh over 85 pounds, a poor skinny little man of 14 years of age. This roping has built him up and added 25 years and over 100 pounds in weight to him. I lay the best part of his tonnage and age to rope spinning. Course, on the other hand, it hasn't done anything for me. I'm as young as I ever was, and am getting lighter every day—so it's hard to tell. So get a rope and start missing—that's about 80 percent of all there is to roping. It's great exercise if you want to get tired. Personally, I don't care to get tired; if I am rested I would rather stay that way."

Will took delight in teaching the children to rope. Each one had his own lasso. Roping was the usual after-supper pastime at our house. Will was always playing at it. It often seemed to me that I had four children instead of three, and that Will was the greatest child of all.

And it was Will of course who always saw to it that Christmas was Christmas at our house. The chil-

dren took turns at being Santa Claus, and Will was
the ringleader who made all the plans. Once when it
was Mary's year, Will fixed up her pony with all kinds
of Christmas trappings. With a huge sack on her
back, in which she and Will had packed all the presents,
she rode the pony into the house.

Will liked to do his own Christmas shopping, but
was ill at ease in the big department stores and smart
shops. I often smiled at the way he did his holiday
buying. He would put it off invariably until the day
before Christmas; then, in the afternoon, he would
hurry away by himself. He bought a tremendous number of presents, remembering everyone who worked
for or with him, and he never asked the price of anything.

In the little village shops where there were no floor-
walkers to bow to him, or carpets to walk on, he would
spend hours over the counters choosing gloves, sweaters,
socks, toys and trinkets for the children, and then, with
face beaming, carry out mountains of bundles to his
car, and spend the rest of Christmas Eve tying up his
Christmas packages.

The only Christmas he ever spent away from us was
that Christmas in Shanghai in 1931. Having cabled
home and shipped off a box of all sorts of presents, he
found the day lonely. Deciding that the famous Astor
bar should be filled with homesick American sailors, he
fortified himself with plenty of loose silver and set out
to cheer the boys in blue. Will found "the longest bar
in the world" deserted, except for one customer, a man
drinking a whisky-and-soda at its far end. Will walked

the length of the bar, explained that he was alone and invited the stranger to join him in a Christmas drink. The stranger turned slowly, adjusted an eyeglass, looked Will over from head to foot, and drawled in an almost stage English accent: "I don't believe we've met."

With a wave of his hand, Will replied, "Forget it, brother," and walked out of the Astor House.

As Will never asked the price in his Christmas buying, so it was in everything. The result of course, was that our bills were two or three times what they might have been under careful planning. But Will never made plans. He knew that life was uncertain, and when he wanted anything he wanted it right away.

With more patience he could have been a pretty good horse trader. He knew horses and their value. And when he bought a horse and paid the owner's price he was usually well aware that he could have had him for less by holding off and waiting a day or so. But that was not Will's way; he couldn't wait to enjoy what he wanted.

A wealthy Los Angeles businessman bought a large plot of land near our ranch. Sunday after Sunday he would ride over his own hills, and once he confided to Will that some day he expected to build a beautiful home there—probably would start building within four years, by which time he hoped to have satisfied himself as to the most desirable site and be sure that his house plans were absolutely perfect. Will was dumbfounded.

"How does he know where he will be in four years?"

he demanded of me. "If he loves the site and wants a home there, why doesn't he build it and enjoy it now?"

I could have answered that he was a careful planner and a foresighted man, but I am glad that I did not, for four years later the depression had wiped him out and he never did live in his perfect house.

CHAPTER XIX

IN SPITE of the time he spent away from it, our little ranch in the Santa Monica hills was one of Will's most absorbing interests. He was always improving it, putting in something new or changing something that was already there. Work went on constantly while he was at home, and when he left there were always plans to be carried out in his absence. Even when he was flying around the country or traveling abroad, the ranch was not out of his mind, and he was seldom gone for any length of time without sending back long telegrams and letters of instructions about things he wanted done.

The never-ending work of improving the ranch had been started many years before. Our first California home was in Beverly Hills, but the little corral and eight stalls there had soon seemed too small to accommodate the family's growing string of ponies. And after our Beverly Hills home was paid for, Will began to talk of needing a larger place for the horses. But of course it wasn't just the horses. Will liked a lot of room to live in; he had always dreamed of owning a ranch.

In the Santa Monica hills he first bought one hundred and fifty acres at $2,000 an acre, making a down payment at the time and stringing along with the rest. This was far out on what is now Sunset Boulevard, but at that time, long before the University of California at Los Angeles was built, the boulevard did not run out that far. There was no paved road of any kind. On our hundred and fifty acres almost nothing had been touched. A little patch of clearing had been made by a Japanese truck gardener, and there was a road, almost impassable, leading up to the mesa. The rest was simply scrub growth over the rolling foothills of the Santa Monica Mountains.

Then the work began. A lot of sagebrush and grease-wood was cleared away and burned. A corral fence and temporary stables were built. Work went on con-stantly—teams of mules and plows clearing and dig-ging, and workingmen camping on the place. Finally, ground was leveled off for a polo field—the first one in that section.

From the very beginning Will loved the little ranch in its picturesque setting, from which there was a beau-tiful view of the Pacific Ocean, Santa Monica Bay, and far-off Catalina Island. Gradually we added more acres, until there were some three hundred in all. Then Will started building. There was cutting, sawing and pounding, and finally our ranch house was built—three small bedrooms, one great big room and a patio. There was no dining room. Will liked eating out of doors and only on damp days would he agree to our having meals inside.

As we found ourselves spending more and more time there, we disposed of our Beverly Hills property and enlarged the little ranch building into a beautiful ram-bling house, the kind of a house Will liked.

The ranch lies high on a mesa above Sunset Boule-vard. From the gate on the boulevard to the house is

about one mile, and we built our own circling driveway
up the hill. The house itself stands on a gentle slope.
Directly below and stretching out in front is Will's
polo field, and near the house is the first tee of a four-
hole golf course that Will put in, but which was seldom
used, as I remember, except by our friend Oscar Lawler.
He spent many Sunday mornings visiting with Will,
and as he knocked the ball over the course Will would
follow him around on Soapsuds. Will used to say,
"I'd play golf if a fellow could play it on horseback."

Back of the stables and in a little draw was the
roping corral, a big circle enclosed by a solid seven-
foot board fence. A chute connected the roping ring
with the calf corral. I think Will liked calf roping
best of all the things he did. He had worked at it in
the early days and he had practised it and played at it
the rest of his life. A lasso and a piggin' string were
tied to his saddle, and he always kept a bunch of little
wild calves grazing over the hills and on the grass of
Rustic Canyon.

With Buddy Sterling, a cowboy who worked for
Will, he would pen the calves and rope in the corral
for hours at a time, and nothing pleased him more than
when one of his old friends, Ewing Halsell, Eddie Vail
or Big Boy Williams, would drop in to rope with him.

The little wild calves soon caught on, after a few
weeks of lassoing, throwing and tying. And when the
gate of the chute was opened, instead of running
frightenedly to the other side of the corral, they'd trot
calmly out and right up to Soapsud's feet. Will would
have to slap them on the back with the end of his lasso

to make them start running away. At this point, and much to the amusement of the boys at the stock yards, the tame little calves would be sent back and another bunch of wild calves ordered.

But there was one calf, Sarah, a purebred Brahma that grew up on the ranch and almost in the house. Raised on a bottle after her mother had been killed in an accident, she was a present to the children from Sarah Kleberg, who shipped her in a padded crate all the way from the great King Ranch in Texas. She was a pet and followed the children around like a big dog. Sitting out on the lawn, the first thing we'd know Sarah would come and curl herself up comfortably at our feet.

With his polo field, his stables, his roping corral, his horses and the bridle trails back in the hills, Will now had just about everything he wanted. But the work went on and on. Will kept adding a new fence, a new corral, a new bridle trail; he cut out new roads; he changed this and that; and the digging, clearing, building and pounding never slowed down while he was here. The ranch was the joy of his life. Every tree and shrub on the place was planted under his direction. He used to drive home followed by a rickety truck driven by a Japanese and loaded with climbing roses, bougainvillea vines and pots of blooming flowers for the patio.

The big living room in the west end of the house, with its Indian blankets, saddles and ropes, tells a story of Will. Even the stones in the fireplace came from off the ranch and were selected and placed in the mantle under his direction. And hanging on the old stone chimney just over the fireplace is a longhorn **Texas** steer head, a present to Will from Amon Carter of Fort Worth, Texas. One of the light fixtures was made from an old wagon wheel that he picked up on the trails back in the hills when he first bought the property. The old wheel no doubt was from a wagon that did duty when our acres were a part of the old Spanish grant known as Rancho Boca de Santa Monica. The tiger skin and black leopard were sent from Singapore by the Sultan of Johore, and the old wooden Indian that stands guard in one corner was a gift from Frank Phillips of Bartlesville, Oklahoma. Will's hurdy-gurdy is there, too, and his barrel of ropes. And tucked back under the stairway, ready to be pulled out into the middle of the room when Will wanted to rope in the evening, is a little stuffed calf on rollers.

The room has a high ceiling. "I raised the roof while Mrs. Rogers and Mary had gone to the Holy Land," Will once wrote. "She said I just did it so I could rope in the house without hitting the ceiling. Well, maybe she was right. Anyhow, I got an old stuffed calf in there that I get out and practise on. I am without a doubt the best dead-calf roper in the world, but when I try it on a live one, it don't work. But I am death on dead calves."

He bought the Navaho rugs in Arizona and New Mexico. The blankets on the walls he brought home with him from Chile and the Argentine. He brought blankets, baskets and little figures from Mexico. Most of the pictures in the room were by old friends of his, the cowboy artists, Charlie Russell and Ed Borein.

He had been years making a collection of quirts and saddles. Will loved horses, everything about them; the room says this right away.

The big landscape window, seven by nine feet, in the west end of the room, was a present to Will from Mr. Ziegfeld. Will's special table and chair were in front of this window, and it was there that he had his breakfast every morning and read his morning paper. As he read, he planned his daily article. He would thresh it through on the way to the studio and peck it out on his typewriter during the lunch hour. Or perhaps he would go upstairs to his study and write the piece before he left the house, leaving it sticking in the typewriter for me to file at the telegraph office later in the day.

Will's study was next to our room upstairs in the east end of the house. Books of cowboy songs and old ranch poetry were there. He bought every one he heard about. It was easy for him to memorize and he liked to recite "Sam Bass," "Hell in Texas," and "On the Banks of the Cimarron." Will loved to sing, too. In the old days he always sang the cowboy songs, *The Dying Cowboy, Bury Me Not on the Lone Prairie* and *The Chisholm Trail—Coma Ti Yi Youpy.* "Cowpunchers had some pretty good old songs," he once wrote. "Course they was sung pretty bad, but the cows seemed to like 'em, and after all, that is what they was made up to be sung to."

Will's desk was in front of a large window that looked out toward the stable and the exercise ring and the hills he loved so well.

The west wing was the first part of the house Will built. The east wing with our bedrooms and a den came later. Between the two wings was a patio where we often entertained. Will hated large formal parties and we entertained with informal outdoor barbecues and buffet suppers if there were many guests. More frequently there were small informal dinners with intimate friends.

If Will had a free day, he liked to hop in a car and drive off without any plans. He would call to me, "Come on, Blake; let's get going," and away we'd go. He loved to prowl around in the car, and I did too. I think I had my happiest times with him on these expeditions. We were alone; I had him all to myself. There was no reading, no calf roping, no hundred and one other things that he always seemed to be doing. Just the two of us driving around the country exploring the beauties of California. Even the daily wire didn't spoil our wanderings. If a deadline was near, he drew up somewhere on the side of the road, and sitting on the running-board of the car with the typewriter on his knees, he would hammer out his daily, sometimes laboriously and sometimes without effort. It meant a short interval for me, when I could take a walk or sit quietly with my knitting if I had remembered to bring it. When the comment was finished, we drove off to the nearest telegraph office to file it.

Sometimes we took a box of sandwiches and ate them in the car as we drove along. Or better still, Will would drive up to a little out-of-the-way grocery store. Like a book hunter in a library, he would move from shelf to shelf, collecting an assortment of cans and boxes which usually included a can of salmon, a can of sardines, a can of tomatoes, cheese and a box of crackers. Then he would stand at the counter and chat with the owner of the store while he ate his lunch.

To get off the highway on a strange dirt road was what Will liked best. I suppose there are few trails or cowpaths in California wide enough for a car to get through that we weren't on at one time or another. Late one afternoon, I remember, he discovered an old, dim road that curved around and up a mountain, and once started on it, we found there was no going back. On either side were outcroppings of stone and red earth, and no place on the road was wide enough to turn our car. Will shifted gears hopefully as the car began to strain its way up the steep hill, and finally we made the top.

There we found an old grizzled ranger and his cabin. Recognizing Will, he exclaimed with a broad grin, "Man alive! Will Rogers! How in the world did you ever get up here?"

The two of them talked for a while and then the ranger helped Will to turn his car around. It was a heavy roadster and never before had any but a light car attempted the climb. Nor was there much room even at the top of the mountain to make a turn. I began to get nervous and hopped out of the car. But Will drove a car just like he rode a horse and could usually make it do what he wanted. Finally the car was turned around and we started back.

Will always had a good time on these trips. Country

storekeepers and such men as the ranger were among the thousands of men he talked to with genuine interest. Sometimes we would spend the night in a little town off the main boulevard. Will liked the small country hotels and liked talking to the people he met in out-of-the-way places. He had a human, friendly way with strangers and a warm curiosity about what other people were doing and thinking.

I was aften nervous and sometimes a little afraid on these drives over forsaken roads and to out-of-the-way places. All Will knew about a car was how to drive it; if something had gone wrong on a deserted road we would simply have had to sit there or walk back. I doubt that Will even knew how to change a tire. And he never carried a gun, although he had grown up among Indian Territory cowmen when most men and boys owned guns and were always hunting.

I know that once when Fred Stone was visiting us he rigged up a little one-man skeet shoot in front of the house. Fred was a great shot and was practising there. Will rode Soapsuds across the lawn while Fred was throwing up the targets and shooting at them.

"Come on, Will; try a shot," Fred said. "I'll throw up the target and you see if you can't hit one."

Will answered, "You know, Fred, it's a funny thing, but I guess I'm about the only cowboy who never owned a gun. When I was a kid I used to go jack-rabbit hunting with the boys, but they did all the shooting. I never killed anything in my life."

When he wasn't exploring California in a car, he was exploring the Santa Monica Mountains on Soapsuds. I think he would have been satisfied to spend his entire life astride a horse. He used to say, "There is something the matter with a man who don't like a horse."

Back of the stables and farther to the north are the Santa Monica Mountains, where Will loved to ride. One year I bought him a machete, and for a long time afterward he went out alone, riding through the underbrush and chopping the thick growth away, laying out new horseback trails for the Mexican boys he always had working on bridle paths over the hills.

CHAPTER XX

WILL's public career was never brought into our home.
It was simply a job at which he worked. A job at which
he worked in his spare time, it almost seemed. For
Will was very casual about it. He was also skeptical;
in his own words, he always felt "they would catch
onto" him sooner or later. I have told how Will intended, at the time of our marriage, to give up the
theater after one more season in vaudeville, and how we
kept putting it off as he received better and better
offers. Through our first years together, both of us
definitely felt that Will's theatrical career wouldn't
last—that we would be going back to Oklahoma soon.

Something of this feeling persisted, not only during
Will's swift rise in the theater but long afterward.
With a good contract and everything set for the immediate future, Will would think himself very lucky.
He was always doubtful that things would be so good
next year. But these were not problems the family
worried over or lengthily discussed. We were pleased
and full of congratulations when Will had done well,
equally we were unhappy when he fell into difficulties.
But over the family dinner table there was always more
talk of the afternoon's polo or calf roping, than of the
theater, the radio, movies or politics.

Thinking his popularity a lucky accident, and feeling
that people would tire of him eventually, Will refused
to consider himself a "public figure." Called a sage, a

philosopher and a statesman, his own estimate of his position never changed. His brand of entertainment happened to consist of "watching the Government and reporting the facts"; nevertheless it was as an entertainer that Will thought of himself. He was irritated and embarrassed by the various drives to run him for office.

At the Democratic Convention of 1924 two Arizona delegates had favored him for the nomination. In his last Convention dispatch Will thanked them for their "unwavering support during the entire fifteen minutes which they struck so staunchly by me." In the 1928 campaign Will had a fine time running as the Presidential candidate of the Anti-Bunk Party, writing campaign promises and oratory for the humor magazine *Life*. And at the Democratic Convention of 1932 he was given twenty-two votes for one round when Alfalfa Bill Murray released his Oklahoma delegation to "that sterling citizen, that wise philosopher, that great heart, that favorite son of Oklahoma. . . ."

"Politics ain't on the level," Will described this last presidential boom. "I was only in 'em for an hour, but in that short space of time somebody stole twenty-two votes from me. I was sitting there in the press stand asleep and wasn't bothering a soul when they woke me up and said Oklahoma had started me on the way to the White House with twenty-two votes. I thought to myself, 'Well, there is no use going there this late in the morning,' so I dropped off to sleep again, and that's when somebody touched me for my roll, took the whole twenty-two, didn't even leave me a vote to get breakfast on."

All this was good-natured fun. But when the idea was seriously advanced, and reports came out that Will was taking it seriously, that was something else again. Several times he was earnestly urged to become a candidate for Governor of Oklahoma. I remember well a committee that called on us in Beverly Hills and tried to persuade him to run, in California, for Senator on the Democratic ticket. Of course he would have nothing to do with such offers. And when it was suggested that he might actually run for President, Will was outraged.

"Will you do me one favor, [he wrote in 1931] if you see or hear of anybody proposing my name for any political office will you maim said party and send me the bill? My friend on *Collier's* (George Creel it is by the way that writes that clever 'Keyhole Column') says that I am taking this running serious. George, that's the worst slam you ever took against my sense of humor. I certainly know that a comedian can only last till he either takes himself serious or his audience takes him serious and I don't want either one of those to happen to me till I am dead (if then) so lets stop all this d—— foolishness right now.

"I hereby and hereon want to go on record as being the first Presidential, Vice-Presidential, Senator, or Justice of Peace candidate to withdraw. I not only 'Don't choose to run,' I won't run. Now I hope in doing this that I have started something that will have far reaching effect. Who will be the next to do the public a favor and withdraw? What is there to worry anybody over the next nominations anyhow? It's one year away but the candidates will be Hoover and Curtis versus Franklin D. Roosevelt and some Western or Southern Democratic Governor. . . ."

When Franklin D. Roosevelt came to Los Angeles, on his speaking tour in the campaign of 1932, the Republican mayor refused to welcome him. Will was annoyed by this lack of sportsmanship. "I'm a former mayor of Beverly Hills," he told the Roosevelt managers, "and if you want me to, I'll welcome him to Southern California." And at the Electric Pageant in the Olympic Stadium that night he told the crowd, "There must be a hundred thousand people here tonight. This is the biggest audience in the world that ever paid to see a politician. Franklin—I can call you Franklin, for I knew you before you were Governor or even Assistant Secretary of the Navy. I knew you when you first started in your career of nominating Al Smith for office. As a young man, you used to come to the *Follies,* and I would call on you from the stage to say a few words, and you would get up and nominate Al Smith for something."

Standing near Governor Roosevelt that night, I noticed that he led the crowd in laughing at the jokes on himself. "Now, I don't want you to think that I am overawed by being asked to introduce you," Will continued. "I'm not. I'm broadminded that way and will introduce anybody. And if this introduction lacks enthusiasm or floweriness, you must remember you're only a candidate yet. Come back as President and I will do right by you. I'm wasting no oratory on a prospect."

Will never predicted the outcome of political campaigns. Until the last minute, he always insisted that he, for one, wasn't sure who'd win. This was a rule of

Will's; people were a little crazy during an election and he didn't want to lay himself open to accusations, however preposterous, that he had influenced the result. But at the Democratic Convention of 1932, in an impromptu speech, Will had told the delegates not to go home and say they had nominated their weakest man and that he couldn't win: "I don't see how he could ever be weak enough not to win. If he lives till November, he's in."

Will's impromptu speech, incidentally, had come on the third day of the Convention when there was a recess to give the Committee on Resolutions time to decide on a platform. As Will explained when he mounted the rostrum: "I'm supposed to stand up here until the Democratic Party agrees on prohibition. I'll be here from now on." And he adlibbed for a solid hour—the first orator, according to Heywood Broun, "to leave the platform with shouts of 'More! More!' ringing in his ears."

The 1932 campaign, as it got under way, was even more bitter than the Smith-Hoover battle of four years before—of which Will had said that it would "take two generations to sweep up the dirt." And early in October, feeling it necessary to escape for a while, Will decided on a trip to South America. "I am leaving for everything south of the equator," he wired October tenth from San Salvador. "Am flying down the west coast to Chile, then to Argentina for a week, and up to the east coast by Brazil. I want to get back just before election. I think people would like to read something in the papers besides 'Hoover said this' and

'Roosevelt says that.' I think it's a good time to go. In fact, I am gone."

In his daily wire on the thirteenth Will told about an old man at a little Peruvian village where the plane had stopped for gas, who came up and began talking about the radio address Calvin Coolidge had made the night before. Will was surprised, and thought Mr. Coolidge might be surprised too. "I'll bet he'll be all broke up," Will said, "when he hears he wasted his speech on people away down here that can't vote."

Back in Coral Gables, Florida, on the twenty-seventh, Will decided to go on to New York. "Was going to stop in Washington," he said, "but the newspaper boys said there wasn't a soul there. 'Ain't Mr. Hoover there?' 'No, he has gone to save Indiana.' 'Well, I know my old Injun friend Charley Curtis is there.' 'No, he is saving Kansas.' 'Well, then I will just drop up and see some of the boys in the Cabinet.' 'Why, there is none of the Cabinet that's been here since early in the spring.' 'Well, who is running the country?' 'Why, nobody, that's why things are kinder picking up.' "

In New York Will decided that he had arrived back "in the midst of the most colossal rodeo of applesauce in the history of our national pastime." But he guessed that, after all, it was what they called a clean campaign. "A clean campaign," he said, "is where each side cleans the other side of every possible vestige of respectability. The opposition are just horse thieves and that's all there is to it. Well, they are, but aren't we all?"

In spite of his efforts to be neutral and fair to both sides, Will received a great deal of indignant criticism in the heat of political campaigns—and never more than in this 1932 campaign. A piece he wrote November first, during the last vitriolic days, was particularly resented by partisans of both sides:

"There should be a moratorium called on candidates' speeches. They have both called each other everything in the world they can think of. From now on they are just talking themselves out of votes. The high office of President of the United States has degenerated into two ordinarily fine men being goaded on by their political leeches into saying things that if they were in their right minds they wouldn't think of saying. Imagine Mr. Hoover last night, 'any change of policies will bring disaster to every fireside in America.' This country is a thousand times bigger than any two men in it, or any two parties in it. This country has gotten where it is in spite of politics, not by the aid of it. That we have carried as much political bunk as we have and still survived shows we are a super-nation.

"This calamity was brought on by the actions of the people of the whole world and its weight will be lifted off by the actions of the people of the whole world, and not by a Republican or a Democrat. So you two boys just get the weight of the world off your shoulders and go fishing. Both of you claim you like to fish, now instead of calling each other names till next Tuesday, why you can do everybody a big favor by going fishing, and you will be surprised but the old U. S. will keep right on running while you boys are sitting on the bank."

When the returns were in and things had quieted down a little, Will replied to his wrathful readers:

"Now that the election is over and people can't write in and complain about my 'Remarks,' why I figure that this department of the paper will be withdrawn," he wrote in the letters-to-the-editor column of the Los Angeles *Times*. "One day when I thought I had written a good article (by accident, I suppose, it certainly wasn't through habit), well, it seems that this one sensible article that I wrote was such a change from the usual bunk I had been dishing out that even the *Times* themselves rose up in protest.

"What surprised me was that I said a hundred fool things day after day that I knew didn't have any sense to 'em. But the only truthful one I happened to stumble on was the one they took the hide off me for, that was the one about telling 'em to go fishing.

"The one thing that I am proud of is the fact that there is not a man in public life today that I don't like, most of them are my good friends, but that's not going to keep me from taking a dig at him when he does something or says something foolish. Mr. Hoover knows that grass is not going to grow on any streets, no matter who's President. You can't get it to grow on your lawns. He knows disaster is not going to be at every fireside; those were said in the heat of a campaign, but that don't keep 'em from being foolish. Roosevelt saying Hoover was responsible for all our depression was just as bad. He knows that's not so, but he said it, all in the heat of a campaign.

"And when I said that they both were taking themselves too serious, that the U. S. was bigger than any two men or any two parties, why that's the way I feel about it."

Which was the way Will had always felt about it. He knew "neither one of 'em is going to save us.

Neither one is going to ruin us." The only thing about Presidential campaigns that seemed to him worth losing his temper over was the bitterness and bad sportsmanship with which they were conducted.

"And by the way," he said, "here is one thing I want somebody to explain to me, why is it during a campaign, after a campaign, or at any other time, why can't our Presidents speak of each other by name and say, 'Well, I wish Mr. So and So well, he is a fine man and will make you a good President,' or to have the victors say, 'He had a hard time, and did the very best he could have under the circumstances.' Even small town mayors have been known to speak of each other complimentary, but if Presidents ever did it I think we would drop dead."

Though Will might arouse the ire of sideline partisans, he almost invariably remained on good terms with those he kidded, the politicians themselves. Will was proud of this, as he said, and a gesture of friendship and esteem from the Senate in 1933 pleased him very much indeed. "I make a living telling jokes about those fellows," Will said, "and then to have them come along and do this. Gee, I don't hardly know what to say."

Will had been making a series of Sunday night radio talks during the first half of 1933, and was spending a good deal of time in Washington where things were happening fast after Roosevelt's inauguration that March. The broadcasts, if notice was given a day or so beforehand, could come from almost any large city, and a few weeks before he finished the series he asked that one of them be scheduled from the capital. Will's Washington friends decided to make the broadcast an event. The ballroom of the Mayflower Hotel was arranged for, and with the Senate attending in a body, Will conducted the broadcast as a mock session of that legislative body.

About a month after the Washington Broadcast, when it was announced that he was concluding his series of weekly radio talks, Will received a message from the Senators asking him to stay on the air. Signed by Vice-President Garner and almost every member of the Senate, the message said:

"Dear Will:
What is this we hear about your radio retirement? Does that mean that you will not preside over the Senate again? We have enjoyed your recent talks on the air and want your assurance that you will soon return with your humorous and wholesome comment on national affairs."

Will read the message in his last broadcast. "You Senators," he said, "you know, it is terrible for me to have to compliment you, but I am going to have to do it. This is one of the most wonderful things that I have had happen to me in many a day. It shows that you can tell jokes about people and still retain their friendship. I am very very proud of that."

CHAPTER XXI

EARLY one morning in 1933 Will heard King George's speech opening the World Economic Conference in London. It came over the radio at five o'clock just as Will, who was making a picture then, was going to work on location. This seemed an inconvenient hour at which to hear the King, and Will, in his wire that day, suggested the Conference fix it so all parts of the world would have the same time. "They can do that just as easy as they can agree on anything else," he said. "Different nations have different problems, just like different nations have the sun shine on 'em at different times."

The unsatisfactory relations between big nations Will could take as a matter of course, a subject for good-natured comedy. But not the behavior of big nations toward the weak and undeveloped ones. Will was indignant at this sort of interference; he thought the "so-called backward" countries should be left alone to work out their problems in their own way. "America and England, especially," he said, "are regular old busybodies when it comes to telling somebody else what to do. We are going to get a kick in the pants some day if we don't come home and start tending to our own business and let other people live as they want to. What degree of egotism is it that makes a Nation or a religious organization think theirs is the very thing for the Chinese or the Zulus?"

Our interference in Mexico, Cuba, and the Central American countries was always a sore spot with Will. He insisted there was plenty for us to do at home, without regulating the affairs of other nations—even if they were weak and defenseless nations. "America has a great habit," he said, "of always talking about protecting American interests in some foreign Country. Protect 'em here at Home! There is more American Interests right here than anywhere. If an American goes to Mexico and his horse dies, we send them a note wanting American Interests preserved and the horse paid for. We don't guarantee investments here at home. Why should we make Mexico guarantee them?"

His feeling about the future of world peace Will summed up in 1934 with the sad observation that "Chile is selling nitrates; Europe is fertilizing again." A major war was coming sooner or later, he was sure. Personally, Will hoped it was later. "The consensus of opinion," he said, "is that 'so-and-so has to fight so-and-so sooner or later.' Well I believe if I had to fight a man 'sooner or later,' I would fight him later. The later the better."

But to tell the truth, Will was surprised and gratified that a fair measure of world peace had lasted that long. As early as 1930, in an article entitled "Wars, and Rumors of Wars," he had written:

"We can't pick up a paper that from one to a hundred don't prophesy that Prosperity is just around the corner. But let me tell you that war is nearer around the corner than prosperity is. Germany is harboring a terrible lot of dissatisfaction; that Hitler has got 'em all stirred up over there. Then those little Balkan Nations, they are like a mess of stray Terriers anyhow—they just as well be fighting as like they are. This has been about the longest they have ever been between wars.

"I see the other day where Russia was just on the verge of invading Roumania. Then Russia and Poland are always on the verge of war. I remember when I was over in both countries in the summer of '26, why they were growling at each other like a couple of Fat Prima Donnas on the same opera bill.

"All this whole mess have no more love for each other than a litter of Hyenas. If we keep our nose clean and don't start yapping about somebody else's honor, or what our moral obligations are, we might escape it. But it's going to take better Statesmanship than we have been favored with heretofore. The way we are now we are mighty lucky to have nothing but a little business depression that is bothering us. Think what those other poor Devils are up against."

Will was persistently opposed to our getting involved in the family affairs of Europe. And he found most Americans of the same opinion. As for Europe's attitude toward America, Will knew it well from his travels. He once explained that he was often asked what Europe would do if this country was in trouble and needed help. What Europe would do, Will thought, was "hold a celebration."

"We ought to set by a day of thanksgiving," Will often said, "blessing the Atlantic and Pacific Oceans for their splendid judgment in locating where they did." But it was never his idea that those two oceans were all we needed for defense. One day in 1934, on location in Sonora, California, Will reported: "Walked into a barber shop in this beautiful and historical little mountain town. I heard the radio going and somebody raising Old Ned with somebody. I says 'Who's that?' They says, 'Why, that's the President giving some folks fits for being against military preparedness.' I says, 'Amen.' Sic 'em, Franklin, pour it on 'em. If they want to know what 'Not having a gun will do for you' they can point out China and India."

What worried Will was that after years of economizing on the Army and Navy we would "wake up some morning with a war on our hands," then the mad rush would be on and "we will go through that silk-shirt buying period again."

For military aviation, as for commercial aviation, Will boosted loudly and at length. He wrote several articles on Colonel William Mitchell's valiant but losing fight to make our War Department realize the importance of aviation. The Colonel was a good friend of his. Mitchell's last flight as a Brigadier-General, just before being demoted to Colonel and sent to an obscure post in Texas, was a sightseeing trip over Washington with Will in the second cockpit. Will admired Colonel Mitchell and thoroughly agreed with him. "When we nearly lose the next war," Will wrote, "as we probably will, we can lay it onto one thing, and that will be the jealousy of the Army and Navy toward aviation."

Will's theory on military preparedness was that "if we build all we can, and then take care of nothing but our own business, we will never have to use it." But even if we did have to use it, he still thought we ought

to have it. As he wired from Washington, January 30,
1934: "Been visiting and listening to speeches in both
ends of the Capitol all day. Debating on the Big Navy
Bill in the House. Was talking to a Lady Congress-
man and she said to me: 'Why do all those men say
that a big Navy will bring peace?' I told her, 'Well,
even if it don't bring peace, it will come in mighty
handy.' "

This was the attitude, though not the official one,
that Will found at all the Disarmament Conferences.
Of every disarmament plan he saw that "nations that
have none say, 'It's fine,' but the ones that are well
armed say, 'It's terrible.' " At the London Naval Disarmament Conference in 1930, for which he had left so
hurriedly with the $19.75 blue serge suit, Will, in the
words of the *Outlook and Independent,* "did himself
proud." Of his work there, a current issue of the magazine had this to say:

"Doubt rather than certainty, suspicion rather than
confidence prevailed as the conference opened, and
Rogers duly suggested the fact while other correspondents described the pretty speeches. As the King left
after his opening-day address, Will declared, 'he happened to think, so he sent four men back and they
carried the gold throne chair out.' The irreverent
fancy—a cautious King, nervous lest his chair be
stolen—pressed the whole atmosphere of the meeting
into one short sentence. . . .

"While assignment-bound reporters strained their
wits to make much out of little or nothing, Rogers
reported blandly and truthfully: 'If any American correspondent sent any news home today, he has made it

up.' . . . Whoever calls this mere irresponsible jesting cannot have followed developments very closely. Truth is, Rogers, day by day, got deeper under the surface of the Conference than almost any of the other correspondents beating their typewriters in London."

If Will took himself at all seriously as a writer, it was as a reporter—a dealer in current, topical facts. He insisted that for comedy all he had to do was report the facts. It might be necessary to exaggerate a little, or to shift the emphasis; but the important and basic element in his humor was factual. Consequently it was in current facts that Will was mainly interested. He got them by traveling to see things and to see people; but chiefly he got them from the newspapers.

Will seldom read books. "I am fifty-two years old," he once wrote, "sound of body, but weak of mind, and I never did read hardly any books. I like to read but I don't have the time. If I got any spare time I like to get on a horse and ride around, or sit and blather with somebody. But I do a lot of newspaper reading. I try to get all breeds, creeds, and every single different political one. If they would just quit printing newspapers for about a year, I could get some books read, but by the time I go through the daily papers, I am sound asleep. I am kind of a slow reader anyhow, and a lot of the stuff I have to read is not delivered in what you would call a straightforward or lucid vein, so I have to go back over it a few times to catch the meaning, and then I don't always grasp it. I just got started in wrong. All educated people started in reading good books. Well I didn't. I seem to have gone from Frank Meriwell and Nick Carter, at Kemper Military Academy, right to the Congressional Record, just one set of low fiction to another."

Will always regretted that he hadn't taken advantage of his opportunities to get a good education; there wasn't a day of his life, he said, that he didn't regret it. The public insistence of his friend Arthur Brisbane that Will was an Oxford graduate in disguise was simply a gag, of course. Will's formal education had ended that "cold winter" when he departed from Kemper.

Having earned no college degree, Will refused all efforts to give him honorary degrees. "I have had this same play come up a time or two," he once wrote of such an offer, "and I think these guys are kidding. If they are not, they ought to be. Degrees have lost prestige enough as it is without handing 'em around to comedians, and it's this handing 'em out too promiscuously that has helped to cheapen 'em. Let a guy get in there and battle four years if he wants one."

Will always wrote hurriedly, and usually, I'm afraid, he wrote carelessly. With his daily wires he would often take considerable pains, fussing and worrying to get them right. But his weekly articles—and some of them as a result were very bad indeed—he would rush through and get rid of as quickly as he could. This was particularly true in his later years when Will really wanted to drop this long article; he would have preferred then to do no regular writing except the daily piece. But in spite of the slap-dash way they were done, the articles remained a popular syndicate feature, and the Mc-

Naught people always talked him out of it when he tried to quit.

In the early days Will wrote in longhand and I did his typing. Later when he began using the typewriter himself, he had a lot of trouble with it. Typing, Will felt, was a nuisance, and when Arthur Brisbane explained to him the ease and convenience of using a dictaphone, Will was elated with the idea. There was nothing easier for Will than talking, so he bought a little machine and sat down hopefully to talk out an article. But with the dictaphone started, Will got all excited. He couldn't think of anything to say; he couldn't think at all.

He tried the dictaphone several times. But finally gave it up and went back to wrestling with the typewriter—hitting the wrong keys, strewing commas all over the place, and using capitals almost at random. Eventually Will developed a two-finger technique that was fairly fast; but the copy he turned out was always untidy. The syndicate editors often must have torn their hair over it, for some of Will's original manuscripts, with their confusing revisions, are really outrageous.

Will never retyped anything. When he revised he used a lead pencil on the original draft. And he simply refused to bother about grammar, spelling, or correct construction. Sometimes he didn't even read the material over; and with the exception of the daily wires, he rarely looked at what he had written when it was published. "When I write 'em I am through with 'em," he said. "I am not being paid reading wages. You can always see too many things you wish you hadn't said, and not enough that you ought to."

Will's early writing efforts were apt to be strident with slang. He thought it was what the public expected of him. But when he got over that and began to write simply as he talked, the style Will naturally fell into— much as he would have snorted at the term "style"— became ideally suited to his purpose. For just as Will's careless manner on the lecture platform and the stage softened the occasional sharpness of his spoken words, so his written words were softened by poor grammar, slipshod construction and an amiable excess of words.

Of the big word and the strange word, Will was always leary. "I got me a dictionary one time," he said, "but it didn't last long. It was like looking in a telephone book. I never called up anybody in my life if I had to look up their number. Nobody is worth looking through all those numbers for, and that's the way it was with my dictionary. I could write the article while I was trying to see what the word meant. But here's one good thing about language, there is always a short word for it. 'Course the Greeks have a word for it, the dictionary has a word for it, but I believe in using your own word for it. I love words but I don't like strange ones. You don't understand them, and they don't understand you. Old words is like old friends—you know 'em the minute you see 'em."

In spite of his neglect of grammar and spelling, and his occasional downright carelessness in making himself clear, Will could write beautifully and well when he chose. His introduction to *Trails Plowed Under*, a posthumously published book written by the cowboy artist Charley Russell, has been called "one of the most beautifully simple, most moving and lovable tributes that ever was penned in memory of a departed comrade."*

Will and Charley Russell had been friends for many years. They became acquainted in Great Falls, Montana, when Will was playing a vaudeville engagement there, and liked each other immediately. Later, just after Will and I were married, we met Charley and Nancy, his wife, in New York, where they had come for an exhibition of Charley's pictures at the Tiffany Galleries. And long afterward in California we always saw a great deal of them during the winter months which the Russells spent at their home in Pasadena.

Charley loved horses as much as Will did, and together, or with Ed Borein, also a Western artist and a great friend of both, they had many rides over the hills back of our Santa Monica ranch. Both Charley and Ed had been cowpunchers in their youth, and both knew the old West they pictured. Will's one great extravagance, and the extent of his art appreciation, was Ed's etchings and water colors, and Charley's bronze and his oils.

"Hello Charley old hand, [Will wrote for *Trails Plowed Under*] how are you? I just thought I would drop you a line and tell you how things are working on the old range since you left. Old Timer, you don't know how we miss you, Gee but it's been lonesome since you left, even to us away down here in California, where we didn't get to see near as much of you as we wanted

* Irvin S. Cobb, *Exit Laughing*.

to anyhow. But think what all them old Montana Waddies are thinking. Why some of those old Birds would miss their wives less than they do you. . . .

"There aint much news here to tell you. But after we realized that you had rolled your Bed and gone, it sure would a done your old hide good to a seen what they all thought of you. You know how it is yourself with a fellow leaving an outfit and going over to another—in talking it over after he had gone, there is generally a BUT to it somewhere. Some old 'Peeler' will unload some dirt about him, but there sure wasn't any after you crossed the skyline. Why it would a been almost worth your going to a new Outfit just to have heard all the fine things said about you.

"Why you old Rascal you would a thought you was somebody. You never was much for swelling up, but I tell you your old hat band would be busted if you had heard. It was wonderful Charley, and it did please your old friends that the world recognized you. But somehow that didn't seem to repay us. It wasn't what you had done, it wasn't because you could paint a horse and a cow and a cowboy better than any man that ever lived, I don't know, it was just you Charley, We want you here if you couldn't whitewash a fence.

"But we all know you are getting along fine. You will get along fine anywhere. . . . You will run onto my old Dad up there Charley. For he was a real Cowhand and bet he is running a wagon, and you will pop onto some well kept ranch house over under some cool shady trees and you will be asked to have dinner, and it will be the best one you ever had in your life. Well, when you are a thanking the women folks, you just tell the sweet looking little old lady that you know her boy back on an outfit you used to rep for, and tell the daughters that you knew their brother, and if you see a cute looking little rascal running around there, kiss him for me. Well can't write you any more Charley, dam paper's all wet, It must be raining in this old bunk house.

"Course we are all just a hanging on here as long as we can. I don't know why we hate to go, we know it's better there. Maby it's because we haven't done anything that will live after we are gone."

Will was, by nature, a deeply religious man, though he belonged to no church, and in later years rarely attended any. "Statistics show how church attendance is sorter falling off on Sunday mornings," Will once wrote. "But it's no lack of religious inclinations, it's just that you can't beat Sunday morning to get the old car out and ramble. Folks are just as good as they ever were, and they mean well, but no minister can move 'em like a second hand car."

When we first moved to Beverly Hills, there was no regular church nearer than Hollywood. Beverly Hills was not a city then—hardly a community—there was no market, not even a drugstore. We attended services, and the children went to Sunday School in the Hawthorne Grammar School, which every Sunday became the Community Church under Dr. Robert S. Donaldson. Will was quite indignant about this lack of a church; and before long, with donations from Will and other early citizens of Beverly, the little Community Church, which is still in use, was built.

All through his career, ministers of the gospel were interested in Will and kind to him. One of his earliest weekly articles had been reprinted in several church papers. Many times he was invited to speak from the pulpit. I remember, long ago, a good-natured and amusing debate he held with a minister on the question of whether cowboys or ministers had done the most for civilization. Texts for sermons were often taken from his writings. Some two years before his death Will quoted in a weekly article his reply to a minister who had written to say that he wanted to discuss him and his philosophy in a sermon.

"I was raised predominately a Methodist, [Will said] but I have traveled so much, mixed with so many people in all parts of the world, I don't know now just what I am. I know I have never been a non-believer. But I can honestly tell you that I dont think that any one religion is *the* religion. Which way you serve your God will never get one word of argument or condemnation out of me.

"I got no 'Philosophy.' I don't even know what the word means. The Fourth Reader (McGuffys) is as far as I ever got in schools. I am not bragging on it, I am thoroughly ashamed of it, for I had every opportunity. Everything I have done has been by luck, no move was premeditated. I just stumbled from one thing to another. It might have been down. I didn't know at the time, and I dont know yet, for I don't know what 'Up' is. I may be lower than I ever was, I dont know. I may be making the wrong use of any little talent (if any) that I accidentally have. I dont know."

Neither Will's philosophy of life, nor his religion, were of the formal type that can be organized into a definite creed. He had both a religious belief and a deep-seated philosophy. But they were a part of him, coloring his whole process of living and thinking; not put away into a compartment of his being, from which they might be withdrawn and explained at need.

And they served him well. Yielding to no rules and
conforming to no standards but his own, Will was very
sure of himself in many ways. He was seldom doubtful in matters of right and wrong. Will had with him
always an inner feeling of right and a conscience free
of guilt. He had this by knowing, and being confident
that he did know, what was right and what was wrong,
and by always doing what he felt was right for him
to do. He tried not to offend, but Will was sure of
his motives. And once he had said a thing or done a
thing, he ceased to consider the possibility that it might
have been actually wrong. I think he never had to justify to himself a single act or word of his.

Will never said a mean thing; he refused to gossip,
would have nothing to do with such talk. When an
absent person was being raked over the coals by a
group, Will invariably found something to say in his
favor. Will wouldn't pick on anyone who was down,
and he always resisted when others were doing so.

Time after time in the old vaudeville days, I saw
him save acts that were dying by going out on the stage
and kidding with the performers. Will did the same
sort of thing in pictures; he spent half his time on the
movie lots thinking up new lines and bits of business
for actors whose parts were being whittled out of the
script.

In after-dinner speaking, where Will was usually
last on the program, it sometimes happened that an
earlier speaker had been nervous and confused, or had
rambled pointlessly on and on. Getting up to talk
later, Will would always mention the unlucky speaker
with some joke or other. The poor fellow, thinking he

was in for a ribbing, would sink lower and lower in his seat. But Will would go on to say something good about him; how, after all, he had brought out one point, or had given them a new slant on this. And before Will had finished, the inept speaker would perk up and feel that maybe he hadn't been so bad at that.

Lending a helping hand or doing what he could to pick up the spirits of anyone feeling low was simply a natural reaction with Will. And because of the off-hand, kidding way in which he performed them, his acts of kindness had nothing of condescension. It was of such things and the spirit that prompted them that Will's natural, living philosophy of helpfulness, honesty and tolerance was composed.

This was not the sort of philosophy of which you could talk; and when asked by Will Durant to contribute to his book, *Living Philosophies,* Will was at a loss.

"I can't tell this doggone Durant anything [he replied]. What all of us know put together don't mean anything. We are just here for a spell and pass on. Any man that thinks civilization has advanced is an egotist. We have got more tooth paste on the market and more misery in our Courts than at any time in our existence.

"So get a few laughs and do the best you can. Don't have an ideal to work for. That's like riding towards a mirage of a lake. When you get there it ain't there. Believe in something for another World, but don't be too set on what it is, and then you won't start out that life with a disappointment. Live your life so that whenever you lose, you are ahead."

CHAPTER XXII

In THE early summer of 1935 it seemed to me that for the first time in his life Will showed signs of weariness. He was in his middle fifties now and the heavy schedule he was carrying had begun to pall on him a little. This summer particularly he was looking forward to a vacation. His contract with the Fox Company provided that he make three pictures a year, and these he had managed to crowd into half a year's work so that he could have the other six months to himself. There was, of course, a series of radio programs in the fall, but now he would be free for a while at least. He was like a small boy with a vacation coming up and not knowing what to do with it.

He had many ideas for a long trip. The plan we discussed most was to fly to Rio de Janeiro and catch the German Zeppelin—which at that time was on a regular schedule—for a flight up the coast of Africa. Because of Will's distaste for planning ahead, even this idea remained in a rather vague state. He was still undecided about what to do and still working on his last picture, *Steamboat Round the Bend,* when Wiley and Mrs. Post arrived in Los Angeles.

Will had great affection and admiration for Wiley Post and felt that his achievements had never been properly recognized. Many pilots had been able to capitalize on lesser deeds, but Wiley, in spite of his two round-the-world flights—one of them alone, on which he had broken the record previously set by himself and Harold Gatty—had never been able to cash in on his exploits. And Will had always been a booster for his fellow Oklahoman.

Wiley had recently conceived the idea of surveying and establishing a mail-and-passenger air route between this country and Russia, one which would avoid the hazards of the long flight over the Pacific by taking the Alaska-to-Asia land route. He had sold one of the great air lines on the idea and the plan was so far advanced that he had letters from the Soviet Ambassador, maps and credentials of all sorts, and permission from the Moscow Government to travel wherever he pleased in Russia. But now, at the last minute, the great air line decided that it didn't want the survey. Wiley, however, was still determined on the trip. His new plane had just been assembled and he intended to put pontoons on it and give it a last going-over in Seattle and then from Nome to fly over the Bering Sea and on across Siberia.

We had crossed Siberia only the year before. Will had intended then for us to fly a part of the way. After the boat trip from Japan to Korea, we traveled across Manchuria to Harbin where we stopped for a few days before taking the Chinese Eastern Railway to Manchouli. Then at Manchouli we changed to the Trans-Siberian train de luxe for the beginning of the long journey. Before we left Tokyo, the Soviet government representative there had promised Will faithfully that we would be met at Novosibirsk by a plane which would carry us on to Moscow. But when the train arrived at Novosibirsk there was no plane, nor was there a message from Moscow.

So for six days we were cooped up in a tiny compartment with a big basket of oranges, a purchased stock of canned goods and a little canned-heat outfit for brewing tea. Our luggage was piled high beside us. Jogging along like this on a slow train behind a wood-burning locomotive was not Will's idea of traveling. Nor was it the way he liked to do his sightseeing. This wild country had great charm for Will. He wanted to see more of it. He wanted to get out and into it. He wanted to see it in the only way one can really see such a vast country—from the sky.

So, when Wiley explained his plans, Will couldn't help remembering Siberia and his disappointment at having been forced to see it from a car window. Still it was a long, hard trip that Wiley had in mind, and Will wasn't sure. But anyway they could fly over Alaska in a leisurely fashion and see a lot of country that was new to him. And so the idea of the Alaskan flight took form.

Wiley made a test flight, taking Will and Mrs. Post along with him. They flew over to Albuquerque and then to visit Mr. and Mrs. Waite Phillips on their New Mexico ranch. Will returned enthusiastic about the plane's performance, but even when Wiley left for Seattle a few days later Will had not definitely decided to make the trip. He was still busy at the studio with *Steamboat Round the Bend,* and Wiley was to telephone from Seattle to learn his final decision.

There was nothing unusual about this vagueness.

Our trips were nearly always made that way, and after
we had our tickets we didn't plan beyond the first stop.
I had tried to adjust myself to the thought of having
Will go. Flying around Alaska seemed safe enough;
it was only Siberia that I dreaded. I could see that
Will wanted me to want him to go. He was always
happier about anything he did if he felt that I wanted
him to do it. And so I tried to be happy about this.

We took a long ride over the ranch the Sunday morning before he left. We talked of some new trails he
wanted made and of a few small things that were to
be attended to. Then we turned off the bridle path,
ducked our heads and rode through the brush to a
hidden trail that led down into the canyon, where Will
had built a little log cabin, just completed a few days
before.

We wound our way to the cabin, drew our horses
up, dismounted and went in. I remember Will was
sorry that he hadn't had a chance to stay there. The
little wood cookstove was up and even the bunks and
the mattresses were there. I tried to persuade him to
postpone his trip for a few days. We'd take our bed-
rolls down and camp for the night, I told him. But
he said, "No, let's wait till I get back."

He had said that same thing so many times before.
And now his desk was piled high with papers, pictures
to sign and unanswered letters. There were two auto-
graph albums on his desk that belonged to Amon
Carter's children; I begged him that afternoon to sign
the books so that I might return them. I wanted him
to get everything cleared away before he left. But he

seemed to have a sort of superstition about it and said, "No, I don't want to do that now. Let's wait till I come home."

In the early afternoon he packed two bags, discarding nine-tenths of the things laid out for him to take. I walked in and out of the room several times, and once he called me back. He had a characteristic, rather sheepish, small-boy look as he said, "Say, Blake, you know what I just did? I flipped a coin." When I said, "I hope it came tails," he laughed and held out his hand. "No, it didn't. It's heads. See, I win."

We saw the last part of a polo game at the Uplifters Ranch, and afterward he and Buddy Sterling penned the calves and roped until suppertime. Bill was with us for supper, and that evening went with us to the rodeo at Gilmore Stadium. After the rodeo and on our way to the airport where Will was to take a regular passenger plane for San Francisco, we stopped at a little open-air restaurant for a sandwich.

The next day Will telephoned from San Francisco. He was rushing to get his passport and everything in order so he could leave on a plane that would reach Seattle that afternoon. Then he called me several times from Seattle. He stayed there a couple of days, playing one game of polo on a new field which has since been named in his honor. Will spoke to me for the last time Thursday, August eighth, about noon. It was just before they took off for Juneau, and although he was not yet definite about going beyond Alaska with Wiley, I was a little worried.

A few days later I flew to New York and joined

Mary and my sister Theda in Skowhegan, Maine.
Mary was playing in summer stock there and they had
taken a cottage near the Lakewood Theater. Jimmy
and his cousin, Jimmy Blake, had been working with
the Mashed O outfit on the Ewing Halsell ranch at
Amherst, Texas, but they were at that moment in their
little car, driving cross-country to join us in Maine.
Only Bill was in California, and he was about to leave
on a Standard Oil tanker for the Philippine Islands.

Will's first daily from Juneau reported the 1,000-
mile hop from Seattle, through mist and rain, and
Wiley's fine navigation. "Nothing that I have ever
seen," Will added, "is more beautiful than this inland
passage to Alaska."

In Juneau Will met his old friend Rex Beach, and
the two of them, with Wiley and Joe Crosson, another
fine flier, had dinner together that night. Rex and Will
had a grand visit talking over old times.

Will and Wiley made a trip to Anchorage and flew
over the highest peak on the North American continent,
Mount McKinley. Then in Fairbanks Will sent his
last daily wire on August fifteenth. It was handed to
Joe Crosson just before Will and Wiley took off to
Point Barrow, and along with it was this telegram to
Mary in Skowhegan:

"GREAT TRIP. WISH YOU WERE ALL ALONG. HOW'S
YOUR ACTING? YOU AND MAMA WIRE ME ALL THE
NEWS TO NOME. GOING TO POINT BARROW TODAY.
FURTHEST POINT OF LAND ON WHOLE AMERICAN
CONTINENT. LOTS OF LOVE. DON'T WORRY.
"DAD"

Reading this, I was sure they had decided to go on, for Nome was the point from which Wiley had planned to take off for Russia. I was disappointed and a little unhappy; I had hoped that after flying around in Alaska for a week or so, Will would join me in Skowhegan. We had discussed this and planned that if he decided not to go on with the flight, we would motor through the Cape Cod country. I dreaded for them to cross the Bering Sea and fly over the great Siberian waste, where they might be forced down and be out of touch with the world. I had no thought of real danger; just the dread of their suffering unnecessary hardships. Now I would have to fly back to California, pack and start for Europe. Will and I had agreed that if he made the trip, I should meet him somewhere, possibly Moscow.

I was telling all this to the Arthur Byrons, who lived near our cottage in Skowhegan and with whom my sister and I were visiting that Friday morning, when we saw a car coming up the road. It was Mr. Miles, the manager of the Lakewood Theater, and his manner alarmed us at once. He spoke only to my sister, and when she walked down from the porch with him and around the corner of the house, my alarm turned to panic. I thought of Jimmy and his cousin in their car. I ran after them. Something had happened to Jimmy. The boys had been in an accident—I was sure of it.

When I said, "Has something happened to Jimmy? Tell me," Mr. Miles did not answer.

My sister said, "No, Betty, it's Will. Will has had an accident."

For a moment I felt only relief. Nothing could happen to Will. A forced landing or an exaggerated report of some trouble with the plane. Jimmy was safe and nothing could happen to Will.

The story of the tragedy above the Arctic Circle has been told many times. Will wanted to go to Point Barrow to visit Charles Brower, a trader and whaler who had lived there for fifty years. Will knew the hazards of flying through a country that was fog-ridden in summertime. Wiley Post, who talked little but was accepted by fellow-pilots as one of the greatest aviators of his time, knew the hazards too. He had flown in Alaska twice on round-the-world expeditions.

Will and Wiley took off from Fairbanks about 11:00 A.M. They were flying over the Endicott Mountains and probably intended, as was usual on this trip, to pick up the coast line southeast of Barrow, and then follow it on to the Point. That afternoon Gus Massick, a white trader, was en route to Barrow in an open motorboat when he heard a plane overhead. Because of a dense fog, he could see nothing. He heard the plane circle above, leave the coast for the tundra and then return, circling once again. Evidently the plane was seeking some clear field or landmark. It flew out over the sea and back again. Massick was perhaps one hundred miles southeast of Barrow when, he said, "the plane seemed to leave for the west."

It must have been about two hours later that Wiley, with some sort of pilot's magic, found a little inlet where they made their landing, just fifteen miles from Barrow. And as a result of the same magic, there was an Eskimo there to give directions. Having apparently overshot their mark in the fog, they had gone beyond Barrow and down-coast to the south. It was in the take-off from the safe little river that the tragedy occurred. The Eskimo, Clare Okpeaha, carried the news to Point Barrow, and from there by radio it was broadcast to the world.

On his way Clare Okpeaha met his companions—they had all gone to Barrow for the day—and after telling them of the accident, he had hurried on. He reached Point Barrow about 8:00 P.M. Sergeant Stanley R. Morgan of the United States Army Signal Corps began at once trying to identify the plane. Within a few minutes he and Mr. Dougherty, the government school-teacher, were in two boats filled with men and boys.

I quote from a little paper that was sent to me, the Point Barrow *Northern Cross:*

"En route to the scene of the accident, Sergeant Morgan quizzed Okpeaha in an effort to learn more. Asked as to how he knew there were two men in the plane, Okpeaha replied, 'Me talk with mans.'

"Sergeant Morgan said, 'When? After they fell?'

" 'No,' answered Okpeaha, 'when they came down on water and asked me how go Barrow, where Barrow is, how far.'

" 'Did they tell you their names?'

" 'No,' replied Okpeaha, 'mans no tell name. But big mans. One man sore eye. He go inside plane and mans with sore eye start engine and go up. Engine spit, start, then stop. Start some more little. Then plane fall just so.'

"And with his hands Okpeaha indicated a bank, a

fall on the right wing, a nose dive in the water, followed by a complete somersault.

"When Sergeant Morgan asked if he waded out to the plane after the crash, Okpeaha said, 'No, me stand on sandspit, forty feet away, and holler to mans. No answer, and so me hurry quick to Barrow to tell people come quick.'"

When the party from Point Barrow arrived at the camp, they found that the other Eskimos had removed Will from the plane, which was nosed down and partly submerged in the crystal-clear water, a little more than three feet deep. Dr. W. H. Greist, the medical missionary at Point Barrow, told me of it when he and Mrs. Greist visited Los Angeles. He told me how they started back with Will and Wiley a few hours later in the boat, the Eskimos chanting their songs for the dead, the strange, solemn words echoing across the still water and into the night.

On Friday I talked with Colonel Lindbergh. He called me several times and continued to keep in touch with Point Barrow, assuring me he would take complete charge and make all necessary arrangements. Joe Crosson in the meantime had flown through dense fog to Point Barrow, and while he was snatching a few hours' sleep in the little hospital there, before taking off with the boys for Fairbanks, Mrs. Greist hurriedly wrote this note and pinned it to Joe's pocket:

"It was a little after 2 A.M. that 100 Eskimos, Sergeant Morgan, and the Government schoolteacher, Mr. Dougherty, arrived on the lagoon just in front of the hospital, with the bodies of your dear husband and Wiley Post in a great skin boat, pulled high on the shore by the many Eskimos. They were tenderly and carefully placed on stretchers and carried into the hospital, where we had made every preparation to give them aid, if alive. I could recognize Mr. Rogers by his pictures I have seen. Both men carried faint smiles on their still faces.

"Mr. Morgan has worked every five minutes since the radio messages have poured in by the hundreds. Impossible to answer each one. All preparations have been made to take the bodies to Fairbanks by plane, piloted by Joe Crosson, as per wire from Colonel Lindbergh. This must go to you in pencil, as I have finished it the last few minutes before the plane leaves."

We left Lakewood Friday night, and Will's old friend Jesse Jones met me in New York. He stayed at the hotel with us until we left the next day for California. And there was a telegram from Amon Carter asking if he might be permitted to fly to Seattle and sit in the plane with his old friend on the flight to Los Angeles.

Messages from friends poured in by the thousands. A letter from Ben Ames Williams in Maine told of a scene his aunt described.

"It must have been multiplied thousands of times [he said]. She had gone to buy some groceries in a little town in New Hampshire near her summer place. The clerks were busy—half a dozen of them—and there were perhaps a dozen customers being served or waiting to be served, when a boy came in from the street and said, loud enough so that everybody heard, that

Will Rogers was dead. Aunt Pearl said that after the first incredulous exclamations, no one spoke at all for a full minute. Three or four of the customers left the store. The clerks stopped what they were doing and one woman, as though she were not able to stand, looked down helplessly and found a box or something and just sat down."

There were so many beautiful letters—hundreds of them—and telegrams and cables from all over the world. People everywhere seemed to have known him.

But I think I liked best what one of his old cowboy friends said to me: "I can just shut my eyes now and see Willie on Comanche, a-ridin' through the broom weeds with his rope in his hand and a-sayin', 'Come on, Jim, let's go over to Musgrove's and beat Clem and Bill a-ropin'.' "

Because I, too, can see the same boy—grown older, but not grown up; though a little gray and a little stout. And it's not Comanche he's on—it's old Soapsuds. But he still has a rope on his saddle and he still wants to go somewhere.

THE END.

INDEX